D1206865

ISAIAH BERLIN

ISAIAH BERLIN

A Celebration

Edited by
Edna and Avishai Margalit

The Hogarth Press
LONDON

Published in 1991 by
The Hogarth Press
an imprint of Chatto & Windus Ltd
20 Vauxhall Bridge Road
London SW1V 2SA

A CIP catalogue record for this book is available from the
British Library.

ISBN 0 7012 0925 9

Typeset by Rowland Phototypesetting Ltd
Bury St Edmunds, Suffolk
Printed in Great Britain by
Mackays of Chatham plc, Chatham, Kent

CONTENTS

Preface

Towards Isaiah Berlin's 80th birthday, there were plans for a conference in his honour that was to take place in Jerusalem. The idea was to gather people close to him, who would deal with subjects dear to him: liberty and nationalism, art, music and opera, religion and secularism, philosophy and the history of philosophy. The conference, however, was not to be, and this volume is its transfiguration. In the nature of things, a book takes longer to gestate. So here it is, presented in celebration of Isaiah's 82nd birthday, and in celebration of his life and work.

The hedgehog, in the fable he made still more famous, sees one big thing, and the fox many small ones. The philosopher Nelson Goodman once asked Isaiah which animal most resembles us mere human beings, who most of the time can see only one small thing. Whatever the zoological answer to that question, the contributors to this collection saw before their eyes one very big thing.

With the following exceptions, the essays presented here were written especially for this volume. The exceptions are: Joseph Brodsky's, which appeared in the *New York Review of Books* (17 August 1989), and Sidney Morgenbesser's (written jointly with Jonathan Lieberson), which appeared in the *New York Review of Books* (10 March 1980). In addition, an expanded version of Alfred Brendel's essay constitutes the second chapter of his *Music Sounded Out* (Robson Books, 1990).

Our deep thanks go to Mr Arthur W. Fried of *Yad Avi Hayishuv*, to Mr Robert Silvers, the editor of the *New York Review of Books*, to Dr Martin Weil of the Israel Museum for permission to use David Hockney's drawing from the Israel Museum Collection, and to Jenny Uglow of Hogarth Press for overseeing the book to completion.

Edna Ullmann-Margalit
Avishai Margalit
Jerusalem, December 1990

CHAPTER 1

*Isaiah Berlin**
Sidney Morgenbesser and Jonathan Lieberson

Encounters with Isaiah Berlin were always pivotal for Jonathan Lieberson and myself. He opened up new intellectual territories, redrew old ones, caused us to rethink our fundamental beliefs and moral commitments and to revise our expectations and sensibilities. When we wrote the essay we were trying, among other things, to express both our admiration and thanks.

Isaiah Berlin remained a fixed point in our lives until Jonathan's early and tragic death. We returned to the themes of the essay and thought of possible emendations and additions. But we knew that we could go on without end in light of new essays and books from Isaiah Berlin that we read with delight and instruction, especially about, but not only about, the legitimate demands that can be made upon a moral and political theory, upon human ideals, and upon a decent and humane society. Encounters with Isaiah Berlin remain for me, as for so many others, somehow wondrous.

Edmund Wilson once described Isaiah Berlin as 'an extraordinary Oxford don, who left Russia at the age of eight and has a sort of double Russian-and-British personality. The combination is uncanny but fascinating.' But even these words from such a usually restrained source fail to do justice to the variety of gifts of this civilised and widely admired man who at one time or another has been a philosopher, a political theorist, an acute practical analyst of American and European politics, a historian of ideas, a biographer of Marx and translator of Turgenev, an active and influential participant in Jewish affairs, a longtime director of the Royal Opera House, a founder of Wolfson College at Oxford, and President of the British Academy. Those who have been in his presence have witnessed his intellectual gaiety; he is a learned and justly celebrated conversationalist, a man who enlarges the lives of his colleagues, his students, his friends.

Berlin is an imaginative philosopher and historian of ideas who has repeatedly reminded us not to underestimate the influence of abstract ideas in human affairs, however harmless such ideas may appear when detached from their historical settings and microscopically analysed by philosophers. He has reminded us that we cannot live without explaining the world to ourselves; that such explanations always rest on a conception of what is and can be; that whether we know it or not, insofar as we care about ideas at all, we are all participants in debates once familiar only to coteries of intellectuals.

Berlin sees his task as one of contributing to our self-knowledge by exhuming, clarifying, and criticising the main ideas and values that lie behind our current conceptions of ourselves – of understanding historically whence we came and how we came to be where we are now, thereby diminishing the dangers of being at the mercy of unexamined beliefs. This task requires rare psychological sensitivity, the capacity to enter into the consciousness of men far removed in space and time, and Berlin discharges it with grace and skill in his essays in the history of ideas.[1]

Berlin's portraits of thinkers from Machiavelli to Sorel are neither chronicles nor exegetical exercises; he approaches ideas as incarnated in the men who conceived them; his subjects are never mere vehicles. Berlin is thoroughly at home with ideas in their personal and emotional, social or cultural embodiments – whether his subject is a fanatical reactionary like Joseph de Maistre or a fastidious dandy like Benjamin Disraeli, he manages to achieve an astonishing directness of contact with it.

His intellectual preoccupations and gifts of imaginative reconstruction are brought together in his essays on men who dissented from shallow views of human nature: the ambiguous Machiavelli, the heroic and profound scholar Vico, the celebrated savant Montesquieu, as well as lesser-known men, eccentric fanatics like Georges Sorel and J. G. Hamann, and the gentle visionary Moses Hess. Berlin appreciates how all these men were treated by their contemporaries, more often than not, as 'immovable, isolated rocks with their absurd appearance of seeking to arrest or deflect the central current'. All of them struggled with, or timidly grasped, or celebrated human freedom and the diversity of human values and patterns of life.

I

According to Isaiah Berlin, one of the deepest assumptions of Western political thought, found in Plato and scarcely questioned since, is 'the conviction that there exist true, immutable, universal, timeless objective values, valid for all men, everywhere, at all times; that these values are at least in principle realisable, whether or not human beings are, or have been, or even will be, capable of realising them on earth; that these values form a coherent system, a harmony which, conceived in social terms, constitutes the perfect society.'

We may desire, for example, both expensive missiles to protect 'national security' and freedom from burdensome taxation; an excellent secondary educational system for all but not an admissions policy which overlooks merit or the effects of past discrimination; equal rights for all but not unwanted neighbours. These conflicting sentiments are expressions of more abstract values we prize – justice, freedom, happiness, security, loyalty. It is a common conviction (or hope) that these conflicts are apparent, that our various values can be somehow harmoniously realised – or at least ranked in importance – perhaps by the efforts of some especially clever thinker, a politician or religious saviour or sociologist, or by the use of some method, scientific or philosophical, or some technological invention.

This conviction is familiar enough, but is it true? Berlin thinks that it is not, and his criticism of it is expressed – as so often in his work – through inspection of the ideas of the historical figures he believes were especially prominent in undermining it. His essay on Machiavelli is an eloquent portrait of a man who questioned this psychologically attractive doctrine in uncompromising fashion. As Berlin claims, 'It is this rock, upon which Western beliefs and lives had been founded, that Machiavelli seems, in effect, to have split open.'

In Berlin's view Machiavelli's central aim was to provide a set of therapeutic maxims designed to help the statesman in restoring Italy to a position of security and stability, vigour and magnificence, to create 'a state conceived after the analogy of Periclean Athens, or Sparta, but above all the Roman Republic'. To do so, the statesman must be realistic, 'pagan': he must be prepared to use terrible measures to ensure the general good, be willing to kill the innocent to create a show of strength, to deceive and betray and falsify. Once he has embarked on the course of transforming a diseased society, he cannot be squeamish. As Berlin expresses Machiavelli's point,

3

to be a physician is to be a professional, ready to burn, to cauterise, to amputate; if that is what the disease requires, then to stop half-way because of personal qualms, or some rule unrelated to your art or technique, is a sign of muddle and weakness, and will always give you the worst of both worlds.

The code of behaviour the statesman must apply is not a game of skill unconnected with morality but a new ethic concerned exclusively with the good of all, with public, not personal, morality – and certainly not with the popular Christian personal morality of Machiavelli's time, which dictated humility, kindness, compassion, sanctity and the quest for salvation in personal life.

Berlin finds much to criticise in Machiavelli's thought: 'His human beings have so little inner life or capacity for co-operation or social solidarity that, as in the case of Hobbes's not dissimilar creatures it is difficult to see how they could develop enough reciprocal confidence to create a lasting social whole, even under the perpetual shadow of carefully regulated violence.' But Machiavelli's 'vision of the great prince playing upon human beings like an instrument' with the aid of a novel morality condoning murder, hypocrisy and fraudulence raises a disturbing question, which Berlin regards as 'the nodal point of Machiavelli's entire conception'. Can these different moralities – the public 'paganism' of the prince and the personal ethics of the Christian – be held by the same man at the same time?

Berlin believes that Machiavelli rightly held the two moralities to be not merely in practice but in principle incompatible. He thus posed a problem of choice: 'One can save one's soul, or one can found or maintain, or serve a great and glorious state; but not always both at once.' Two moralities, two sets of virtues, two ethical worlds – with no common ground – are in collision. Each is coherent and integral; we cannot have both. Machiavelli shocked his contemporaries (and many others since) by frankly renouncing Christian morality, but, Berlin claims, he did so 'in favour of another system, another moral universe', 'a society geared to ends just as ultimate as the Christian faith, a society in which men fight and are ready to die for (public) ends which they pursue for their own sakes.'

Machiavelli's problem of choice, Berlin suggests, has outlasted the specific conflict to which it was addressed and lives with us still, not merely in its obvious applications to such questions as the propriety of

4

the conduct of our statesmen, or indeed any officials authorised to protect the public good, but more pervasively, in a wide variety of cases in which he claims we must, like Machiavelli's men, choose between incompatible values.

Suppose, Berlin has asked on another occasion, we were placed in charge of a hospital's supply of kidney machines, costly machines vastly outnumbered by those who suffer from diseases from which they would provide relief: 'If there is a great scientist who suffers from a kidney disease, should the only machine we have be reserved for him alone? Should we use the few machines we have only for gifted or important people who, in our view, confer a lot of benefit on society? If some child is dying whom the kidney machine might save, how do we decide between them?'[2] In deciding, should we think only of the happiness of mankind and therefore reserve the machine for the scientist, who is more likely to confer greater benefits on humanity than the child? But then doesn't this clash with the view that all human beings have certain fundamental rights, that we cannot grade lives in importance, that all have an equal claim to be saved? We must decide and yet what are we to do?

Berlin is careful to point out that this kind of conflict is not like the familiar ones we encounter in daily life; it is not like the business of adjusting the demands of work and leisure, or of choosing between a trip to the beach and remaining at home to watch a television programme – a conflict that might be removed by a technological innovation (like a television set one could take to the beach). The kind of choice in question is radically unlike that in common speech and thought, where we choose among different courses of action – what school to attend, what stock to invest in – with the help of stable, previously held, values and standards: living near our families, getting the best return on our money. Such values serve as a secure basis for determining the merits and demerits of the options.

In the dilemma posed by Machiavelli, we are dealing with a less familiar, more radical, kind of choice: There is no stable background of standards against which we can appraise the alternatives, no common criterion whereby a rational decision between them can be made. There are just the competing alternatives; we must somehow settle for one of them. As Berlin expressed it, such 'choices must be made for no better reason than that each value is what it is, and we choose it for what it is, and not because it can be shown on some single scale to be higher than another.' No alteration of our circumstances, no new technology or scientific knowledge can remove such conflicts. 'Whom shall I save, the scientist or the child?' is not a *fact* to be discovered but requires a decision, a spiritual movement making one moral attitude to the problem *ours* – an 'invention', as Berlin puts it, obedient to no pre-existing rules. This radical kind of choice can be protracted and painful precisely because it concerns alternatives we care deeply about.

Machiavelli, says Berlin, 'helped to cause men to become aware of the necessity of having to make agonising choices between incompatible alternatives in public and private life (for the two could not, it became obvious, be genuinely kept distinct).' But, as this remark suggests, the 'agony of choice' discovered by Machiavelli is double, not single: The moralities of the personal and public spheres of life are distinguishable; and they can collide. But a choice of the one affects the choice of the other. If we must have 'dirty hands' in public life, we may find it impossible to remain Christians in personal life; if we are humble seekers of salvation in personal life, we may find it impossible to pursue the realisation of the successful state. We are agonised in two ways: We must choose what we are to consider virtuous not merely in the personal sphere, but in the public sphere as well, and these choices may clash.

And of course the same problem of choice arises *within* these spheres in addition to arising between them. We could well be forced, for example, to make the sort of choice described by Machiavelli as a part of public morality – to choose, for example, between values like freedom or security. Is not the man who is troubled whether taxation is compatible with individual liberty concerned with a problem of this kind? As for personal life, do we not face Machiavelli's problem of choosing between incompatible values and ways of life when we ask ourselves whether we should become involved in social issues or 'drop out'; whether we should devote our lives to active involvement in a consuming cause or to scholarly research; whether, like Gauguin, we should dismiss our responsibilities to our family and flee to an undisturbed paradise in order to cultivate our genius?[3]

As Berlin sums up, Machiavelli discovered that 'ends equally ultimate, equally sacred, may contradict each other, that entire systems of value may come into collision without possibility of rational arbitration, and that not merely in exceptional circumstances, as a result of abnormality or accident or error – the clash of Antigone and Creon or in the story of Tristan – but (this was surely new) as part of the normal human situation.'

If what Machiavelli wrote is true, 'the idea of the sole, true, objective, universal human ideal crumbles. The very search for it becomes not merely Utopian in practice, but conceptually incoherent.' As Berlin interprets him, Machiavelli planted 'a permanent question mark in the path of posterity' by his discovery of the diversity and incompatibility of human values – of 'pluralism'.

These themes arise again and again, not merely in these essays, but throughout Berlin's work. 'If, as I believe,' he writes,

> the ends of man are many and not all of them in principle compatible with each other, the possibility of conflict – and of tragedy – can never be wholly eliminated from human life, either personal or social. The necessity of choosing between absolute claims is then an inescapable characteristic of the human condition.[4]

These contentions are of immense importance for that branch of philosophy called 'moral theory', many of whose practitioners continue to seek ways to harmonise or systematically order our deepest values. Berlin nowhere, so far as we know, claims that all systems of this kind are necessarily false. Nor, on the other hand, does he merely assert that some such systems have been false. In agreement with the fundamental insight of Machiavelli, Berlin views conflict among values as a permanent feature of life, which no system or theory is likely to remove.

To reduce such conflict hastily and artificially by logical or theoretical means is for him a species of self-deception that could be dangerous; as he has written, the notion that 'it is in principle possible to discover a harmonious pattern in which all values are reconciled . . . seems to me invalid, and at times to have led (and still to lead) to absurdities in theory and barbarous consequences in practice.'[5]

II

If the 'permanent question mark in the path of posterity' planted by Machiavelli is closely scrutinised, important consequences for our conception of human beings – of 'human nature' – seem to follow from it. For example, if it is an 'inescapable characteristic' of our lives that we make choices among absolute claims, choices that may have fruitful or ruinous consequences for human life, then must we not in some sense be unconstrained, undetermined, 'free'? And if so, then doesn't this indicate an important fact about 'human nature', about man and his actions, individual or collective, past or present? Berlin's essays on 'The Counter-Enlightenment' and on Giambattista Vico explore the historical growth and consolidation of the 'pluralist' insights he commends in Machiavelli as they were extended by other thinkers to address this question.

The eighteenth-century French Enlightenment philosophers – Voltaire, Diderot, Helvétius, Condorcet – further developed, according to Berlin, the 'ancient and almost universal' philosophical doctrine of the harmony of human values by combining it with a theory of human nature and by invoking the promise of new 'sciences of man':

> The central doctrines of the progressive French thinkers, whatever their disagreements among themselves, rested on the belief, rooted in the ancient doctrine of natural law, that human nature was fundamentally the same in all times and places; that local and historical variations were unimportant compared with the constant central core in terms of which human beings could be defined as a species, like animals, or plants, or minerals . . .
>
> It was further believed that methods similar to those of Newtonian physics, which had achieved such triumphs in the realm of inanimate nature, could be applied with equal success to the fields of ethics, politics and human relationships in general, in which little progress had been made; with the corollary that once this had been effected, it would sweep away irrational and oppressive legal systems and economic policies the replacement of which by the rule of reason would rescue men from political and moral injustice and misery and set them on the path of wisdom, happiness, and virtue.

In other words, on this view human nature is fixed and determined; underneath the apparent diversities of men lies an unchanging 'nature', endowed with identical needs, motives, values. On this view, Machiavelli must have been in error; ultimate ends could not be in conflict; they are identical throughout the 'species' of man, for is it not true that all men seek the satisfaction of hunger and thirst, the realisation of security, justice, happiness? If Mongols, Hottentots and Semites ostensibly differ from Parisians, the Enlightenment thinkers held, the new sciences of man will show this difference to be merely apparent. Human beings can be studied as ants or bees are; what can be

8

applied with success to nature can be applied with equal success to human nature. Everything that exists on this view can be explained and possibly even predicted by general laws.

In opposition to this body of beliefs, a great stream of dissident thought evolved in the late eighteenth and early nineteenth centuries, reaching its most eccentric, angry, and eloquent expression in the work of the German Romantics – J. G. Hamann, his pupil J. G. Herder, F. H. Jacobi, the *Sturm und Drang* poets, and their assorted idealist and irrationalist successors. These men, who form the core of what Berlin calls the 'Counter-Enlightenment,' protested the facile transfer of scientific methods from the inanimate realm to the human: Could Newton's methods for plotting the movements of the planets, they asked, explain the efforts of an original artist? Could mechanics or indeed any general scientific theory offer understanding of a moral dilemma, the aspirations of those touched by God, the radical choices performed by the free and creative self – in short, the complex inner life of the spirit? In the case of some of the Counter-Enlightenment thinkers, like the strange Königsberg sage Hamann, the preoccupation with the inner life led them to demand the total destruction of Enlightenment values. In his essay on Hamann, Berlin vividly describes how that thinker violently attacked not merely the claim that science has something to say about human nature but its claim to do anything useful at all.

According to Berlin, Hamann saw analysis, classification, deduction and system as 'infantile' efforts to 'confine the unconfinable'; nature, he thought, could not be caught by the simple nets laid out by the French and English scientists. Hamann held that only the man who feels and loves, the artist and the poet, can fully understand nature; that faith in things unseen was the foundation of true knowledge; art or religion provide truth, not the 'stuffed dummy' called 'reason', which creates foolish rules – 'walls of sand built to hold back the waves of an ocean' – and systems that ignore 'the teeming variety of the living world, the untidy and asymmetrical inner lives of men, and crush them into conformity for the sake of some ideological chimera.'

Berlin writes, 'No system, no elaborate construction of scientific generalities, will, in Hamann's view, enable a man to understand what is conveyed by a gesture, a look, a style, or to understand a line of poetry, a painting, a vision, a spiritual condition, an *état d'âme*, a form of life.' Hamann's challenge in his fulminations against the

9

Enlightenment was, in Berlin's words, 'How dare these pathetic pedants impose on the vast world of continuous, fertile, unpredictable, divine creation their own narrow, desiccated categories?'

Hamann's celebration of natural variety and the free, rich, spontaneous patterns of the will and the inner life was shared by other German Counter-Enlightenment figures – Herder, and later Schelling, the Schlegels, Novalis, Fichte – and indeed artists and thinkers in other countries like Coleridge and Wordsworth, Blake, Chateaubriand, Stendhal and Emerson, Carlyle.

Berlin is sharply aware of the excess of the Counter-Enlightenment thinkers – their haste, their gross errors of detail, their eccentric prescriptions, their wild mythologies – but he sees in their work sound intuitions, expressed perhaps most fully and coherently by Herder, but anticipated, with far greater force and depth, a half-century before him by the 'obscure, poverty-ridden Neapolitan recluse' Giambattista Vico, a lonely professor of rhetoric 'who might have had a decisive role in this countermovement if anyone outside his native country had read him.'

According to Berlin, Vico was the most powerful of the Counter-Enlightenment thinkers, a man who in a single, complex vision discredited in advance the Enlightenment conceptions of human nature, the perfect society, the progress of humanity, the nature of history, a thinker who has a claim to be the founder of the history of ideas, of comparative cultural history, comparative anthropology, law, religion, aesthetics – indeed, of the modern 'social sciences'. Vico set in train the idea, as Berlin puts it, that

> history did not consist merely of things and events and their consequences and sequences (including those of human organisms viewed as natural objects) as the external world did; it was the story of human activities, of what men did and thought and suffered, of what they strove for, aimed at, accepted, rejected, conceived, imagined, of what their feelings were directed at.

Vico argued that history is neither a tissue of gossip and travellers' tales (as Descartes had argued a century earlier), nor 'a collection of factual beads strung on a chronicler's string', nor (as his younger contemporary Voltaire thought) a disparate mass of instructive and entertaining truths retrieved from the past.

Closely linked to this view of history, Berlin claims, was Vico's bold idea that human nature is not unchanging – as the Enlightenment held, that human nature is not like a fan (or a peacock tail) that opens out over the centuries, showing now one, now another, colour, with all its qualities and properties present (but hidden) at the beginning. In place of these views, Vico appealed to a radical new principle, that the 'nature' of man is his history. Moreover, for Vico, man's history reveals that human beings have changed over time in vitally important respects: Men were once savage brutes; now they are democrats; but – in his famous 'cyclical theory of history' – they will be brutes again.

In Vico's view, shared by Berlin, men have had different values at different times and in different circumstances. They have employed different concepts or categories of interpreting their experience; as these patterns have changed, so have men's reasons for acting, their ruling conceptions, of good and evil, happiness and humour, their duties, their song, art, dance. The values men cherish have changed over time, in this view, as the interests, needs, desires in which these values are rooted change, as the ideas men formulate in response to the questions they ask of the world become obsolete.

History, then, for Vico and Berlin, is a process of man's self-creation, a transforming and correcting process; 'a changing pattern,' Berlin writes, 'of great liberating ideas which inevitably turn into suffocating straitjackets, and so stimulate their own destruction by new, emancipating, and at the same time enslaving conceptions.'[6] Each integral culture or age generates its own unique mode of expressing its response to the world, which is intelligible only to those who understand its own internal rules and style. Historical change is a sequence of births and deaths of forms of life, with valuable modes of expression lost irretrievably along the way, with others cropping up continually, not necessarily more valuable than their predecessors: There is no sense, in this view, in speaking of 'progress' in history. There is no need to compare and grade on some single scale of merit each cultural phase and its creations and forms of life and action; indeed, it is not possible to do so, for they are evidently 'incommensurable'.

These pluralist views were remarkably original, as Berlin persuasively argues by comparing them to those of the reigning arbiter of intellectual taste in Vico's time, Voltaire. But Vico also boldly challenged the claim that scientific method as it was conceived in his time could dominate the entire sphere of human knowledge, by asserting that it was not applicable to history and humane studies. As Berlin puts it, Vico thinks that

> to understand history is to understand what men made of the world in which they found themselves, what they demanded of it, what their felt needs, aims, ideals, were: he seeks to discover their vision of it, he asks what wants, what questions, what aspirations determined a society's view of reality; and he thinks that he has created a new method which will reveal to him the categories in terms of which men thought and acted and changed themselves and their worlds.

The 'understanding' yielded by Vico's new method is entirely different from that offered by the natural sciences: The new method is not just a matter of raising hypotheses and testing them by simple observation or the use of refined experimental techniques, as geographers or micro-biologists or mineralogists do. We have, Vico and Berlin claim, a special relation to the objects of our investigation in the humane studies – in history, literary criticism, political theory, in much of anthropology and sociology, and indeed in much of what passes under the name of 'social science'. We are, like our subject matter, human; we can claim the understanding that participants in an activity possess, as observers cannot.

If we are to understand a text, an instance of behaviour, a historical event (such as Xerxes' conduct at the Hellespont); if we wish to know why a financial panic took place, why bureaucracy diminishes produc-tivity, why a people rebelled against their authorities; in short, if we wish to understand anything human, we need to do more than exercise our simple perceptions – discriminating differences of pitch and colour; we need to do more than examine the physical states of our subjects – their weight, or blood pressure. As Berlin has written, we need also

> the capacity for conceiving more than one way of categorising reality, like the ability to understand what it is to be an artist, a revolutionary, a traitor, to know what it is to be poor, to wield authority, to be a child, a prisoner, a barbarian.

This capacity, Berlin claims, is distinct from, and possibly more complex than, that exercised by a physicist in gathering observational evidence, or testing a theory, in registering points of light, or tracing the tracks of invisible particles. Unlike 'simple' perception grasping empirical facts, this capacity is part imagination, part memory, part intuition, always governed by the conceptual patterns in which we think of other human beings, and never reducible to inductive or deductive rules of scientific research.

In the humane studies, Berlin claims, the understanding of subject matter (and possibly some ways of testing – as against discovering – of hypotheses concerning this subject matter) consists to a large degree in the exercise by investigators of distinctive, imaginative capacities of this kind, capacities – or, as Berlin sometimes calls them, 'knacks' – which allow these investigators to enter into the lives and outlook of other human beings and cultures, past and present, to acquire the sense of what 'fits' and what does not in an interconnected body of human activities, to acquire the sense of anachronism they employ when, upon reading a passage in Shakespeare, they know straight off that it could not have been composed by a Manchu or a Sumerian.

The investigator using this 'new method' is able to obtain an 'inner', direct grasp of events akin to self-knowledge because he, like his subjects, is a thinking, planning, acting being. The 'knowledge' that results from his efforts

> is quite different from that in which I know that this tree is taller than that . . . In other words, it is not a form of 'knowing that'. Nor is it like knowing how to ride a bicycle or to win a battle, or what to do in case of fire, or knowing a man's name, or a poem by heart. That is to say, it is not a form of 'knowing how'. It is more like the knowledge we claim of a friend, of his character, of his ways of thought and action, a species of its own, based on prior personal experience, memory, imagination and communication with other human beings.

In *Against the Current* and in the more abstract writings collected in *Concepts and Categories* Berlin claims that the discovery by Vico of this special 'mode of perception' – he admits that 'knowledge' might be too strong a word for an activity 'so obviously fallible' and in need of 'empirical research to justify its findings' – marks the discovery of a central difference between the natural sciences (which need not employ it) and the humanities (which inescapably do), and confutes the possibility of a 'scientific history'.

Is this so? Berlin is, of course, entitled to claim that there may exist *particular* modes or capacities of cognition unique to the humanities. If the historian must understand what it is to be poor, the physicist is not concerned with what it is to be an electron. Still his account may be contested, and not only because he has not, as he acknowledges, explained exactly how people with radically different categories of thought 'enter into' and 'inwardly grasp' each other's views. (Nor did Vico.) It may be that Berlin is tacitly assuming too superficial a conception of the natural sciences when he draws a sharp distinction between scientific 'experience' and that brought into play in humane studies. If recent researches in the philosophy of science by T. S. Kuhn, Karl Popper and others are correct, even ordinary experimental interpretations in science are laden with preconceptions and categories that may undergo radical change in the course of scientific development. To understand different comprehensive scientific theories or deal with new data, natural scientists might also have to use 'the capacity for conceiving more than one way of categorising reality' and perform efforts of 'resurrection' and reconstruction similar to those cited by Berlin as distinctive of humane studies.

If even natural scientists can, and indeed may have to, grasp radically different ways of interpreting the natural world, and if even their observations are 'theory laden', the objectivity of science in some of the senses described by Berlin is open to question. Berlin himself in his earlier writings attacked the oversimplified accounts of historical knowledge as objective that were in vogue between the 1930s and the 1950s. It seems ironic that some philosophers would argue that this earlier account could in part be transposed to scientific knowledge as well and thereby challenge some of the distinctions Berlin draws between the natural sciences and the humanities.

The issues are far from settled and often not even clearly understood. Berlin might claim that whatever difficulties there may be in the understanding of new scientific theories they can, once understood, be objectively tested; not so for all theories and hypotheses in the social sciences and humanities. There is much current debate about the kinds of cognitive skills and commitments that are involved in the understanding, testing and accepting of scientific theories and hypotheses. The old empiricist claim that essentially the same methods can be used to test hypotheses in both the natural and social sciences is far from dead.

Whatever the outcome of these debates, it should be clear why the

14

Counter-Enlightenment thinkers, taken together, are of such importance to Berlin. They, more than any other group of thinkers, saw how
intellectual confusion can result from the deliberate or unconscious
application of scientific (or pseudo-scientific) methods and doctrines
where they do not apply; and, despite their obvious shortcomings, they
clearly saw that scientific methods could not adequately answer fundamental questions about human values. But perhaps even more important, they first set in motion ideas which provided the philosophical
underpinning – the reasoned justification – for the facts Berlin claims
were pointed out by Machiavelli: If men can choose, by their own
lights, among incompatible alternatives, then their behaviour could not
be explained by appeal to a set of general laws – as some Enlightenment
thinkers believed. They could not be the 'mechanical' systems Condillac and perhaps in our own day B. F. Skinner take them to be; they
could not be like computers or calculators. Their history must be an
open process of self-creation, without a large strategy or inevitable
trend.

This idea lies at the heart of Berlin's work, and he has often
expressed it with eloquence – the idea, as he once put it, that man is

> incapable of self-completion, and therefore never wholly predictable: a
> fallible, a complex combination of opposites, some reconcilable, others
> incapable of being resolved or harmonised; unable to cease from his
> search for truth, happiness, novelty, freedom, but with no guarantee,
> theological or logical or scientific, of being able to attain them: a free,
> imperfect being capable of determining his own destiny in circum-
> stances favourable to the development of his reason and his gifts.[7]

But if human beings are, as the combined insights of Machiavelli
and Vico suggest, free, spontaneous, choosing beings, with widely
diverse values and cultural embodiments of these values, what political
arrangements are best suited to their nature? How ought they to live in
political association?

III

Berlin's views on pluralism, the necessity of radical choice and on
human nature interlock in his well-known writings in defence of
liberalism, not merely in the essays on nationalism, on Georges Sorel

and on Alexander Herzen in *Against the Current*, but also, and more fully, in his *Four Essays on Liberty*, which is the main subject of *The Idea of Freedom*,[8] a collection of essays by distinguished scholars in honour of Sir Isaiah's seventieth birthday.

As Berlin noted long ago, political ideas always rest on a conception of what man is and can be; the philosophical ideas behind liberal doctrine and practice were, along with more arcane matters, a ground of battle between the Enlightenment and the Counter-Enlightenment. 'European liberalism,' he wrote, 'wears the appearance of a single coherent movement, little altered during almost three centuries, founded upon relatively simple foundations, laid by Locke or Grotius or even Spinoza; stretching back to Erasmus and Montaigne, the Italian Renaissance, Seneca and the Greeks.'[9] The demands for tolerance, freedom of speech and thought and assembly, for a minimum amount of liberty to be granted each individual, for the cultivation of choices available to men (as opposed to the coercion of choice), for the divorce of the content of justice from any specific doctrine of goodness – of the Right from the Good – these were the characteristic demands of liberals.

Liberals often also added theories about 'natural rights' which were not obviously compatible with the 'tentative empiricism', as Berlin puts it, that usually characterised their views. Rational morality, they thought, would secure universal truths and, when combined with acceptable economic theories, would encourage freedom, happiness, economic growth and the decline of economic misery.

But, as Berlin continues this narrative, the nineteenth century saw disturbing developments which led thinkers as different as J. S. Mill and Nietzsche to rethink or modify or reject the simple philosophical underpinnings of liberalism inherited from Condorcet and Helvétius. Such developments included unbridled private enterprise, the rise of industrialisation, the appearance of unexpected forms of concentrated political and economic power, the failure of education and legislation to ensure a just social order, the conformism and monotony of modern life. However, as Berlin adds, one antiliberal development 'dominated much of the nineteenth century in Europe and was so pervasive, so familiar, that it is only by a conscious effort of the imagination that one can conceive a world in which it played no part.' This movement is nationalism, and none of the aforementioned prophets – or their fellow futurologists Tocqueville, Weber, Jakob Burckhardt, Marx,

Durkheim – 'predicted for it a future in which it would play an even more dominant role.'

The great German Counter-Enlightenment philosopher Herder, to whose ideas Berlin has devoted much attention, apparently coined the word 'nationalism' and created the notion that 'men, if they are to exercise their faculties fully, and so develop into all that they can be, need to belong to identifiable groups, each with its own outlook, style, traditions, historical memories, and language.'[10] Like Vico (and, as Berlin's essay in *Against the Current* shows, like Vico's famous French contemporary Montesquieu, who dimly perceived the point), Herder argued against the Enlightenment belief in the unity of man. What Machiavelli had noticed about warring moralities, he said of cultures: They are 'comparable but incommensurable', incapable of being arranged on a single scale of progess or retrogression, each having its own style of law, music, dance, gesture, handwriting. Men, he suggested, need to belong to such a culture just as much as they need to eat or sleep.

The groups Herder spoke of were not groups of men formed by focusing on attractive features of the world and then inviting others to join in preserving or contemplating them – like a film club or the hypothetical groups we find in some simple theories of social contract. They resembled more a family, or a clan or tribe: Jews, Kurds, Turkomans owe their very sense of identity, on this view, to their membership in their race or tribe; they do not choose to belong to them any more than they choose to love or identify with their parents. Their group values, according to Herder, are neither portable nor exchangable, but unique, historical, irreplaceable. This is why Herder thought imitation or transplantation of alien standards harmful and why he thought nothing more false than the idea – espoused by enlightened and zealous reformers of every age – that members of disparate groups, communities and cultures could be transported *en masse* to a utopia on the outskirts of civilisation, Oneida perhaps, or Red Bank, or Nauvoo, or Jonestown, there to create a politically perfect social mixture. As Berlin quotes him, 'whom nature separated by language, customs, character, let no man artificially join together by chemistry.'

Yet according to Berlin, Herder was not a 'nationalist' in any dangerous sense; he valued, rather, the individuality and diversity of cultures (and thus his own, German, culture). His idea of 'belonging' was posed as a social, not a political idea. Moreover, Berlin claims,

17

Herder believed that different nations or cultures can emerge alongside one another, respecting each other's activities, without engendering conflict; he held a

> view of men and society which stressed vitality, movement, change, respects in which individuals or groups differed rather than resembled each other, the charm and value of diversity, uniqueness, individuality, a view which conceived of the world as a garden where each tree, each flower, grows in its own peculiar fashion and incorporates those aspirations which circumstances and its own individual nature have generated, and is not, therefore, to be judged by the patterns and goals of other organisms.

Although these ideas were not justifiable grounds for it, Berlin argues, they were developed into aggressive nationalism by German thinkers as a result of complex factors, among which was unquestionably the wounded collective pride experienced in Germany after the Napoleonic wars. They were distorted into not mere pride of ancestry but a consolidated movement of intolerant chauvinism, led by men in search of a base for power or 'a focus for loyalty', and asserting the supremacy of their culture and sensibility. Such movements were to appear again, for example, among the Slavophils in Russia. Eventually they arose in Africa, the Balkans, the Middle East and Southeast Asia.

Much as he deplores this development and is concerned to know why its rise was unforeseen or treated merely as a symptom of the craving for self-determination that would pass with time and social change, and how its more inflammable forms may be curbed or avoided, Berlin agrees with Herder that eliding or denying the need to be rooted in a particular group robs men of dignity and self-identity. He thinks this is confirmed in the case of Jews by the twisted self-perception of men like Disraeli and the 'Jewish self-hatred' of Karl Marx – as his essay comparing 'the search for identity' of these two deracinated Jews amply documents.

Berlin also hopes that Herder's idea may be confirmed in a different, more fruitful and tolerant way by the outcome of Zionism, which was virtually invented by another of his subjects, the nineteenth-century 'communist rabbi', Moses Hess. In his youth this sensitive and truthful man had held the fashionable and 'enlightened' belief that his fellow Jews, having served their historical mission, should 'disperse and assimilate'. He looked forward to a new, socialist world. As Berlin summarises his view, 'there was no room in the universal society of the future for sectional religions or interests. The Jews must scatter and vanish as a historical entity', suffer a 'dignified dissolution'. But by middle age, Hess regarded his earlier views as fallacious, arguing that the Jews had a historic task – to unite communism and nationality – and that they must find a homeland. As Berlin quotes him, 'You may don a thousand masks, change your name and your religion and your mode of life, creep through the world incognito so that nobody notices you are a Jew', yet 'neither reform nor baptism, neither education nor emancipation, will completely open before the Jews of Germany the doors of social life.' Instead, the Jews must realise they are a separate nation and try to establish a home on the banks of the Jordan.

Berlin does not pretend to draw the line between beneficial and dangerous expressions of the idea of 'belonging' but he sees this as an acutely pertinent question that must be faced for, as he writes, 'no political movement today, at any rate outside the Western world, seems likely to succeed unless it allies itself to national sentiment.' Nationalism is but one of the movements in the modern world that may endanger the existence or maintenance of liberal societies. To identify such movements, to understand their causes, and perhaps their justifiable ingredients (and to accommodate to these as best one can), to create means for protection from them: these are for Berlin prime responsibilities of the liberal. Indeed, Berlin's more theoretical work on liberalism is a sustained attempt to furnish a more truthful and effective philosophical defence of it. By making this attempt, he hopes the decay of liberal institutions may be stopped rather than unwittingly fostered.

IV

Berlin's most famous contribution to this end has been his effort to clarify or define the concept of liberty itself. Common sense and thought, he wrote in his 'Two Concepts of Liberty',[11] have no single meaning for the term, but there are two central senses of it, which have been distinguished and which he claimed are worthy of further analysis and classification – 'negative' and 'positive' liberty. 'Negative' liberty he characterised very roughly as the absence of interference – by the state, a class, a corporation or another individual – with what one wishes to do. As he wrote, 'political liberty in this sense is simply the area within which a man can act unobstructed by others'; it is often understood as being left alone by others to act as you desire, so that the larger the range of your potential choice, the greater the extent of your 'negative liberty'. (He has also noted that this is not all that is involved in negative freedom, however. It cannot be *defined* as the lack of obstacles to the fulfilment of your present desires, for this would lead to the consequence that the person who has no desires at all is the freest.) 'Positive liberty,' on the other hand, is self-realisation, bringing into active service our potentials and powers in order to pursue a goal we identify with; it is self-direction, the acquisition of a share in the authority ruling one:

> the 'positive' sense of the word 'liberty' derives from the wish on the part of the individual to be his own master. I wish my life and decisions to depend on myself, not on external forces of whatever kind. I wish to be the instrument of my own, not of other men's, acts of will . . . I wish, above all, to be conscious of myself as a thinking, willing, acting being, bearing responsibility for my choices and able to explain them by references to my own idea and purposes. I feel free to the degree that I believe this to be true, and enslaved to the dgree that I am made to realise that it is not.

The distinction between positive and negative liberty is, for Berlin, of crucial importance for theory and practice, even though he writes that 'the freedom which consists in being one's own master, and the freedom which consists in not being prevented from choosing as I do by other men, may, on the face of it, seem concepts at no great logical distance from each other – no more than negative and positive ways of saying much the same thing.'

'Negative liberty', he thinks, is at least tolerably clear: Although there are of course subtle exceptions, we can tell with relative ease whether a man's actions are physically obstructed by another or by the state, and, perhaps less easily but in general accurately, whether he is being intimidated or threatened or otherwise prevented from doing something he wishes to do by these same agencies. The man may be an illiterate, a pauper, a victim of a crippling disease, a psychotic; he may lack the means, will, knowledge, confidence, to *use* his freedom – he may, in other words, lack what Berlin calls the 'conditions of liberty' – but he is free in the 'negative' sense if he is not interfered with or can legally regain his freedom if it is infringed. Defenders of negative liberty, he believes, should try to specify the conditions under which we are free to act. Specific desires and preferences should not be brought into the definition of negative liberty – rather, they are best regarded as presupposed by a claim that a person is in fact free; similarly for capacities or powers. This approach comports with common sense. Most of us, for example, are negatively free to walk on our ears or eat books; there is no law prohibiting us from doing these things; yet to be able to do them generally does not count as 'freedom' precisely because most people do not have those desires or capacities, and accordingly it does not occur to us to speak of a corresponding freedom.

By contrast, the 'positive' concept of liberty is opaque: Whether a man is free in this second sense depends on more than his having 'negative liberty', on more than the absence of impediments to his action. But what more? One answer might be: having the right to participate in the sovereign authority. But there are others as well. It could be said that man does not possess 'positive freedom' unless he possesses whatever means – money, success, friendship, luck, security – are necessary for him to realise his ambitions, just as it could be said that a man who has a low income, or who has never had a university education or who has never been psychoanalysed, is not 'free'.

Berlin suggests that this 'positive' sense of freedom has repeatedly been debased, turned into a denial of present, negative liberty in the name of a 'true' or 'real' or 'ultimate' freedom by specious argument. He agrees that we all wish to realise a variety of values – health, freedom from penury, leisure, wealth – and he shares these values; but he says that nothing good will come of confusing these with liberty. It is easy enough to gather all of these values together and call them 'liberty', but we would still have to distinguish between them eventually, and failure to do so only encourages the illusion that they can somehow be combined into a single, coherent pattern.

Moreover, he thinks, we court dangerous consequences in theory and practice if we employ those interpretations of 'positive liberty'. To use an example of Berlin's, the German philosopher Fichte argued that even though men are in some sense rational, their rationality is often undeveloped; they are not self-directed because they fail to think, to discover their own real desires; they must be educated, as children are, for their own good; they will not recognise the reasons for such education now, but they will later. There are, of course, more recent examples of the same kind of fatal argument: True 'freedom' has often been defended by authoritarian regimes in both advanced and developing nations.

Critics such as C. B. Macpherson and Charles Taylor in his essay in *The Idea of Freedom* argue that we do not desire merely freedom from external 'obstructions to action'. We wish liberty to pursue activities that are significant to us. We may not care much if we are prohibited from driving at 80 miles an hour, but we care deeply if deprived of religious liberty. Taylor also seems to argue that defenders of negative liberty are wrong to believe that people are uniquely privileged to know what is significant for them in ways that others cannot improve upon – in the way, for example, that they are in the best position to know whether they are in pain. If a person is neurotically unhappy or obsessed by emotions such as revenge or spite, his grasp of what is important for him may be so distorted that his freedom is thereby diminished.

We may imagine Berlin's response to such objections: First, it is not true that we desire liberty simply in order to realise ideals we currently have. We might develop new interests and new ideals, and we cherish liberty for allowing us to realise these possible values – which could include having some negative liberties for their own sake. Second, while agreeing that sheer lack of obstruction to our actions by the state is not all we desire, Berlin would add that liberty may very well be a prerequisite for the accomplishment of many of our desires, for example to communicate freely with others and to learn through them about ourselves. And he might argue that although some defenders of negative liberty held the views about self-knowledge that Taylor rightly attacks, he himself does not.[12]

In any case, the central question for the liberal throughout the history of liberalism has been one of how and where the frontiers are to be fixed between individual freedom and state interference. How does Berlin conceive the answer to this question? Is negative freedom (however it is to be precisely defined) for him an absolute value that is to be ensured before any other? Or is it a value among many that must be taken into account in the constitution of a state?

As might be expected from even a cursory knowledge of Berlin's complex conception of human values, one cannot find a simple answer in his work. On the one hand, he sometimes writes as if negative liberty is just one among the many 'ultimate' values human beings possess;

'positive liberty' is another; none is 'absolute' or to be favoured over the others; each is an ingredient (and only that) in the pattern of life we desire. This is the pluralism we have seen Berlin praise Machiavelli for discovering: freedom is not the only value human beings have; it is not 'superior' to, or more 'true' than, other values, such as happiness or loyalty or economic security. 'The issue,' Berlin writes,

> is more complex and painful. One freedom may abort another; one freedom may obstruct or fail to create conditions which make other freedoms, or a larger degree of freedom, or freedom of more persons possible; positive and negative freedom may collide . . . But beyond all these there is an acuter issue: the paramount need to satisfy the claims of other, no less ultimate values: justice, happiness, love, the realisation of capacities to create new things and experiences and ideas, the discovery of the truth.[13]

On this view, then, the distribution of these many, competing values is a matter of balance, of intelligent adjustment, case by case, as each situation demands, with no guarantee that each value will be satisfied to the same degree as the others. This is presumably the reason why Berlin could write that the New Deal was 'the most constructive compromise between individual liberty and economic security which our time has witnessed'.[14] Even if negative liberty – freedom from interference by others – was lost to some degree under the New Deal by the rich and by businessmen, the situation as a whole realised a blend of values which was preferable as a total pattern to that offered by other blends, such as one which would preserve existing negative liberties and contain uncontrolled private enterprise and mass un-employment.

On the other hand, Berlin also seems to sympathise with the position that freedom should be ensured before other social values are. Free-dom, he writes, is valuable because, as we saw earlier, 'the necessity of choosing between absolute claims is an inescapable characteristic of the human condition' and is therefore not just a means but an end in itself: 'to be free to choose and not to be chosen for, is an inalienable ingredient in what makes human beings human'; this fact 'underlies both the positive demand to have a voice in the laws and practices of the society in which one lives, and to be accorded an area, artificially carved out if need be, in which one is one's own master.'

If one has less than this amount of freedom from interference one is 'dehumanised': This is a fact, Berlin claims, not perhaps like a fact that can be verified by observation, but a truth about the concepts and categories we use to interpret the world. Sheer indifference to freedom is not compatible with being human. This conception has not always prevailed – Vico has shown that our concepts and categories of interpretation have changed over time – but it is a fact about how we now happen to conceive the world.[15]

When Berlin speaks in this way, as he does often, it seems he is claiming that freedom is *not* on a par with other values we treasure. On this view, freedom is of prior importance, a more fundamental aspect of humanity; values other than freedom may override freedom only in order to secure greater freedom; the realisation of values like happiness, mercy, efficiency could not compensate for the loss of liberty.

In other words, Berlin does not claim that negative liberty in general must be preserved at any cost. His answer to the question of the place of negative liberty in a desirable society seems to be, rather, that at any time *some* negative liberties must be preserved – an example might be the freedom from arbitrary arrest – but that some of these may be overridden for the sake of other, more pressing values. There is no general answer available to the question of which negative liberties should be present at any given time. For example, developing countries that lack productive resources might understandably claim that the negative liberties granted by them to entrepreneurs should differ from those in an advanced country like the United States.

Berlin's view expresses a distrust of general formulas and principles which pretend to offer universal – as opposed to concrete and specific – and final or permanent – as contrasted with temporary and tentative – claims or solutions. None of this implies, however, as some of his critics have urged, that Berlin is an indecisive liberal who distrusts efforts to solve political problems. Berlin is claiming, instead, that different, unpredictable problems arise in different circumstances and at different times and that they demand solutions that are appropriate to their situation; solutions that purport to be permanent and general, he thinks, are rarely 'solutions'. Each situation, he thinks, calls for its own policy, not the automatic application of abstract 'keys' or theoretical principles that are supposed to be 'guaranteed' to solve all political problems wherever they arise. Nor does his view entail that no radical or fundamental changes should be undertaken in society. It is of course not clear what the radical's call for 'fundamental changes' means; nor does Berlin analyse in detail what he means by a 'solution' to a deep human problem. But if Berlin's claim about social and political problems does not exclude the attempt to introduce broad changes in social arrangements, then the issue turns on what concrete information we possess about the political situation under discussion. As such, Berlin's point about the complexity of social problems might be helpfully applied both to the arguments of those who seek 'radical' change and of those who seek social reform, and might act as a corrective or an encouragement to both.

V

Still, there are important questions that remain to be answered within the liberal tradition advocated by Berlin. The complex social arrangements of the modern liberal society have often compelled its members to lead unimaginative and mechanical lives, filled with drudgery and monotony. Doesn't such a state of affairs mock liberal ideals? In *Against the Current*, the essay on Georges Sorel discusses a recent thinker – he died in 1922 – who closely examined this problem. According to Berlin, Sorel realised that the eighteenth-century confidence in 'scientific', rational politics – once a progressive faith used to attack conservatism – had, in his day, itself become the orthodoxy, expressed in the triumph of the technocratic society, with its experts and specialists, in Berlin's phrase its 'bureaucratic organisation of human lives'.

Sorel deplored this development: As Berlin describes him, he loathed the bourgeoisie, the flatness of their lives, their materialism and hedonism; for him they were 'squalid earthworms', sunk in vulgarity and boredom in the midst of mounting affluence.' He hated the technological disciplines that were beginning to dominate business and politics in his day, run by narrow specialists and dedicated to adjusting men to the new social order; he felt that humanitarian democracy robbed men of their most distinctive characteristics, their need to express themselves, to rise above the norm, to find dignity in fulfilling work.

The desire to satisfy this need is what Berlin claims underlay Sorel's continuous search for a group, or a class, which would 'redeem humanity, or at least France, from mediocrity and decay' – what Berlin points out is now called a 'counterculture'. The desire drove him, with 'the moral fury of perpetual youth', from one extreme to another in the service of this cause. He was successfully a Marxist, a Dreyfusard, a royalist, an anti-Dreyfusard, a Bolshevik and an admirer of Mussolini. He eventually discovered that the proletariat was the only truly creative class of society and thenceforth struggled to formulate the energising social myth of a general strike that would

> call for the total overthrow of the entire abominable world of calculation, profit and loss, the treatment of human beings and their powers as commodities, as material for bureaucratic manipulation, the world of illusory consensus and social harmony, or economic or sociological experts no matter what master they serve, who treat men as subjects of statistical calculations, malleable 'human material, forgetting that behind such statistics there are living human beings'.

Although Sorel was largely ignored by the workers, he spoke to them above all of defiance, resistance against devitalising forces of mechanisation and technology, against 'those who turned every vital impulse into abstract formulas, Utopian blueprints, learned dust.'

Berlin's essay skilfully retrieves Sorel from his reputation as an eccentric, a fanatic, an intellectual misfit; it establishes that Sorel's ideas anticipated those of later men like Franz Fanon and Che Guevara, as well as the disaffected 'grimmer dynamiters of the present', that 'his words still have power to upset.' Berlin has written elsewhere of his own reaction to the social developments denounced by Sorel, which he believes have intensified in the vast totalitarian regimes of our time, as well as in some of the new sovereign states of Africa and Asia, governments that hold that individuals are incapable of making choices, of raising upsetting questions, governments that employ 'the calm moral arithmetic of cost effectiveness which liberates decent men from qualms',[16] and that treat the solitary questioner as 'a patient to be cured'.[17]

To be sure, Berlin does not condone Sorel's remedy: He is aware that violent means or the loss of existing liberties, or of habits of courtesy and decency, can spoil laudable ends. He is aware that, as he once expressed it,

> a humane cause promoted by means that are too ruthless is in danger of turning into its opposite, liberty into oppression in the name of liberty, equality into a new, self-perpetuating oligarchy to defend equality,

26

justice into crushing of all forms of nonconformity, love of men into hatred of those who oppose brutal methods of achieving it.[18]

We must not, he says, be magnetised to security or to happiness at the expense of existing liberties; we must be tolerant of idiosyncrasy, even inefficiency; we must live with 'logically untidy, flexible, and even ambiguous' political adjustments: These will, he says, 'always be worth more than the neatest and most delicately fashioned imposed pattern'.[19]

Berlin seems to sympathise with the social perceptions of thinkers like Sorel (and Bakunin) who make a devastating case against the miserable lives people are often forced to lead – in spite of their possession of liberty. It is commonly argued that the remedy for such developments lies with government, that private associations will fail to provide solutions. But here Berlin might balk. He deeply fears the mentality that looks to government to solve human problems, and indeed much of his political writing is addressed to the classical question of the individual's rights against the state. The emphasis in the writings of anarchists on achieving desirable social results through cooperation and voluntary means seems more congenial to him than the insights of some socialists and 'planners', provided that individual liberties are secure. More generally, greater respect for charity, openness, decency – as against a tradition that views society as 'a trading company held together solely by contractual obligations' – might permit, he thinks, the liberal society to remould its institutions so that the continual agony of balance and compromise is lessened. But these will not disappear altogether. We must therefore be prepared to endure the agony of political choice, which, he thinks, is just a special instance of the lesson, sprung upon the Western intellect most vividly by Machiavelli, that in both our personal and social lives, beneath the surface of an apparently clear pattern of moral values lie contradiction, collision, conflict.

This conclusion, as Berlin's essay in *Against the Current* shows, is strikingly like the ideas of that nineteenth-century radical Alexander Herzen, the 'Russian Voltaire' as Berlin calls him, the great populist who, twice imprisoned by tsarist authorities, fled Russia in 1847 and spent the rest of his life wandering about Germany, Italy, France and England, composing sharp analyses of European political affairs in the turbulent years following the revolution of 1848, in journals he founded and subsidised.

As Berlin describes him, Herzen was equipped with unusual independence of mind and an exceptionally keen and self-critical awareness of the twin agonies of choice analysed by Berlin: He occupied throughout his life a thankless, middle ground of moderation amid the political convulsions surrounding him, and was morally offended by both the callous men to his right and the boorish and hysterical young revolutionaries to his left. He fought all of his life for freedom and yet he permitted himself to wonder whether men, after all, really did want freedom, or whether the men who did were not, in contradiction to his deepest convictions, exceptions in their species, like fish that fly.

His ideas were constantly tested and refined by self-questioning and by events themselves. He consistently believed, as Berlin quotes him, that 'art, and the summer lightning of individual happiness' are the 'only real goods we have'. It is indeed irresistible to compare Herzen and Berlin in a less superficial manner. Both are sharp, urbane, multiply talented writers, 'talking' writers resistant to academic classification. Both are highly self-critical, sceptical of their scepticism, combining deep respect for learning and a sense of the great importance of ideas in our lives, with a concern for dignity and decency. Both are thinkers who rest their views on common sense and experience and who are willing to accept the metaphysician's taunt that they are abdicating their responsibilities in favour of 'brute facts'.

Both fear 'the despotism of formulas' and continuously stress the diversity and incompatibility of human values and the inescapable predicament of choosing between them. Both are moralists who openly respect the free play of individual temperament, exuberance, variety, independence, distinction. Both recognise that, as Herzen wrote, 'one must open men's eyes, not tear them out', and ask that men be content with piecemeal, fallible, gradual solutions to their most pressing problems and not be fooled by metaphysical nostrums that require brutal methods of social reform.

Indeed, seen in this light, their works – ostensibly those of 'foxes' (to use the terminology of Berlin's famous essay on Tolstoy), or marvellously scattered intellects dispensing interesting and informed judgments on unconnected topics – have a striking affinity. An ironist would remark that they are indeed not foxes (who 'know many little things') but hedgehogs (who 'know one big thing') and the one thing they say again and again is that questions such as 'What is *the* goal of life?' or 'What is *the* meaning of history?' or 'What is *the* best way to live?' can receive no general answer – that is, that there is not, or should not be, any hedgehog's thesis about human affairs to expound.[20]

VI

We have already noted some of Berlin's central points that require further elucidation. In addition, several of his analyses of the freedom and unpredictability of human choice appear to undermine psychological determinism – the view that all our actions can be explained by general laws and information about our desires, preferences, and beliefs. He does not (nor does he intend to) disprove or conclusively refute psychological determinism. But this point is in need of refinement. We may be able to explain one aspect of a person's choice but not another. To take a common example, a young friend may be torn whether to become a poet or a mathematician. We may not be able to explain why our friend chose to become a poet rather than a mathematician, but we can explain why he did not become a clown or a pilot. In view of his background, certain choices were not plausible for him. In his writings Berlin emphasises freedom, but his view of the interplay between freedom and the conditions that restrain freedom deserves further development.

Another element in his thought that needs clarification concerns the nature of history. Berlin rarely fails to denounce interpretations of history as conforming to laws or rules or inexorable trends; this, he says, would run counter to our view of man as free, creative, and responsible for his actions. Yet when he comments sympathetically on the work of Vico, Berlin himself agrees that history is an account of gradual changes in ideas, ideals, forms of life and cultures, along with the self-transformation of humanity. History can be understood, he seems to say, as a process of self-correction, for men seek ideas and patterns of life that are adequate to their needs and their dominant questions; when these outlooks begin to collapse, men discard them in favour of better ones. This, he adds, is a fact we can discover with the help of imaginative reconstruction and empathy. How do we reconcile these views? It seems Berlin is not offering us a general theory of history in the sense that Newton offered us a general theory of matter; he is, rather, giving us a picture or general approach to history. The issue of when general pictures (as against theories) of history are acceptable, tenable, or indeed indispensable needs clarifying.

A final issue in Berlin's thought that might be usefully amplified also derives from his discussion of Vico. Berlin agrees with Vico that we can grasp the values of alien cultures with the help of sympathetic imagination. He can be interpreted as suggesting that once we do this, we realise that these values are not random preferences; they are rooted in deep human interests and needs, and expressed in different cultural settings. A theory of ethics based on shifting and often conflicting human interests seems implicit in Berlin's work and might be developed further as an alternative to theories grounded on a fixed or eternal 'human nature'.

However this may be, we must be grateful to Isaiah Berlin: as a philosopher, for puncturing shallow theories of man that ignore our freedom; as a historian of ideas, for exploring, with resilience, sympathy and lack of dogmatism, neglected ideas about man, and thereby reanimating misunderstood intellectual undercurrents of the past. In his recent as in his earlier work, Berlin presses home a conception of life that is at once morally invigorating and hopefully true, a view he himself admirably summarised when he once wrote that

> the principal obligation of human beings seems to me to consist in living their lives according to their own lights, and in developing whatever faculties they possess without hurting their neighbours, in realising themselves in as many directions as freely, variously and richly as they can, without worrying overmuch whether they are measuring up to the peaks in their own past history, without casting anxious looks to see whether their achievements reach the highest points reached by the genius of their neighbours, nor yet looking at other nations, or wondering whether they are developing precisely as they expect them to develop.[21]

CHAPTER 2

Philosophy and the History of Philosophy
David Pears

Oxford philosophy, when I returned to finish reading Greats after the war, was a confusing scene. In 1941 my tutor had led me through the history of ideas, starting with Plato. At first we took giant strides – the Greeks, Aquinas, Spinoza, Kant – but as we got closer to our own times, our steps became progressively shorter, and after two essays on F. H. Bradley I began to fear that we would never reach the present day. It was as if the tortoise had decided to put Zeno's thesis to the test. So one week I asked if I could write an essay on the verification principle. My tutor confessed that he had never read anything by Ayer, but he added that a friend of his had explored that avenue and had come back with the report that there was nothing at the end of it. I did not write the essay, but I enjoyed our leisurely review of the philosophers of the past. Even if I did not understand their problems, I could, at least, give their solutions a neat, systematic arrangement.

After the war my predicament was reversed. Most of my weekly essays were now about identifiable problems, but I no longer felt that I knew what counted as solutions to them. There were, of course, brilliant philosophers around, who seemed to know the answer to this central question, but they disagreed about the criterion of adequate solutions, except on one point – whatever it was, it was new. Austin and Ayer (whose works I was determined to study this time) both lectured on perception, Ayer defending, and Austin attacking phenomenalism, and, more interestingly for a student, Ayer offering systematic logical analysis, while Austin took his stand on undoctored ordinary language. Ryle was giving lectures which were soon to be published as *The Concept of Mind*, and in Cambridge Wittgenstein was reputed to have found an altogether new way of philosophising. But how were all these innovations related to one another? I did not know, and I felt like a

31

spectator in a crowd at an air show, watching extraordinary things going on above my head, but unable even to tell whether they were part of the same act.

Isaiah Berlin's role in this period of transition was a special one. He was involved in the controversy about verificationism, but he was able to distance himself from it and see it in its place in the history of ideas. So when we argued about it, he would punctuate the discussion with asides, like certain jazz pianists, or like those characters in Roman comedy, who, without withdrawing from the action, interpret it in oblique remarks addressed to the audience. Now philosophers who are committed to a philosophical thesis seldom care about its precursors, while those who have a sense of history often suffer from what Wittgenstein calls 'loss of problems'. But it was obvious to Berlin's pupils and friends that the natural tenor of his thought avoided both these extremes. His concentration on a finely formulated problem would always be informed by his awareness of its place in some larger system of ideas and ultimately of its place, if it had one, in human life. There was none of the desiccation and brittleness which have made analytical philosophy so unpopular with those who do not understand it.

His involvement in the controversy about verificationism had begun in the 1930s. Towards the end of that decade he, Austin and Ayer had belonged to a group which discussed the question whether all our knowledge of the world and of other people in it could be reduced to our knowledge of our own personal experiences. If phenomenalism can be believed, each of us starts alone with his or her own sense-data, which we then have to use in prodigious feats of construction in order to avoid solipsism. However, this dilemma – construction or solipsism – would be ill founded if there were something wrong with the phenomenalist's account of our original predicament, or, perhaps, with the very concept of a sense-datum. So the pre-war discussions focused on the way in which sense-data were introduced and the use which was then supposed to be made of them.

In 1946, at the end of one of Austin's lectures, I overheard one undergraduate saying to another, 'Well, he has made phenomenalism impossible for us, but what has he left us in its place?' They expected another theory and they failed to see that Austin had no theory, unless the classifications that had proved themselves over the centuries and had won recognition in ordinary language amounted to a theory. All this, no doubt, had been thrashed out in those discussions in the 1930s, but the war had interrupted the downward percolation of ideas and that was one of the reasons why we found the transition to the new philosophy so baffling. Another reason was Wittgenstein's secretiveness. He was by then a legendary figure, with one enigmatic book to his name, the *Tractatus Logico-Philosophicus*, but he was known to have since worked out another philosophy, which he shared with a small circle of pupils and friends but had not revealed to the rest of the world. Iris Murdoch and Elizabeth Anscombe had attended his classes and we expected some revelation from them.

Soon after the war Berlin gave a seminar with Austin on sense-data. It was the kind of event that occurs more often in fiction than in real life, because it neatly pulled together several different lines of development and sent them on, with certain deflections, into the future. Anthony Powell uses a party for this purpose in *The Music of Time* and the seminar was equally dramatic. It offered the spectacle of a vehement confrontation between Anscombe and Austin which was sustained week after week. They both opposed the kind of phenomenalism that Ayer was defending at the time in his lectures and they both subscribed to the vaguely formulated thesis that 'sense-data are not objects'. But they meant quite different things by it.

What Austin meant was that the subtle differences marked by qualifying verbs in ordinary language were lost when the verbs were replaced by the single, levelling noun, 'sense-data'. If, as Berlin put it, 'things don't always look what they seem', the verbs should be retained and the translation into the language of sense-data should be resisted. Anscombe rejected this line of argument and attacked Ayer's theory from a different angle. When she denied the status of objects to sense-data, she meant that they were not basic objects which could be described independently of any connection with the physical world. So while Austin regarded Ayer's building-blocks as a crude philosophical fabrication, Anscombe accepted them, but not their proposed function, because, according to her, they depended on the very structures that they were supposed to be used to produce. Her criticism was an application of Wittgenstein's still unpublished Private Language Argument.

Berlin attacked Ayer's theory from a third angle, different from both Austin's and Anscombe's. If physical objects really could be reduced to sense-data, then unobserved physical objects with observed effects would be sets of possible sense-data causing sets of actual sense-data.

But how could a mere possibility cause anything actual? A theory with this absurd consequence must surely be rejected.

This criticism of phenomenalism can be seen as part of Berlin's general rejection of positivism, or it can be taken more narrowly as a deep objection to a particular theory of perception. In the 1930s he had gone along with positivism only to this extent: as an instrument with a limited use, puncturing intellectual inflations, it was salutary, but as a general ontological theory it was unacceptable. But does this particular argument achieve its specific goal, the refutation of phenomenalism? That is the question.

It was an argument which had been used before against Ayer, but Berlin generalised it and deployed it on a broader front. How could a statement about an unobserved tree in the quad be equivalent to a hypothetical statement about the sense-data that we would get if we looked at it? Surely there must have been something already going on out there before we went to look at it, if only to give us an *it* to go and look at? And when we did go and look at it, how could that suddenly change its status from the merely possible to the actual? Even a philosopher who believed that something could be produced out of nothing would hardly be prepared to say that it was produced by something else acting on nothing. So the phenomenalist's hypothetical statements about sense-data could only be ascribing dispositions to us as observers rather than to the objects observed by us. Instead of expressing the tendencies of objects to produce sense-data in us, they must really be expressing our tendencies to generate them. But in what circumstances? If there were not already a stone out there for Dr Johnson to kick, why should he expect to feel the shock of impact in his toes?

This criticism was published by Berlin in an article, 'Empirical Propositions and Hypothetical Statements', which appeared in 1950 when he was well on the move away from the rather arid zone in which British analytic philosophy remained for so long. The printed version does not capture the sharpness and exuberance of his objections as he developed them in live discussion. When I argued the point with him on a beach in Italy, he asked me if I really believed that a friend, who had just swum out of sight behind a rock, now amounted to no more than our own possible sense-data. That, he said, would be hard to believe even about his body, but he also had a mind and a point of view from which it was *me* who had disappeared behind the rock. I had been defending Ayer and arguing that one must not interpret the sense-datum language in exactly the same way as the physical object language. At least, when we see a wave sink a boat, our later sense-data depend on, but are not directly caused by, our earlier ones, and actualities can depend on possibilities even if they cannot be directly caused by them.

I realised later that my defence had been inadequate. No doubt, phenomenalism is not immediately destroyed by the rhetorical question, 'How can the actual be caused by the merely possible?' But behind this question there were, as Berlin had seen, other deeper issues. Can anything possess nothing but dispositional properties? If so, what would sustain them in existence, as the molecular structure of a metal sustains its disposition to expand when heated? More fundamentally, could such an object ever be located in space? If at this point the phenomenalist concedes Berlin's point, that they would really be *our* dispositions, the same questions arise about us.

These criticisms of phenomenalism were rich in implications which were to be worked out in the next two decades. At the time it was not clear to most of us how much lay latent in them waiting to be developed. One of the things that makes the history of philosophy so difficult is that, when new ideas first begin to make their influence felt, they often remain partly in the air and have not yet fully taken up their abode in a particular thinker's mind. In this case there was also something else which added to the general difficulty: the ideas served to support the common-sense view that the world consists of physical objects in space, and it is not easy to separate a philosopher's refusal to abandon that view (Dr Johnson) from his understanding of the elaborate theory that is needed in order to defend it from the sceptic and from that false friend, the reductionist.

Certainly, Berlin saw further than his critics. But there was at that time a great reluctance among British philosophers to theorise in defence of common sense, a reluctance which owed much to the example set by Moore and Austin. It took the work of Strawson, Evans and many others to show exactly what was wrong with the phenomenalist's attempt to give us phenomenological space without physical space, or, as Berlin himself would put it, to make phenomenological space basic. It is interesting that in his article Berlin does not question the mentalisation of the subject which is presupposed by the phenomenalist's description of our original predicament. Yet the question was implicit in our conversation about the swimmer. If Berlin found the dispositions of physical objects unintelligible with nothing to sustain them, why not also the dispositions of our minds? Wittgenstein had long been arguing that the solipsist must admit that his body is one physical object among others in physical space, but the full development of his ideas on this matter was not yet available in print.

It is widely believed that Berlin abandoned analytic philosophy around this time and that his simultaneous publication of his final criticism of phenomenalism and of another article, 'Logical Translation', which questioned the whole programme of logical analysis, was a kind of clearing of his desk. He himself said, later, in his preface to the first volume of his selected writings, that he left philosophy for the history of ideas, and that the impetus for his move came from a conversation with H. M. Sheffer, the logician. He meant that he left *analytic* philosophy, because his interest in the philosophy of history, which started with his book on Marx in the middle 1930s, was something that he never abandoned. Sheffer had maintained that there are only two areas in which a philosopher can hope to add to the sum of human knowledge, logic and psychology. But, of course, Berlin's was no sudden conversion. I remember his telling me that he had contemplated the move while he was flying between London and Washington during the war. The planes were Dakotas, a successful transport with a very unreassuring appearance, and thin air just did not seem to offer enough resistance to keep them flying (like Kant's dove), and that, he realised, was what he felt about analytic philosophy.

However, he never made a complete break with it. Liberty, the topic of his Inaugural Lecture as Chichele Professor in Oxford (1959) could hardly be discussed without an analysis of the various meanings of the word and their interrelationships. His later article, 'From Fear and Hope Set Free' (1964) is a sustained analytical investigation of the often exaggerated connection between increased knowledge and increased freedom of action. More generally, the study of ideas of any complexity without an analysis of their contents or of the problems and solutions in which they figure is plainly impossible. In philosophy there is no straight choice between recording the history of ideas and analysing them and even having them. My experience as a student had soon taught me this obvious truth. So Berlin's description of his move, 'from philosophy to the history of ideas', should be taken as a short way of saying something that is really more complicated.

Consider, first, a well-known pattern into which philosophical problems tend to fall: some lie close to the centre of human life, while others lie further out and are often dismissed by the uninitiated as 'irrelevant'. People care about the problems in the inner ring – for example, about philosophical theories of liberty, because they shape their political systems, and about philosophical theories of freedom of action, because they determine the incidence of punishment. But philosophical theories of perception lie far out on the periphery. Imagine phenomenalism starting a war! Well, of course, one can imagine a theory of perception starting a war of religion, if it had been seen as incompatible with some received doctrine. So the placing of philosophical problems in concentric rings is really relative to people's changing conceptions of the heart of the matter, but the fact is that philosophical theories of perception have always lain far out on the periphery.

Now the analytic philosophy in Britain in the mid-1930s was largely an import from Vienna, positivistic in tone and primarily concerned with the philosophy of perception and of science. So when Berlin moved away from it, he was moving towards the centre, where the connections between ideas and actions are denser and stronger. This is a move which any historian of ideas would naturally make, and, at least, as I have described the situation so far, it does not essentially involve the rejection of the analytic *method*. To put the point in another way, the analytic school did eventually extend its operations to more central topics, and if it had done so sooner, Berlin would have had one less reason for his move.

However, he would still have had other reasons which were not quite so closely connected with his abiding interest in history. Consider the fundamental question, why philosophers are impelled to pursue the peripheral problems which strike the uninitiated as 'irrelevant'. Presumably, they are not just teasing their uninformed critics and the force that drives them outwards from the centre cannot just be centrifugal, an affectation, perhaps, or just an experiment. To formulate the question in another way, what is the real nature of philosophy? If we put aside the historical by-products of this strangely marginal mode of thought, what is its residual essence?

Berlin's answer to this question, given in his paper 'The Purpose of Philosophy' (1962), indicates that he had more reasons than one for his move away from analytic philosophy. He accepts the Kantian view that all experience and thought are shaped by the categories we impose on them, and that the philosopher's task is to record these structural patterns and to analyse them. It is also – and here he differs from Kant – to trace their gradual changes from one age to the next. For example, today we categorise all events as at least non-purposively caused and so we find it hard to explain how a special class of events, human actions, can be independently originated; but this was not seen by Aristotle as a problem because it is one that could not be framed in his categories. Now Berlin's view of the philosopher's task still maintains something in common with the view that he was abandoning – it still involves analysis – but there are also two differences, each of which is connected with a further reason for his move away from analytic philosophy.

First, Berlin's interest lies not in the minutiae of language and thought but in their larger structural features. The function of these features is to express those modes of construing our experience which are so pervasive that we hardly notice them until philosophy identifies them for us. His investigations are, therefore, appropriately holistic, sweeping searches rather than narrowly concentrated scrutinies. This is one conspicuous difference between his work and both Ayer's and Austin's. There is also another, equally important, holistic trait which distinguishes his work from theirs: he believes that the way to understand any structural feature is to trace its development from earlier forms of thought. So a philosophical inquiry, as he conceives it, spreads itself on two distinct planes – laterally across a time-slice of human consciousness and backwards into the past. History has the last word.

His writing and, even more, his conversation is stamped with the same holistic pattern. The main point that he is making will be linked to many others, perhaps on both planes of the inquiry, and it will call on them, one by one, for support. The method is not linear argument but cumulative presentation. Listening to him is like watching an artist painting a picture with breath-taking rapidity. You want to say, 'Wait a moment; I don't quite understand what is going on in this corner', but each brush-stroke immediately helps and is helped by the next one. This is not just a stylistic trait but an essential feature of his thought.

Evidently, there were many reasons for his move away from the analytic philosophy of the 1940s. About one of them, the remoteness of its problems from central human interests, there is more to be said. When I look back on my conversations with him forty years ago, I am struck by two antithetical facts. First, the depth of his understanding of

38

contemporary philosophy was unequalled and I know that I did not really see what was going on until I talked to him about it. That was also the experience of several of my contemporaries. The second fact was that his understanding of the peripheral issues, with which the analytic philosophy of that period was preoccupied, was, from an emotional point of view, an achievement of sympathy. He himself did not feel compelled to follow the trail of a philosophical investigation however far it might lead him from the centre.

A philosopher who does feel this compulsion, as Wittgenstein evidently did, will, of course, place it at the centre with the other basic drives which he shares with the rest of humanity. He will, therefore, have a different conception of what counts as peripheral, and his response to the frequent complaint, that analytic philosophers waste their time on trivialities, will be that the goal of any commoner basic drive would appear trivial to someone who lacked it. What he has, and others lack, is something which makes it impossible for him to accept their explanations as final. He is, as Wittgenstein says, like a child who goes on questioning where adults see no room for a question. They, of course, will be irritated, because, though they too may have started life with this drive, it is forced into latency by education, and there are few in whom it manages to surface again later.

Berlin perfectly understood the shift in the concept of centrality which is experienced by those in whom this instinct does re-emerge, but it is doubtful whether he himself had experienced it. In the articles in which he discusses contemporary analytic solutions to fundamental problems in the philosophy of language and logic, there is a certain aloofness, or, at least, a detectable coolness, and I remember conversations in which he seemed to be distancing himself from the philosophy of the desert. He understood it perfectly, and his explanations of it were marvellously illuminating, but his understanding of it was intellectual and, on the emotional side, it was the product of sympathy rather than direct passion. So though his analyses of it were second to none, they were, to this extent the reactions of a historian rather than a complete participator, and his move away from it was natural and, perhaps, inevitable.

(1990)

CHAPTER 3

The Importance of Herder
Charles Taylor

I

Isaiah Berlin has helped to rescue Herder from his relative neglect by philosophers.[1] His seminal role in the creation of our post-Romantic thought and culture has gone largely unnoticed, at least in the English-speaking world. The fact that Herder is not the most rigorous of thinkers makes it perhaps easier to ignore him. But deeply innovative thinkers don't have to be rigorous to be the originators of important ideas. The insights they capture in striking images can inspire other, more philosophically exigent minds to more exact formulation. This was exemplified, I believe, in the relation of Herder to Hegel. The consequence has been that the earlier thinker drops out of sight, and the later has become the canonical reference point for certain seminal ideas, such as what I have called, following Berlin, the 'expressivist' understanding of the human person.[2]

This losing sight of the origins can be of more than historiographical significance. It may also be that we have still something important to learn from the original statement of certain foundational ideas that has yet to be captured in the recognised 'philosophical' formulations. I think this is true of another one of Herder's crucial contributions, his 'expressivist' theory of language. My (perhaps over-dramatic) claim is that Herder is the hinge figure, who originates a fundamentally different way of thinking about language and meaning. This way has had a tremendous impact on modern culture. It has not quite swept all before it, because there are still important segments of contemporary thought which resist these insights, but even they have been transformed in ways which can be traced to the Herder revolution.

I can't make good this claim across its whole extent here. My strategy will be rather to focus on a key passage of Herder, his rejection of Condillac's theory of the origin of language, and the related invocation of 'reflection' (*Besonnenheit*) as essential to language. I hope to be able to make visible in this microcosm certain basic themes and assumptions of our contemporary understanding of language.

I have called Herder a hinge figure. He swings our thought about language into a quite different angle. And as so often happens, the resultant change of perspective makes it hard to grasp just what has happened. People in the old and new perspectives tend to talk past each other, constantly translating the interlocutor's claims into their own terms, and thus distorting them.

The old perspective, which has a venerable pedigree, is the one which Wittgenstein attacks in the form of an influential statement by Augustine.[3] It can be defined in terms of its approach to the question of meaning. I'll call it 'designative'.[4] Words get their meaning in being used to designate objects. What they designate is their meaning. This age-old view gets a new lease of life in the seventeenth century with the theories of Hobbes and Locke, where it gets interwoven with the new Way of Ideas, and from the amalgam emerges a powerful and influential picture of the place of language in human thought.

In the following century a new question arises. In keeping with the eighteenth-century preoccupation with origins, which we can also see reflected, e.g., in theories of the evolution of society by Smith and Ferguson, there is a growing interest in explaining how language could have arisen. Condillac's answer, one of the most influential, draws on Locke's designative theory. In his *Essai sur l'Origine des Connoissances Humaines*,[5] he offers a fable, a 'just so' story, to illustrate how language might have arisen. It is a fable of two children in a desert. We assume certain cries and gestures as natural expressions of feeling. These are what Condillac calls 'natural signs'. By contrast, language uses 'instituted signs'. Condillac's story is meant to explain how the second emerged out of the first. He argues that each child, seeing the other, say, cry out in distress, would come to see the cry as a sign of something (e.g., what causes distress). He would then be able to take the step of using the sign to refer to the cause of distress. The first sign would have been instituted. The children would have their first word. Language would be born. The lexicon would then increase slowly, term by term.

Herder in his *Abhandlung über den Ursprung der Sprache*[6] zeroes in on this story and declares it utterly inadequate. As an account of origins, it presupposes just what we want to explain. It takes the relation of signifying for granted, as something the children already grasp, or that

41

can unproblematically occur to them: 'ils parvinrent insensiblement à faire', says Condillac, 'avec réflexion, ce qu' ils n'avoient fait que par instinct.'[7] Condillac, says Herder, 'hat das ganze Ding Sprache schon vor der ersten Seite seines Buches erfunden vorausgesetzt.' His explanation amounts to saying, 'es entstanden Worte, weil Worte da waren, ehe sie da waren.'

The problem is that Condillac endows his children already from the beginning with the capacity to understand what it is for a word to stand for something, what it is therefore to talk about something with a word. But *that* is just the mysterious thing. Anyone can be taught the meaning of a word, or even guess at it, or even invent one, once they have language. But what is this capacity which we have and animals don't to endow sounds with meaning, to grasp them as referring to, as used to talk about things?

Here is where the two perspectives come apart, and the two sides can talk past each other. What is not easy is to define just what Herder thinks Condillac presupposes and fails to explain. To get this clear would bring us to the animating centre of Herder's new outlook.

But this is not easy to do, because the rival perspective still has a residual hold on us. To grasp Herder's outlook, we have to do two things, against which there is still some resistance in our intellectual culture.

(1) First you have to place yourself in the standpoint of the speaker, and ask yourself what he has to understand in order to learn a new word. In other words, you have to go beyond the standpoint of the external observer, from which it might seem sufficient to account for the learning as the setting up of a connection between word and thing, such that the subject's use of the word can be correlated to the appearances of the thing. One can remain in this external standpoint, even while developing a very sophisticated theory linking words to things, or descriptions to truth-conditions, which invokes the subject's other meanings, and his beliefs and desires.

These last phrases are meant to evoke the influential theories of Donald Davidson, whom I consider to be a prominent contemporary representative of the camp Herder was attacking. He belongs in a sense to the Locke–Condillac tradition. This tradition has, of course, gone through a profound transformation since the eighteenth century. It has become much more sophisticated, and in some respects it has taken on board certain discoveries of Herder.

Nevertheless, there is an important continuity in this sense: Davidson insists that when I understand you, I can be seen to be applying a theory of the meaning of your utterances, which maps these on to features of the objective world. The descriptive kernel of your utterances maps onto their truth conditions. Davidson is quite clear that once I have such a theory which enables me with tolerable accuracy to make sense of you, and within limits to predict your behaviour, there can be no further question whether you and I understand these utterances in the same way. Subjective understanding of meaning (which Davidson, unlike behaviourists, doesn't want to deny) must be exhaustively grasped in terms of truth conditions, along with illocutionary forces and the apparatus of speech act theory. Questions about it can be answered *only* in these terms.[8]

This is not the relatively uncontroversial thesis that where there is a difference between our subjective understandings of a term, this is almost bound to come out somewhere in a difference between the extensionally-defined truth conditions which we acknowledge for expressions employing this term. It is the much stronger claim that agreement about truth conditions is criterial for agreement in understanding. Put in terms of a popular science fiction scenario, the possibility that some sophisticated robot might be built out of transistors, which matched us in the correlations of 'utterance' to world, and yet might not *understand* anything, makes no sense on Davidson's view. And the same must be said of the scenario of exile, that we might meet up with a people, such that we could attribute truth conditions to parts of their utterances, and in this way co-ordinate our action with them and predict them, while on a deeper level there remains a profound gap between our conceptual schemes.[9]

To understand Herder's objection to Condillac, we have to take the 'inner' standpoint, that of the agent. That is, we cannot accept an account of what it is for a creature to possess language exclusively in terms of the correlations an observer could identify between its utterances, behaviour and surroundings. We have to try to define beyond this conditions of subjective understanding, because Herder's whole argument turns on a particular definition of these conditions.

(2) But this is not enough to get Herder's point. We can focus on understanding, and still take it as something obvious, unproblematical. This is in fact what Condillac and other designative theorists did. That words can stand for things is taken as something immediately

comprehensible. It's just a clever idea which can occur to someone, and after a while in a predicament like that of the children is pretty well bound to occur. What Herder did was to make us appreciate that this understanding doesn't go without saying; that other kinds of creatures would respond quite differently to the correlations between cry and danger; that acquiring this kind of understanding is precisely the step from not having to having language. It is therefore just this step that a theory of origins would have to explain.

Ironically, Herder does no better in explaining this. The objection has often been made,[10] but it doesn't dispose of his criticism. In respect of their common failure, Herder and Condillac are in good company. No one has come even close to explaining the origin of language. But by focusing on the framework understanding which language requires, Herder opened a new domain of insights into its nature. These have enabled us to get a better grasp of the essential conditions of language, which have in turn shown that theories like those of Locke and Condillac are untenable.

What Herder is doing, I want to claim, anticipates (and perhaps distantly influences, through many intermediaries) what Wittgenstein does when he lays out the background understanding we need to grasp an ostensive definition. What Wittgenstein's opponent takes as quite unproblematical and simple turns out to be complex and not necessarily present. Appreciating this fully blows the opponent's theory of meaning out of the water.

II

What then is Herder's point? What is the framework understanding which is necessary for language? I want to try to define this in my own terms, departing at first from Herder's terminology. I think it can best be defined in terms of a contrast. What Condillac's children have to grasp in order to learn a new word is different from what animals grasp when they learn to respond to signals. For instance, rats can be trained to respond differentially to different shapes and colours. And chimpanzees, as is well known, can learn not only to respond to much more elaborate signals, but also to emit them.

This kind of capacity to operate with signals was not always clearly distinguished from human language by eighteenth-century writers; and it is even more clearly assimilated to our language by contemporaries who are in the grip of the external perspective, as the discussion about chimp language attests. Central to Herder's point, if I understand him, is that a crucial distinction has to be made here.

Both responding to signals and speaking are achievements. Some mastery is acquired. We can speak in either case of the animal/human getting it right or wrong. But in the first case, getting it right is responding to or making the signal as appropriate to carry out some task or get some result. It's right to go through the door with the triangle, not the square, because that gets the cheese. Signalling 'want banana' has been made right, because it gets the banana, or perhaps attention. To learn to use the signal is to learn to apply it appropriately in the furtherance of some non-linguistically-defined purpose or task.

The complex hyphenated adjective here is crucial. The rightness of the signal is defined by success in a task, where this success is not in turn defined in terms of the rightness of the signal. The relation is uni-directional.

But this is clearly not the case with some of the uses of human language. Consider a gamut of activities, including disinterested scientific description, articulating one's feelings, the evocation of a scene in poetry, a novelist's description of character. A metaphor someone coins is right, profound. There is a kind of 'getting it right' here. But in contrast to animal signalling, this can't be explained in terms of success in some task not itself linguistically defined.

Otherwise put, if we want to think of a task or goal which would help to clarify the rightness of words which occur in the human activities just mentioned, it would have itself to be defined in terms like truth, descriptive adequacy, richness of evocation, or something of the sort. We can't define the rightness of word by the task without defining the task in terms of the rightness of the words. There is no unidirectional account which can translate out rightness of word in terms of some independently-defined form of success. Rightness can't be reductively explained.

These activities define what I want to call a 'linguistic dimension'. To attribute these activities to some creature is to hold that it is sensitive to some such irreducible forms of rightness in the signs it deploys. A creature is operating in the linguistic dimension when it can use and respond to signs in terms of their truth, or descriptive rightness, or power to evoke some mood, or recreate a scene, or express some emotion, or carry some nuance of feeling, or in some such way to be 'le mot juste'. To be a linguistic creature is to be sensitive to irreducible issues of rightness. This is not to say that they are always, even usually raised. We just talk and understand. But it means that it can raise them, understand them when raised, and frequently defend its unreflecting practice ex post by articulating reasons relevant to this issue ('of course, I used the right word, because I meant . . .'). Whether a creature is in the linguistic dimension in this sense isn't a matter of what correlations hold between the signals it emits, its behaviour and surroundings – the kind of things the proponents of chimp language focus on. It is a question of subjective understanding, of what rightness consists in for it, *qua* what a word is right.

From this point of view, a creature acquires language in the human sense when it enters the linguistic dimension. The rat who learns to get the cheese by going through the door with the red triangle is not yet in this dimension, because the rightness of response is defined by what gets the cheese. And similarly when one bird in a flock emits a characteristic cry of danger on perceiving a predator: if we want to speak of 'rightness' in connection with this unlearned behaviour, it is because cry and response together get the flock out of danger.

The gap between these cases and human language is perhaps clear enough. People are more tempted to believe that the chimpanzees who learn to signal in American Sign Language possess something very much like human language. It would be a mistake here to be prematurely dogmatic, but does the evidence force us to suppose that some sense of irreducible rightness is playing a role here? Or could we just explain the performance as a very elaborate and impressive case of signal learning, where the rightness is to be understood in terms of the responses of the trainer?

The question at least needs to be asked. And to this end, we have to distinguish the issue of irreducible rightness from other features of human language, which chimps undoubtedly do exhibit, but which seem to be separable from it:

(1) Combinatorial relations. What's impressive about the chimps as against lower animals is that they can learn the sign for 'want' and signs for 'banana', 'apple', etc., and then combine these appropriately. Building phrases out of components is a crucial feature of human language, remarked on by Humboldt and Chomsky, and central to theories like those of Davidson. Along with the possibility of endless

46

recursion, it allows us to use finite means to infinite ends, in Humboldt's famous phrase. Impressive as this is, it is not the same thing as operating in the linguistic dimension.

(2) Play. Chimps are sometimes said to play with their repertory. They emit the signals they have been taught even outside a context of communication with the trainer. This kind of activity, running through bits of one's repertory when not using it with serious intent, is common among higher mammals, and involves all sorts of other capacities besides signalling. Once again, it is clearly distinct from the issue of linguistic rightness.

(3) Chimps not only respond to signals, but also learn to produce them, unlike other higher mammals we train. But this achievement also has no necessary connection with the linguistic dimension. It signifies only that whatever signalling means for chimps, they can give them as well as respond to them.

(4) Curiously, there is another feature of human language on which chimps seem further from us than more fully domesticable animals like dogs and horses. This is something I want to talk about more below; it is the way that language creates a kind of bond, of common understanding between those who share it. As Vicki Hearne has pointed out,[11] something similar gets set up between a dog and its trainer, a rapport we don't seem to be able to establish with chimps: the adult Washoe was no friend of her human caretakers, as she tellingly describes.

One of the reasons for doubting that the linguistic dimension plays any role in chimp signing is the absence of any of its other candidate manifestations, beyond just pointing to and calling for the object. For a human language, it is pervasive, and it is a constitutive part of all sorts of activities and purposes beyond the merely designative. Take a ritual, for example, like a rain dance. If we thought of it just as a tool which has proved handy in bringing on rain (or thought to be so proved), then we could construe it as an elaborate signal. But plainly the very sense of its efficacy is bound up with its felt rightness as evocative of, or akin to the forces producing rain. This kind of 'sympathetic magic' can only be practised by creatures which are already in the linguistic dimension.

Or again, think of the expressive dimension of human speech. As we converse, even about the most severely 'factual' matters, we establish our stance, and our footing with the interlocutor, by the way we stand and speak. We take up an 'objective' stance, for instance, coldly examining the objects under review, and this emerges in our style of speech, and the words we use, while at the same time we hold our interlocutor at a distance with our aloof air; or else perhaps we invite him warmly into a brotherhood of the initiate, distinct from the surrounding 'unscientific' world. We both take up and broadcast these stances through our expressive behaviour, and that means that another species of properly linguistic rightness is in play. For we have to distinguish the way in which my severe mien, and choice of neutral words, express my aloofness towards you, from the way in which my facial twitches or trembling may show you my agitation. The first is genuinely expression, and it is a condition on this that, if perhaps at an entirely unarticulated level, these behaviours carry the meaning of aloofness for me; whereas nothing of the sort need hold for the second. In other words, however 'unconscious' I may be of what I'm doing, I must be sensitive to the rightness of this mien as expressing aloofness, my stance must be reflecting this sensitivity, if we are to speak of expression.

But this expressive dimension, which is inseparable from any human conversation, seems utterly absent from the signing of chimps; and this is perhaps another reason to question whether they are beyond mere signalling.

We can bring out the main distinction in still another way. For full language users, even when they are using words just to signal, a question can arise about the intentional description of the thing signalled. I make you aware of mortal danger just in time by calling out: 'Watch out for the bull!', or perhaps on another occasion just 'Tiger!' There is an answer to the question, what the first locution commands you to do, or what the second signal word exclamation describes. That is why Quine can raise the issue he does about the sense of my informant's utterance 'Gavagai'.[12] But there is no sense to the question whether the red triangle for the rat means 'run here', or 'cheese', or 'run here for cheese', or 'forward' or whatever; any more than we can ask whether the bird cry means 'danger', rather than 'skedaddle'. If we want to talk of 'meaning' here, we will be tempted to describe the 'meaning' in terms of the response aroused, as Mead does;[13] but this assimilation just ignores the whole issue of the linguistic dimension (and incidentally causes trouble for Mead, but that would take us too far afield.)

It's a consequence of this that we can speak of human language users as having a gamut of illocutionary forces in their repertoire. For this

requires that we distinguish linguistic meaning from action undertaken, and these in turn from the result encompassed (the 'perlocu-
tionary effect', in Austin's terminology,[14] distinctions which get no
purchase on the bird's cry.

III

I have taken a long excursus from my discussion of Herder, but my aim
has been to explain better the basis for his objection to Condillac. The
connection is this: Herder sees that what is essential if the children are
to learn to take their cries as words is that they come to function in the
linguistic dimension. That is, of course, my way of putting it. What I am
trying to gloss in these terms is Herder's notion of 'reflection'. It is
reflection which enables us to be language users. 'Der Mensch in den
Zustand von Besonnenheit gesetzt, der ihm eigen ist, und diese
Besonnenheit (Reflexion) zum ersten Mal frei wirkend, hat Sprache
erfunden.'[15]

Herder then glosses this notion of reflection in his own 'just so' story
about the invention of the first word. And he does it in a fashion which I
have imitated, by contrasting the language user's response to a target
object from that of pre-linguistic creatures. A particular thing, say a
lamb, figures in the world of various animals in characteristic ways: as
prey for the 'hungry wolf on its scent', or the 'bloodlicking lion'; as a
sexual partner for the 'ram in heat'. For other animals, who have no
need for sheep, the lamb passes by barely noticed. For all these
creatures, the lamb can figure only as relevant to some (non-linguistic)
purpose.

Herder's reflection is the capacity to focus on the lamb in a way
which is no longer tributary to any such purpose. This is its negative
characterisation. Positively, what is it? How does the lamb figure as
object of the reflective stance? It is recognised as a being of a certain
type through a distinguishing mark (*Merkmal*). This mark in Herder's
story is its bleating. And indeed, some onomatopoeic imitation of
bleating could well have been the first word for lamb, he thinks. In
other words, in the reflexive stance the lamb is first recognised *as* a
lamb; it is first recognised as an object rightly classed as 'the bleating
one'. An issue of rightness arises, which cannot be reduced to success
in some life-task. This for Herder is inseparable from language. It is
defined by this capacity to focus on objects by recognising them, and
this creates, as it were, a new space around us. Instead of being

overcome by the ocean of sensations as they rush by us, we are able to distinguish one wave, and hold it in clear, calm attention. It is this new space of attention, of distance from the immediate instinctual significance of things, which Herder wants to call 'reflection'.[16]

This is what he finds missing in Condillac's account. Condillac does have a more sophisticated idea of the move from animal to human signs than Locke. Animals respond to natural and 'accidental' signs (e.g., smoke is an 'accidental' sign of fire, and clouds of rain). Humans have also 'instituted' signs. The difference lies in the fact that by means of these latter humans can control the flow of their own imagination, whereas animals passively follow the connections which are triggered off in them by the chain of events.[17] There is obviously some link between Herder's description of our interrupting the 'ocean of sensations' and this Condillaquian idea of taking control. But what is still missing in the French thinker is any sense that the link between sign and object might be fundamentally different when one crosses the divide. It is still conceived in a very reified way, typical of the followers of Locke, a connection which is there in a thing-like fashion, such that the only issue allowed is whether it drives us or we drive it. Condillac belongs to the mode of thought which conceives language as an instrument, a set of connections which we can use to construct or control things. The point of language is to give us 'empire sur notre imagination'.[18] That a wholly different issue about rightness arises escapes him.

To raise this issue is to swing our perspective on language into a quite new angle. But this issue is easy to miss. Condillac was unaware that he had left anything out. He wouldn't have known where Herder was 'coming from', just as his heirs today, the proponents of chimp language, 'talking' computers and truth-conditional theories of meaning, find the analogous objections to their views gratuitous and puzzling. That is why Herder stands at a very important divide in the understanding of language in our culture.

To appreciate this better, let's examine further what Locke and Condillac were missing, from Herder's standpoint. Their reified view of the sign didn't come from their taking the external observer's standpoint on language, as the people I have just described as their heirs do in our day. On the contrary, they wanted to explain it very much 'from the inside', in terms of the agent's experience of self. They weren't trying out a behaviourist theory à la Skinner, in which linguistic rightness played no role. Rather they assumed this kind of rightness as unproblematically present. People introduced signs to 'stand for' or 'signify' objects (or ideas of objects), and once instituted these plainly could be rightly or wrongly applied. Their 'error' from a Herderian perspective was that they never got this constitutive feature into focus.

This failure is easy, one might almost say natural, because when we speak, and especially when we coin or introduce new terms, all this is in the background. It is what we take for granted or lean on when we coin expressions, viz., that words can 'stand for' things, i.e., that there is for us such a thing as irreducible linguistic rightness. The failure is so 'natural' that it has a venerable pedigree, as Wittgenstein showed in introducing a passage from Augustine as his paradigm for this mistake.

What is being lost from sight here is the background of our action, something we usually lean on without noticing. More particularly, what the background provides is being treated as though it were built in to each particular sign, as though we could start right off coining our first word and have this understanding of linguistic rightness already incorporated in it. Incorporating the background understanding about linguistic rightness into the individual signs has the effect of occluding it very effectively. As the background it is easy to overlook anyway; once we build it into the particular signs, we bar the way to recognising it altogether.

This is a fault of any designative theory of meaning. But the reification wrought by modern epistemology since Descartes and Locke, that is, the drive to objectify our thoughts and 'mental contents', if anything made it worse. The furniture of the mind was accorded a thing-like existence, something objects can have independent of any background. The occluding of the background understanding of the linguistic dimension by incorporating it into reified mental contents prepared the way for an elision of it altogether in those modern behaviourist and semi-behaviourist theories which try to explain thought and language strictly from the standpoint of the external observer. The associations of thing-like ideas were easily transposed into the stimulus-response connections of classical behaviourism. An obvious line of filiation runs from Locke through Helvétius to Watson and Skinner.

In this context, we can see that any effort to retrieve the background had to run against the grain of this important component of modern culture, the epistemology which was most easily associated with the scientific revolution. In fact, some of what we now recognise as the most important developments in philosophy in the last two centuries have been tending towards this retrieval, culminating in this century in different ways in the work of Heidegger and Wittgenstein, to name the most celebrated variants. When I called Herder a hinge figure, I meant that he had an important place as one of the origin points of this counter-thrust, in particular in relation to our understanding of language. This is not to say that he went all the way to this retrieval. On the contrary, as we shall see, he often signally failed to draw the conclusions implicit in the new perspective he adopted; but he did play a crucial role in opening this perspective.

There have been two very common, and related directions of argument in this counter-thrust, both of which can be illustrated in Herder's views on language. The first consists in articulating a part of the background, in such a form that our reliance on it in our thought, or perception, or experience, or understanding language, becomes clear and undeniable. The background so articulated is then shown to be incompatible with crucial features of the received doctrine in the epistemological tradition. We can find this type of argument with Heidegger, Wittgenstein, Merleau-Ponty, in our century. But the pioneer in this kind of argument, in whose steps all the others have followed, is Kant.

The arguments of the transcendental deduction can be seen in a number of different lights. But one way to take them is as a final laying to rest of a certain atomism of the input which had been espoused by empiricism. As this came to Kant through Hume, it seemed to be suggesting that the original level of knowledge of reality (whatever that turned out to be) came in particulate bits, individual 'impressions'. This level of information could be isolated from a later stage in which these bits were connected together, e.g., in beliefs about cause-effect relations. We find ourselves forming such beliefs, but we can by taking a stance of reflexive scrutiny (which we saw above is fundamental to the modern epistemology) separate the basic level from these too hasty conclusions we leap to. This analysis allegedly reveals, for instance, that nothing in the phenomenal field corresponds to the necessary connection we too easily interpolate between 'cause' and 'effect'.[19]

Kant undercuts this whole way of thinking by showing that it supposes, for each particulate impression, that it is being taken as a bit of potential information. It purports to be about something. This is the

background understanding which underpins all our perceptual discriminations. The primitive distinction recognised by empiricists between impressions of sensation and those of reflection amounts to an
acknowledgment of this. The buzzing in my head is discriminated from
the noise I hear from the neighbouring woods, in that the first is a
component in how I feel, and the second seems to tell me something
about what's happening out there. So even a particulate 'sensation',
really to be sensation (in the empiricist sense, that is, as opposed to
reflection), has to have this dimension of 'aboutness'. This will later be
called 'intentionality', but Kant speaks of the necessary relation to an
object of knowledge. 'Wir finden aber, dass unser Gedanke von
der Beziehung aller Erkenntniss auf ihren Gegenstand etwas von
Notwendigkeit bei sich führe . . .' (A104).[20]

With this point secured, Kant argues that this relationship to an
object would be impossible if we really were to take the impression as
an utterly isolated content, without any link to others. To see it as about
something is to place it somewhere, at the minimum out in the world, as
against in me, to give it a location in a world which, while it is in many
respects indeterminate and unknown for me, cannot be wholly so. The
unity of this world is presupposed by anything which could present
itself as a particulate bit of *information*, and so whatever we mean by
such a particulate bit, it couldn't be utterly without relation to all
others. The background condition for this favourite supposition of
empiricist philosophy, the simple impression, forbids us giving it the
radical sense which Hume seemed to propose for it. To attempt to
violate this background condition is to fall into incoherence. Really
to succeed in breaking all links between individual impressions
would be to lose all sense of awareness of anything. 'Diese [sc.
Wahrnehmungen] würden aber alsdann auch zu keiner Erfahrung
gehören, folglich ohne Objekt und nichts als ein blindes Spiel der
Vorstellungen, d.i. weniger als ein Traum sein' (A112).

So Kant by articulating the background understanding of aboutness
sweeps away the empiricist atomism of experience. I want to suggest
that Herder does something analogous. By articulating the background
understanding of the linguistic dimension, he also undercuts and
transforms the designative theory of language dominant in his day. And
to make the parallel closer, one of the features swept away is precisely
its atomism, the view that language is a collection of independently
introduced words. I will return to this below.

The second main direction of argument in the counter-thrust to Cartesianism-empiricism has been the attempt to place our thinking in the context of our form of life. The original early modern epistemologies gave a notoriously disengaged picture of thinking. This was no accident. The foundationalist drive, the attempt to lay bare a clear structure of inference on the basis of original pre-interpreted bits of evidence, pushed towards a disengagement from embodied thinking, and the assumptions buried in everyday custom.[21] The move towards a more situated understanding of thinking is evident enough in the work of Wittgenstein and Heidegger. But Herder is one of its pioneers. He constantly stresses that we have to understand human reason and language as an integral part of our life-form. They cannot be seen as forming a separate faculty which is just added on to our animal nature 'like the fourth rung of a ladder on top of the three lower ones'. We think like the kind of animal we are, and our animal functions (desire, sensibility, etc.) are those of rational beings. 'überall . . . wirkt die ganze unabgeteilte Seele.'[22]

These two directions, retrieving the background and situating our thinking, are obviously closely interwoven. In fact, it is the firm belief in situated thinking which leads Herder to his articulation of the linguistic dimension. Just because he cannot see language/reason as a mere add-on to our animal nature, he is led to ask what kind of transformation of our psychic life as a whole attends the rise of language. It is this question to which 'reflection' is an answer. To see our thinking as situated makes us see it as one mode among other possible forms of psychic life. And it is this which makes us aware of its distinctive background.

IV

It is by embarking on these two related directions of argument that Herder brings about a rotation of our thought about language, so that we see it from a quite new angle. I want to illustrate the significance of this by enumerating some of the important changes which ensue from this rotation. The fact that Herder himself failed on many occasions to liberate his thinking from the older forms, and draw the full conclusions, shouldn't hide from us how many of our contemporary modes of thought are implicit in the steps he took.

(1) The first important insight was to see the linguistic dimension as

constituted by expression. This emerged from his understanding of linguistic thought as situated. Reflexion arises in an animal form which is already dealing with the world around it. Language comes about as a new, 'reflective' stance towards things. It arises among our earlier stances towards objects of desire, fear, to things which figure as obstacles, supports and the like. Our stances to these things are literally bodily attitudes or actions on or towards objects. The new stance can't be in its origins entirely unconnected with bodily posture or action. But it can't be an action just like the others, whose point is definable outside the linguistic dimension. It has to be seen rather as an *expressive* action, one which both actualizes this stance of reflection, and also presents it to others in public space. It brings about the stance whereby we relate to things in the linguistic dimension.

The action which expresses/actualizes this new stance is speech. Speech is the expression of thought. But it isn't simply an outer clothing for what could exist independently. It is constitutive of reflexive, i.e., linguistic thought, of thought which deals with its objects in the linguistic dimension. In its origins it is close to and interwoven with gesture.[23] Later we can detach our thinking over some of its extent from public expression, and even from natural language. But our power to function in the linguistic dimension is tied for its everyday uses, as well as its origins, to expressive speech, as the range of actions in which it is not only communicated, but realised.

This doctrine is obviously contested, first by those who have remained tied to the 'intellectualism' of the old disengaged epistemology, but also surprisingly enough by some thinkers who have explicitly built on post-Herderian themes, for instance, Jacques Derrida.[24] It has, however, been central to those who have tried to give a picture of human agency as embodied.[25] But can we attribute it to Herder? One can contest this, because Herder himself doesn't seem to take the point in the very passage about the birth of language I quoted above. Instead of stressing the crucial role of overt expression, he speaks of the recognition of the animal through a distinguishing mark as the discovery of a 'Wort der Seele'. The new mark is, indeed, a sound, the bleating, but it can become the name of the sheep, 'even though [the human's] tongue may never have tried to stammer it'.[26]

Nevertheless, I want to see the origin of this idea in Herder, not just because it so obviously flows from his concern to situate thought in a life form, but because he himself stresses elsewhere (including elsewhere in this same work) the importance of speech,[27] and vocal expression for the human life form.

(2) One of the most important, and universally recognised consequences of Herder's discovery was a certain kind of holism of meaning. A word has meaning only within a lexicon and a context of language practices, which are ultimately embedded in a form of life. Wittgenstein's is the most celebrated formulation of a thesis of this kind in our day.

This insight flows from the recognition of the linguistic dimension as Herder formulated it. Once you articulate this bit of our background understanding, an atomism of meaning becomes as untenable as the parallel atomism of perceptions does after Kant. The connection can be put in the following way.

To possess a word of human language is to have some sense that it's the right word, to be sensitive, we said above, to this issue of its irreducible rightness. Unlike the rat who learns to run through the door with the red triangle, I can use the word 'triangle'. That means that I can not only respond to the corresponding shape, but can recognise it as a triangle. But to be able to recognise something as a triangle is to be able to recognise other things as non-triangles. For the description 'triangle' to have a sense for me, there must be something(s) with which it contrasts; I must have some notion of other kinds of figures. 'Triangle' has to contrast in my lexicon with other figure terms.

But in addition, to recognise something as a triangle is to focus on a certain property dimension; it is to pick the thing out by its shape, and not by its size, colour, composition, smell, aesthetic properties, etc. Here again, some kind of contrast is necessary.

Now at least some of these contrasts and connections we have to be able to *articulate*. Someone can't be recognising 'triangle' as the right word, and have absolutely no sense whatever of what makes it the right word, doesn't even grasp for instance that something is a triangle by virtue of its shape, not its size or colour. But one cannot have any sense of this, if one cannot say anything whatever, even under probing and prompting. There are cases, of course, where we cannot articulate the particular features peculiar to something we recognise, e.g., a certain emotional reaction to something, or an unusual hue. But we know to say that it is a feeling or a colour. And we can state its ineffability. The zone where our descriptions give out is situated in a context of words. If we couldn't say any of this: even that it was a feeling, couldn't even say that it was indescribable, we couldn't be credited with linguistic consciousness at all; and if we did utter some sound, it couldn't be described as a word. We would be out of the linguistic dimension altogether.

In other words, a being who just emitted a sound when faced with a given object, but was incapable of saying why, i.e., showed no sign of having any sense that this is the (irreducibly) right word, other than emitting the sound, would have to be deemed to be merely responding to signals, like the animals I described earlier. Like a parrot, it has learnt to respond to that thing appropriately, but it can't be attributed recognition of the word's rightness.

What flows from this is that a descriptive word, like 'triangle', couldn't figure in our lexicon alone. It has to be surrounded by a skein of terms, some which contrast with it, and some which situate it, place it in its property dimension, not to speak of the wider matrix of language in which the various activities are situated where our talk of triangles figures: measurement, geometry, design; and where description itself figures as one kind of speech act among others.

This is what the holism of meaning amounts to: that individual words can be words only within the context of an articulated language. Language is not something which could be built up one word at a time. Mature linguistic capacity just doesn't come like this, and couldn't; because each word supposes a whole of language to give it its full force as a word, i.e., as an expressive gesture which places us in the linguistic dimension. At the moment when infants start to say their 'first word', they are certainly on the road to full human speech, but this 'first word' is quite different from a single word within developed speech. The games the infant plays with this word express and realise a quite different stance to the object than the adult descriptive term. It's not a building block out of many of which adult language is gradually built.

But this exactly was the error of the traditional designative view. For Condillac, a one-word lexicon was quite conceivable. His children acquire first one word, then others. They build language up, term by term. That's because Condillac ignores the background understanding necessary for language; rather, he builds it in unremarked to the individual words. But Herder's articulation of the real nature of linguistic understanding shows this to be impossible. Herder rightly says in the passage I quoted earlier that Condillac presupposes 'das ganze Ding Sprache'.

This expression seems happily to capture the holistic nature of the phenomenon. And yet, here too, Herder disappoints in the conclusions he actually draws in his passage on the birth of language. The 'just so' story after all tells of the birth of a single word. And at the end of it, he unfortunately throws in the following rhetorical question: 'was ist die ganze menschliche Sprache als eine Sammlung solcher Worte?'[28] And yet I'd like to credit him again with putting us on the track to holism. Not only because it is clearly implicit in what he did articulate, but also because he himself made part of the mediating argument.

He sees that the recognition of something as something, the recognition which allows us to coin a descriptive term for it, requires that we single out a distinguishing mark (*Merkmal*). The word for X is the right word in virtue of something. Without a sense of what makes it the right word, there is no sense of a word as right. 'Deutlich unmittelbar, ohne Merkmal, so kann kein sinliches Geschöpf ausser sich empfinden, da es immer andere Gefühle unterdrücken, gleichsam vernichten und immer den Unterschied von zweien durch ein drittes erkennen muss.'[29]

So Herder's articulation of the linguistic dimension, properly understood, and as he began to work it out, shows the classical designative story of the acquisition of language to be in principle impossible. This story involves in a sense a deep confusion between the mere signal and the word. For there *can* be one-signal repertoires. You can train a dog to respond to a single command, and then add another one, and later another one. In your first phase, whatever isn't your one signal isn't a signal at all. But there can't be one-word lexica. That's because getting it right for a signal is just responding appropriately. Getting it right for a word requires more, a kind of recognition: we are in the linguistic dimension.

The holism of meaning has been one of the most important ideas to emerge from Herder's new perspective. Humboldt took it up in his image of language as a web. And it takes its most influential form early in this century in the celebrated principle of Saussure: 'dans la langue il n'y a que des différences sans termes positifs'.[30] A term gets its meaning only in the field of its contrasts. In this form, the principle has achieved virtually universal acceptance. It is an axiom of linguistics.

But perhaps its most powerful application in philosophy is in the work of late Wittgenstein. Wittgenstein's devastating refutation of 'Augustine's' designative theory of meaning constantly recurs to the background understanding which we need to draw on to speak and understand. Where the traditional theory sees a word acquiring meaning by being used to name some object or idea, and its meaning as then communicated through ostensive definition, Wittgenstein points out the background of language which these simple acts of naming and pointing presuppose.[31] Our words have the meaning they have only within the 'language games' we play with them, and these in turn find their context in a whole form of life.

(3) These two insights, the constitutive role of expression (1), and the holism of meaning (2), combined are at the origin of a series of further transformations in our understanding of language. These represent, as it were, a further working out of these two seminal ideas. I want briefly to mention four of them here.

(A) On the classical designative view, language is an assemblage of separable words, instruments of thought which lie, as it were, transparently to hand, and which can be used to marshal ideas. This was the principal function of language for Hobbes, Locke or Condillac. It gives us, as Condillac put it, 'empire sur notre imagination'. Ideally we should aspire fully to control and oversee its use, taking care of our definitions, and not losing them from sight in inconsiderate speech, whereby we become 'entangled in words, as a bird in lime twigs'. [32]

But on the new perspective which Herder inaugurates and Humboldt developed, language is rather something in the nature of a web; a web, which, to complicate the image, is present as a whole in any one of its parts. To speak is to touch a bit of the web, and this is to make the whole resonate. Because the words we use have sense only through their place in the whole web, we can never in principle have a clear oversight of the implications of what we say at any moment. Our language is always more than we can encompass; it is in a sense inexhaustible. The aspiration to be in no degree whatever a prisoner of language, so dear to Hobbes and Locke, is in principle unrealisable. So much seems to follow from (2).

But this difference has to be seen in the context of (1). Language cannot be seen as a set of instruments, lying to hand, of words to which meanings have been attached. The crucial and salient feature of language is now that it is a form of activity, that in which through expression, 'reflection' is realised. Language, as Humboldt put it, has to be seen as speech activity, not as work already done; as *energeia*, not *ergon*.[33]

Language as a finished product, as a set of tools forged for future use, is in fact a precipitate of the ongoing activity. It is created in speech, and is in fact being continuously recreated, extended, altered, reshaped. This Humboldtian notion is the basis for another famous contribution of Saussure, his distinction between *langue* and *parole*.

If we combine these two insights, then we will come to see language as a pattern of activity, by which we express/realise a certain way of being in the world, that which defines the linguistic dimension, but a pattern which can be deployed only against a background which we can never fully dominate. It is also a background that we are never fully dominated by, because we are constantly reshaping it. Reshaping it without dominating it, or being able to oversee it, means that we never fully know what we are doing to it. In relation to language, we are both makers and made.

(B) The classical picture of language as a set of designative terms can also be upset from another direction. Early modern theories of language focused on its functions of recording and communicating thought. The emphasis was on the descriptive dimension. Later, in the eighteenth century, interest also turned to the expressive uses of language, but these were conceived after the same model. Certain feelings become linked with certain cries and gestures (or perhaps are so linked by nature), and this allows them to be communicated to others, in both senses: that is, the cry can both impart information to you about what I feel, and/or evoke the same feeling in you. The basis was laid for the later distinction between 'descriptive' and 'emotive' meanings, both conceived in the same fashion as independent contents of thought or emotion associated with a signal.[34]

Herder's discovery (1) opens a new dimension. If language serves to express/realise a new kind of awareness, then it may not only make possible a new awareness of things, an ability to describe them. It may also open new ways of responding to things, of feeling. If in expressing our thoughts about things, we can come to have new thoughts, then in expressing our feelings, we can come to have transformed feelings.

This quite overturns the eighteenth-century view of the expressive function of language. Condillac and others conjectured that at the origin of language was the expressive cry, the expression, say, of anger or fear. This later acquired designative meaning and could serve as a word. But the underlying assumption was that expression was of already existing feelings, which were unaltered in being expressed.

The revolutionary idea implicit in Herder's expressivism was that the development of new modes of expression enables us to have new feelings, more powerful or more refined, and certainly more self-aware. In being able to express our feelings, we give them a reflective dimension which transforms them. The language animal can feel not only anger but indignation, not only love but admiration.

Seen from this angle, language can't be confined to the activity of talking about things. We experience our essentially human emotions not primarily in describing, but in expressing them. Language also serves to express/realise ways of feeling without identifying them in descriptions. We often give expression to our feelings in talking about something else: we give vent to indignation in condemnation of unjust actions, and voice our admiration through praise of some person's remarkable traits. And much of what we feel is actualised and conveyed not in words at all, but in the way we stand and move, in our closeness and distance from others, and the like.

(C) From this perspective, we can't draw a boundary around the language of prose in the narrow sense, and divide it off from those other symbolic-expressive human creations: poetry, music, art, dance. If we think of language as essentially used to say something *about* something, then prose is indeed in a category of its own. But in the light of insight (1), of the constitutive nature of speech, then talking *about* is just one of the provinces it constitutes. Human emotion is another, and in this some uses of prose are akin to some uses of poetry, music and art. The idea that one can get a good grasp of the phenomena by drawing a boundary around descriptive prose comes to seem less probable, and the surmise gains ground that any adequate theory of language must be able to give some account of the whole range of the 'symbolic forms'.[35]

(D) But the post-Herderian view has not only transformed and extended our conception of the uses of language. It has also transformed our conception of the subject of language. If language must be seen primarily as activity (following A), if it is what is constantly created and recreated in speech, then it becomes relevant to note that the primary locus of speech is conversation. We speak together, to each other. Language is fashioned and grows not principally in monologue, but in dialogue or, better, in the life of the speech community.

Hence Herder's notion that the primary locus of a language was the *Volk* which carried it. Humboldt takes up the same insight. Language is shaped by speech, and so can grow up only in a speech community. The language I speak, the web which I can never fully dominate and oversee, can never be just *my* language, it is always largely *our* language.

This opens up another field of the constitutive functions of language. Speech also serves to express/constitute different relations in which we stand to each other: intimate, formal, official, casual, joking, serious. In naming them, we shape our social relations, as husbands and wives, parents and children, as equal citizens in a republic, or subjects of the same monarch, or followers of a war-leader. From this point of view, we can see that it is not just the speech community which shapes and creates language, but language which constitutes and sustains the speech community.

V

I have just been enumerating four seminal ideas, which have defined some major themes in our thought about language in this century. Not that they are agreed. On the contrary, they are not contested only by those who resist the whole drift away from designative theories. They are also a source of division for those who embrace them. We are not clear yet, certainly not agreed, on what to make of them. A and D together helped to inspire the sort of 'structuralist' theories for which Lévi-Strauss's work was paradigmatic, and through them issued in 'post-structuralism'. The confusions, willed and involuntary, of the latter have temporarily obscured some of the important implications of Herder's seminal insights. These remain to be properly defined. In particular, the significance of D, the dialogical nature of language, is still being articulated in fundamentally different ways, by Habermas and other followers of Mead, in one way, thinkers inspired by Heidegger in another, by those working in the wake of Vygotsky or Bakhtine in a third and fourth. The debate will rage for some time.

In describing Herder as a hinge figure, I am saying that he first articulated the insights which have given these multi-faceted debates their point. For better or for worse. One may regret this turn in our thought about language. I for one welcome it, but I can understand others feeling dismay, particularly when one surveys the nonsense that has been generated along the way. My aim here has not been to justify the turn, but to show Herder's role in it. I hope I have succeeded in showing, even in the short passage of the *Ursprung* examined above, how important and seminal this was.

(1990)

CHAPTER 4

The Idea of a Common Human Nature
Richard Wollheim

I

I feel confident that as, over the years, over the decades, the thought of Isaiah Berlin, which we think of as belonging so much to our world, our age, our circle perhaps, gets subjected to that kind of interrogation which is the fate of any body of ideas that outlives its original circumstances, there is one question that will increasingly be asked of it. There is no particular passage, no special crux, which directly poses it, but any attempt to put together the work as a whole, the metaphysics with the history of ideas, the philosophy of history with those startling *éloges*, unique in our time, in which the dead are resurrected, is constantly met by the question: Did Berlin believe, or did he not, in a common human nature?

The question itself has its difficulties. For what this belief is, what it is to believe it, is a debated issue. Beliefs whose content is problematic, so that part of why it is hard to know whether people believe them or not is that it is hard to know what believing them consists in, include both empirical and philosophical beliefs: but where these beliefs abound is in that area which is the overlap of the two. A belief in a common human nature has this character: it is at once part of the science of man and part of the philosophy of mind. The inquiry to which it belongs used to be called 'philosophical anthropology', and that is a revealingly hybrid term.

Today this belief is under a great deal of pressure. It is attacked on all sides. Those who overtly champion it are few. Yet, interestingly enough, we are none the clearer about what the belief asserts. Thinkers who treat the beliefs as manifestly false put no noticeable effort into clarifying what it would be to hold it true.

This is the point at which I shall start, and I shall start negatively.

II

To believe in a common human nature is not to believe that psycho-logically we all *are* identical, any more than to believe in equality is to believe that materially we all *should be* identical. These might be called the 'absolute' interpretations of the two beliefs, and neither belief is attractive on its absolute interpretation. Nor, for that matter, is the absolute interpretation attractive: attractive, that is, as an inter-pretation. Nevertheless when the two beliefs are taken in conjunction, specifically when the first is taken as a justification for the second, which is a reasonable enough thing to do, there is a tendency, altogether misguided, to understand both of them on the absolute interpretation.[1]

What the belief in a common human nature requires us to think is that the nature we exemplify or share in is identical, not that we are identical in virtue of sharing in it. The way we share in it, or the different shares that we have, may make us different. And this is the case.

So what is this nature in which – or so it is claimed – we share? A suggestion is that the commonality of human nature is to be found in the mode of explanation to which we are all susceptible. In other words, we are all comprehensible – comprehensible to ourselves and to others – along the same lines, in the same broad terms. For certain contingent reasons there may well be, for each of us, some people whom we do not, even in some way cannot, understand, but all those whom we do understand we understand in the same way. If there were real discrep-ancies in the way people are made sense of, so that, as we shifted our attention from some to others, this involved a shift in the mode of explanation, then it would follow that there is no such thing as a human nature that we all share. Conversely, there is a common human nature if (the suggestion continues) there is a common mode of explanation to which all persons are amenable.

III

Before examining this suggestion, which I shall do in the next section, let me first fill it in. This is a matter of introducing the most widely-held view about the mode of explanation to which we are amenable. The view is this: Every action that we perform can be explained by referring it back to a paired desire and belief. Such a reference can be effected if (1) the desire is a desire that we actually have, and (2) the belief is a belief that we actually have, and (3) the belief and the desire are at once appropriately related to one another and appropriately related to the action itself. The last of these three conditions is complex. The desire and the belief are appropriately related to one another if the desire is for something (as all desires are) and the belief tells us the best way of bringing this thing about in the circumstances in which the agent finds himself. In other words, the desire and the belief are appropriately interrelated when the belief is instrumental *vis-à-vis* the desire. The desire and the belief are appropriately related to the action if (1) the best way of satisfying the desire according to the belief is the very action that awaits explanation – or, as it is often put, the desire and the belief conjointly 'rationalise' the action for the agent – and (2) it was the desire and the belief that caused the agent to perform the action. It is Donald Davidson to whom in our time credit is due for insisting that, if an appropriately paired desire and belief are to be capable of explaining a certain action, causation is necessary in addition to rationalisation. Rationalisation means that the desire and the belief provide the person with a reason for doing the action. But someone can have a reason for doing an action and yet not do it: or do it but do it for some other reason. It is causation that converts a reason that someone has for doing an action into – what explanation is interested in – the reason why that person did it.[2]

Creatures whose every action is explicable in the mode I have just set out are often said to have a desire-belief psychology: although it should be clear that a desire-belief psychology is not, strictly speaking, a kind of psychology at all. It is more in the nature of a condition that certain psychologies meet. So now back to the suggestion: Is it right to think that a belief in a common human nature at once entails, and is exhausted by, the claim that all humans have a desire-belief psychology?

IV

I think not: for at least two strong reasons.

In the first place, human nature expresses itself – or, more modestly, manifests itself – in so many different ways that it seems highly unlikely that a criterion that concentrates solely upon agency could suffice: too many other manifestations of human nature would, on this basis, go unconstrained. We could differ in so many varied ways, and still be regarded as sharing a nature. To this objection it might be retorted that the slack in the suggestion is more apparent than real, since agency is so central to our humanity. In other words, if we are identical in our agency, then we shall be identical in enough other ways for it to be plausible that we share a common human nature.

This retort would have more force if in the original suggestion itself the term 'agency' were being used in a broad sense: if it were being used to cover everything that we do. But this is not so. The suggestion uses the idea of agency in a narrow sense: it uses it to cover intentional action alone. And there are many, many things that we do that are not intentional actions. We do something, we are agents in the broad sense, when we recall a name, when we repress a desire, when we scowl at an insult, when we learn a new word, when we focus on an object in the far distance, when we find a lost ribbon, when we suckle at the breast: but these are not actions, these are not things that can be explained by reference back to a paired desire and belief. It is then far-fetched to claim that, just because, out of all the things we do, our *actions* are amenable to the same mode of explanation, the theory of a common human nature is vindicated.

The second reason for rejecting the current suggestion is this: If humans possess a desire-belief psychology, this ensures a certain use to which desires and beliefs are put: they cause actions. It also ensures a certain way in which actions come about: they are caused by desires and beliefs. But these requirements are purely structural: they leave (as I have already hinted) the substance of our psychology free-floating or unconstrained. Yet it seems as though a belief in a common human nature must have something to say about what we can desire or what we can believe: it must, somehow or other, impose limits within which our desires and our beliefs will fall. Eighteenth- and early nineteenth-century philosophers were more than likely naive to think that our motives, our 'springs of conduct' as some liked to put it, could be tabulated by content, so that any departure from these tables spelt monstrosity. But that doesn't mean that something along those lines, though far less rigid, is not called for, and perhaps a more promising way of circumscribing our desires and beliefs would be by invoking some characteristic history or histories they must have within the life of the individual to whom they belong. They must be the products of these histories and not others.

Such an historical or 'dynamic' approach to our psychology would inevitably have two aspects to it. It would, on the one hand, stipulate the sources or origins of our desires and beliefs, and, on the other hand, indicate the laws or principles according to which our desires and beliefs develop from these beginnings. Of course, there is no reason to believe, and every reason to deny, that the history of our psychology is a hermetic affair, or that it unfolds, inviolate, within the confines of our minds and bodies. It is fundamental that psychological development is the result of an interaction between the human organism and the environment in which it finds itself. In other words, if we get closer to the idea of a shared human nature by combining the possession of a desire-belief psychology with common sources for our desires and beliefs and their governance by common laws of development, there is nothing in the resultant idea that leads us to anticipate anything other than the incredible diversity of persons we actually find. Similar factors can operate similarly in the different circumstances of different lives to produce the dazzling heterogeneity we know. The urgencies of the body, the nature of experience both early and late, and the ramifications of the intrapsychic world, prime amongst the factors formative of us, make us what we are, and they make us different out of the same materials and under the same laws.

A belief in a common human nature is then a belief that our psychology has its distinctive genealogy: it has a certain ancestry and certain laws of descent. It goes without saying that this belief in a common human nature can far outstrip any positive knowledge on our part of what our origins actually are and how precisely it is that we have emerged from them to be the creatures we are.

V

If this is how we should think about the hypothesis of a common human nature, in what circumstances would someone feel justified in rejecting the hypothesis? To disbelieve it would be to believe what?

There are two broad ways of denying that there is such a thing as a common human nature.

The first way begins by accepting that in all cases human psychology has both its distinctive origins and its particular laws of development. However it denies that the origins or the laws, one or both, hold good for all humanity. As we move, not necessarily from person to person, but certainly from group to group, or from society to society, or from age to age, there are real discontinuities or discrepancies in the genealogy of human psychology. The family tree, as we might call it, which is the person's life, is not necessarily the same for all in its construction: it goes back to different sources, or it observes different laws. On this view there is no such thing as a common human nature, because there are different human natures.

The second way of denying that there is such a thing as a common human nature is more radical, and we hear more of it these days. For it the distinction between the origins of our psychology and the laws according to which this psychology develops is rejected as insignificant. It lumps the two aspects together, rejects them both, and then, taking human nature as a totality, claims that this has no existence over and above some conception of human nature. Human nature is reduced to what adherents of this way of looking at things might call a 'narrative' of human nature. A conception of human nature, or a narrative of the subject, is indoctrinated into us, at (presumably) some sensitive age, by external or (in some broad sense of the term) 'social' factors, and, once this has happened, once the indoctrination has taken, it fixes how we regard ourselves and others. Human nature is, in the accompanying terminology, 'constituted' by a 'discourse' of human nature, and different societies, different ages, different historical moments, generate their own discourses, and they do so in a way that admits of functional explanation. As to what function this discourse serves, today's answer is that it serves the ends of power, but the view can, of course, be detached from any such specificity. Tomorrow's answer might well be different. On this view there is no such thing as a common human nature, not because, as the first view has it, there are different human natures, but because there is no such thing as human nature.[3]

I shall spend a little time on this second way of denying a common human nature, or the 'constitutive' or 'constructive' account of our psychology, before turning back to the first way, which in fact presents a graver challenge to the hypothesis of a common human nature.

Superficially the constructive view might seem to gain credibility from a phenomenon on which philosophers, psychologists, sociologists, linguists, general thinkers of our day, have rightly laid great stress. This phenomenon is the interaction between, on the one hand, concepts that we acquire and, on the other hand, how we think about and how we experience the world. A concept that we have internalised can so colour reality for us that not merely do we see the world differently from others who are without it but in time we cannot remember, we cannot imagine, what the world was like for us before (if there was such a time) we had the concept. This process can happen in the case of a single concept (say, the concept 'genteel' or the concept 'nostalgia'), or it can happen with a battery or schema of concepts (say, colour-concepts, or the orders of architecture), or it can come about through the acquisition of concepts tight-knit into a theory (say, the 'language' of psychoanalysis).

But, at least on reflection, it looks as though the way in which our thought or experience is rightly recognised to be concept-laden, or schema-laden, or theory-laden, gives no credible support to the claims made by the constitutive view of human nature. There are three massive differences.

In the first place, of the ordinary impregnation of experience by concepts, it is always possible to ask – that is, there is always room for the question – And does, in *this* case, or with the possession of *this* concept, the phenomenon lead us to see the world as it is, or does it lead us, perhaps progressively, to see the world as it isn't? Concept-ladenness, in its ordinary manifestation, can be evaluated in terms of truth, something which the constitutive view of human nature can make no sense of. According to this view, there is no fact of the matter about human nature except relative to some conceptualisation of it. Secondly, the impregnation of experience by concepts as it is ordinarily understood explains itself as the result of the interaction of concepts that we acquire with the normal processes of cognition, perception and imagination. In other words, the impregnation of experience presupposes human nature or psychology as we have it, and presses it into explanatory service. The constitutive theory, by contrast, undercuts any such explanation of what it claims to be true, since it cannot permit the explanation of something (our conception of human nature) by reference to something else (human nature) which it (the conception) is alleged to construct. Thirdly, when, in the ordinary course of events, we are told that some concept or set of concepts has a powerful influence over our dealings with reality, we can ask which concept or which concepts it is that has this influence, and we can expect an answer. But with the constitutive view of human nature nothing is so straightforward. On the face of it, it is the conception of, or our discourse about, human nature that constitutes human nature. But this way of picking out the conception or the discourse is, or so it seems, semantic. 'Of' or 'about' are surely semantic notions. But how can this be? How can we use the referent of some conception, of some discourse, to identify the conception or the discourse, when all the while we believe that the referent is the product of that conception or discourse? If we now fall back on a purely syntactical way of identifying the discourse that so moulds our thinking, this trivialises the explanation. What is so potent about the mere words 'human nature'?

I now turn back to the first way of denying a common human nature, or to the view that, though human nature exists, and exists independently of what we say or think 'about' it, human nature is no one single thing. On the contrary, there are different human natures.

One marked way in which this view differs from the constitutive view of human nature lies in the manner of its advocacy. In principle the constitutive view could be advanced as an empirical thesis, but the fact is that invariably it isn't. No factors are cited as causing how we constitute human nature. By contrast, the present view almost invariably is advanced as an empirical thesis. Appeal is made to specific identifiable factors which, it is claimed, account for the significant discontinuities between groups of persons. Of course, these discontinuities have to be evaluated as well as verified if the challenge to the unity of human nature is to be effective. For it might be that, though these discontinuities exist, they might not be sizeable enough to be significant, in which case the hypothesis of a common human nature would survive. For any set of human idiosyncrasies and foibles, however florid they might be, it remains a contestable matter whether they genuinely subdivide human nature.

In the last hundred years or so, there can be little doubt about the direction from which the most persistent, the most dogged, repudiation of a common human nature has come. More strident than the historicist claim that different historical ages, different epochs, have their own human natures, has been the nationalist claim that it is the nation, whether defined geographically, linguistically, genetically, that is the real source, the real well-spring, of those characteristics which a more universalistic form of thought attributed to abstract human nature.

The rhetoric of nationalistic ideologues is familiar. But, if I am right, these thinkers and their arguments cannot be taken totally at their face-value. It might still be possible to admit the claims they make about human differences and yet to incorporate these differences within the universalistic framework against which they fret. There may very well exist the similarities within nations, the dissimilarities between nations, of which these thinkers tell us, but all this might be perfectly compatible with the hypothesis that these facts are supposed to shatter. And, of course, there have always been thinkers highly sensitive to national characteristics, sometimes indeed strident about the rights or claims that these characteristics are said to engender, who have never doubted the ultimate commonality of human nature. They have never claimed to have anything against it.

No one who has read Isaiah Berlin's writings carefully, certainly no one who has known Isaiah, can be unaware that national characteristics, the distinguishing physiognomies (to use this word in the broadest sense) of Frenchmen, of Turks, of Russians, of Englishmen, of Danes and Balts and Jews, above all of Jews, that most legendary of nations, have a large part to play in the way he perceives and responds to the world. No one can forget the excitement with which a forgotten part of someone's ancestry is brought to the light of day, and for a moment this discovery is afforded by Isaiah the kind of significance that the revelation of a vice or a virtue, of a felony committed in obscurity or a child's life anonymously saved, might be expected to play in other people's thinking.

But, as I have suggested, a question remains, and that is: How does this concern with the marks of nationality stand to the belief in a common human nature? It is not a question that is easy to adjudicate either in general or in particular.

I want to introduce into the record a story involving a great modern philosopher whom I call as witness.

VI

In his altogether intriguing memoir of Ludwig Wittgenstein, Norman Malcolm tells a story which has puzzled a whole generation of readers. He is describing his relations with Wittgenstein, which, as he describes them, would seem to have arrived at intimacy, when suddenly the following untoward incident occured:

> One time when we were walking along the river we saw a newsvendor's sign which announced that the German government accused the British government of instigating a recent attempt to assassinate Hitler with a bomb. This was in the autumn of 1939. Wittgenstein said of the German claim: 'It would not surprise me at all if it were true.' I retorted that I could not believe that the top people in the British government would do

such a thing. I meant that the British were too civilized and decent to attempt anything so underhand: and I added that such an act was incompatible with the British 'national character'. My remark made Wittgenstein extremely angry. He considered it to be a great stupidity and also an indication that I was not learning anything from the philosophical training that he was trying to give me. He said these things very vehemently, and when I refused to admit that my remark was stupid he would not talk to me any more, and soon after we parted.[4]

When I first read this passage, my instinct was to sympathise overwhelmingly with Wittgenstein. I still do: over the decades my feelings have not weakened, but I am no clearer in my mind now than then, perhaps less so, about what his reasons were – as opposed, that is, to what mine might have been – for taking the stand that he did.

One thing that Wittgenstein might have thought was that Malcolm took an absurdly idealised view of the British national character. The British have a national character, but there is more of the ruffian and the hypocrite in it than Malcolm had bothered to perceive. Another thing that Wittgenstein might have thought is that Malcolm took too simplistic a view of how national character works. A country's national character may be good, it may be excellent, but, in times of war or danger of war or in any major crisis, it is inevitably fused with more opportunistic, less scrupulous, considerations. Or again Wittgenstein might have thought that Malcolm took far too determinate a view of national character: specifically the British national character. National character is the kind of thing that expresses itself in attitudes, in preferences and prejudices, and in tendencies to behave in this way rather than that, but it is not correctly associated with something so precise as an unconditional ban on the political assassination of the enemies of one's country.

Now if any one of these three thoughts had been not merely present in Wittgenstein's mind at the time but uppermost, he would not be a particularly relevant witness to the issue at stake. He would not show himself to have been a defender of the idea of a common human nature or a critic of the idea of national character: above all, he would have nothing particular to tell us about where the latter idea begins to trespass upon, and to imperil, the former. And finally, if it had been some one of these ideas that constituted the burden of Wittgenstein's charge against Malcolm, then it is impossible to see why he should have thought that Malcolm had shown himself to be impervious to philosophy.

So Wittgenstein must have thought that Malcolm, perhaps inadvertently, almost certainly unreflectingly, had committed himself to some more fundamental error. What I suggest is that, in his invocation of national character, Malcolm, according to Wittgenstein, had in effect appealed to something in the nature of an implant within our psychology: something which had its own sources and its own mode of operation, but these could not be fitted into the way we describe and explain our ordinary doings and thinkings. Furthermore, Malcolm, though perfectly confident that national character existed, made not the slightest attempt to indicate how it came about or how it worked itself out. He introduced the mysterious, and then took it for granted.

If I am right about what it was in Malcolm's thinking that angered Wittgenstein, then we might say that what it was about Malcolm's commitment to national character that Wittgenstein found so offensive was the way that it transgressed against the assumption of a common human nature. Furthermore Wittgenstein implicitly indicated when it was that according to him this assumption was breached. The supposition of an implant, a graft, breached it.

But though we might say this, Wittgenstein wouldn't have. For him the idea of a common human nature would itself have been anathema. Perhaps it would have irritated him as much as Malcolm's references to nationality. But Wittgenstein's reasons would have been different from those I have considered. What Wittgenstein would have objected to in the idea was its deep implication with the principles of Enlightenment reasoning: that our psychology is something that can be studied scientifically, that it will under inspection turn out to have its own laws, and that these laws will expose the deep-seated causal processes of the mind. In other words, Wittgenstein would have thought that an objectionable way of describing the point at which a belief in national character becomes unacceptable would be to say that it is where this belief starts to postulate a new mechanism independent of but incapsulated within the original mechanism, which is our psychology. For to Wittgenstien, the idea of our psychology as a mechanism was worse than objectionable: it was preposterous. The commonality of human nature for Wittgenstein lay in the way in which language – not this or that language, but language – led us to think and talk about human nature, and it did so for no appreciable reason, to no appreciable end.

Indeed for him to say that language led us to apprehend the world as we do *for some identifiable purpose* – and here we come back to the constitutive account – would be to presume to stand outside language in a way that invited ridicule.

Nevertheless there is something that can be purloined, purloined and then learnt from, in this whole incident. For what would surely be common ground between, say, Wittgenstein and myself is – to reverse the argument – that belief in national character is in principle acceptable so long as what is postulated is traceable to certain factors in our lives that operate upon us in the way that things that are recognised to change, to modify, to tinge, our lives ordinarily do operate upon us. These factors might be the influence of, say, parents or teachers, books we read or games we play, injunctions we internalise or rewards and punishments imposed upon us, sights and smells and rhythms of speech, heroes held up to us in childhood, or inadequacies and shortcomings that are ridiculed and reviled. By contrast, once national character is dissociated from these influences, or once the way these influences work upon us is held to be, in some fundamental fashion, dependent itself upon national character, the idea invites the hostility that Wittgenstein vented upon the unfortunate Malcolm.

Where does this leave Berlin? At this stage we need, I believe, to refashion the issue. Now I start to speculate.

VII

In his autobiography, *World Within World*, Stephen Spender writes with great vividness of Oxford in the 1930s. He recalls Berlin, a close friend then and since, in these words:

> Berlin excelled in descriptions of people by metaphor. 'X—', he said to me one day, speaking of a contemporary essayist, 'is like a man who at a certain stage in his career decided that his talents were worth exactly so many pounds. So then he went and changed himself into threepenny bits. He has been publishing threepence a week ever since.'[5]

Friends of Isaiah Berlin's will immediately recognise the typicality of this description, and memories of other descriptions, possessed of a certain similarity, which we have been treated to, will pour in. A crucial fact, which needs to be emphasised, is that, though some of these descriptions are critical, some highly critical, many are not: many identify the virtue of a friend, of an acquaintance, of some public figure, of a character in history or in an opera. They surround it with a glow which serves to sharpen the features of that which it illuminates. Of someone he knew well and admired from close to, he said to me once, 'Many people have sailed close into the wind. Some have sailed very close into the wind. Y—, whenever he could, sailed bang against it.' Of all the traditional virtues, there is none, I believe – though I may hold this belief partly because I share the taste – that Berlin likes more than courage, and this is a striking panegyric to a friend's courage.

Spender is right: most of such descriptions use metaphor. Some coin a metaphor, many take hold of a familiar metaphor and project it. What, Isaiah asked at one time, do you find when the ice breaks? The answers ramify. With A— icily cold water; with B— boiling water; with C— more ice; with D— the bottom of the skating rink; with E— it goes on . . .

But the pervasive feature of these descriptions, which makes them live on in the memory, is something we might easily overlook. It is what allows them to serve as a much-needed corrective to the way we ordinarily think and talk, and it is this: that they set out to capture the surface of life, or to mirror the appearances of people. They describe, they do not purport to explain. But two caveats are necessary. In the first place, surface, appearance, should not be automatically equated with mere behaviour: feelings too play across the surface of life, and effulgent qualities are also appearances. Secondly, in thinking of surface, of appearances, we must not, like a certain kind of philosopher, slip into thinking of them in a dissociated or free-floating fashion; on the contrary, it is always the surface, the appearance, of some solid, three-dimensional, corporeal, sensitive, memory-burdened object, a person in short, that these descriptions of Berlin's invite us to attend to. Interestingly enough, both these caveats connect directly with Berlin's original strictures upon phenomenalism as a philosophical thesis,[6] and what makes this interesting is that it shows how these strictures, philosophical in their original motivation and import, have continued to influence Berlin, explicitly or implicitly, just because they showed themselves to have the virtue of holding true across the total spectrum of experience.

It is, I think, in this new setting that we should situate and assess Berlin's concern with national character – or, as it might turn out better to say, with national characteristics. For, as I read his writings, as I have listened to him over the years, it strikes me that, when he is concerned with nationality, it is less as an underlying explanatory factor, more as a set of nuances that colour the surface of life. Ways of feeling, ways of manifesting these feelings, ways of recording these manifestations in speech and in art: here Englishmen, and Russians, and Turks, and Frenchmen, and Balts, and Jews, might be expected to differ, and to do so for who knows what deep or what shallow reasons, and the adjectives of nationality can catch, at least as well as any other tool that language provides us with, these elusive differences, which nevertheless are precious to those who share them, and which impress us all. I would not wish to claim that this exhausts Isaiah's preoccupation with national character – if it did, some of his commitments might well go unaccounted for – but I am confident that much more of it is of this nature than is generally recognised. In so far as it is, it is, of course, in no way incompatible with the idea of a common human nature: it does not present that idea with even a glancing challenge. What I am saying is that for Isaiah nationality is, for the most part, most like that thing to which, of all that the senses offer us, he is most dedicated, and most exposed: a voice, a human voice in all its poignancy. Nations have voices, and these voices, through upbringing, through training, through the natural sounds by which they have been surrounded, sing differently.

What remains a question is why Isaiah should be as committed as I suggest he is to the capture of appearance, to the description of life's surface, and there is for that matter, a further question, which is why we should think of this commitment as I have spoken of it: as a much-needed corrective to contemporary habits. If I try to suggest an answer to the first question, I hope that the second might answer itself.

In the first place, in our dealings with other persons, it is the surface that means so much to us. Social life – life, as we might say – loses its spontaneity, which is what gives it so much of its intensity, when we fail to respond to appearances, and instead we wait, coldly, calculatingly, to be certain that we know why the surface appears as it does. Friendship at first sight, which accounts for some of the deepest bonds in life, depends upon a certain trust that we put in our perception of others, and that trust in turn depends upon our setting a proper value upon the sharpness, the acuity, of our perception. And not just upon our perception, but also upon our imagination. Once we fail to appreciate, to cultivate, these gifts, we are lost. It would – to take an example from an area close to Berlin's concerns – be a strange but, unfortunately, not an unthinkable kind of historical training which had the result that, should we be magically transported to some period of the past that we have studied, we would not enable us to recognise or to respond to any of the figures whose lives we had in our intellects mastered to the minutest detail.

Secondly, true though it most certainly is that, in order for observation to be finely focused, it ultimately needs to take stock of the interests of theory and explanation, or that in observation there is (as everyone says nowadays) no 'innocent eye', nevertheless there is the ever-present danger that theory can move in too fast, edging observation out of the way, and then we find ourselves offering explanations of what is not there. Particularly is this true in our dealings with people. Even in so well-constructed a context as the psychoanalytic session, the psychoanalyst can fail to hear: it is manifest that, in his analysis of the Wolf Man, Freud failed to hear what, only a short while later, Ruth Mack Brunswick heard very clearly.[7]

Thirdly, in Berlin's own case, we can easily overlook the place that a deep-seated but undogmatic scepticism about fundamental causes, at least as far as human psychology is concerned, plays in his view of the world. It has often seemed to me that it is this that accounts for his reserved attitude towards the art of the novel, except in the hands of a writer whose practice is compatible with scepticism, such as Tolstoy.

The truth of the matter is that the historian and connoisseur of German romanticism, the re-discoverer for our age of Vico and Herder, is a Humean. Whenever we are in doubt in reading Berlin's work, whenever chance associations lead us to impose a Hegelian reading upon his words, a formula that leads us back to his meaning is, Substitute a Humean interpretation. But Berlin is a particular kind of Humean. He is not the kind of Humean who utterly rejects the idea of fundamental or underlying causes as absurd; but he is the kind of Humean who rejects the idea – or, more accurately, treats it with measured diffidence – that our knowledge can actually reach to these causes. Berlin is the kind of Humean that Hume was: at least the David Hume who so scandalised the atheistic *philosophes* of Paris whom he met around the table of the Baron d'Holbach. Berlin's concern with observation, with what I call the surface of life, is something that he might well be ready to justify as preparing the ground for theory, for

78

explanation, but, as to the chances of our ever finding theories, at any rate about the human world, that are likely to retain their hold over us after the first flush of excitement, I believe that his most encouraging response would be: Wait and see. Perhaps, but who knows? Maybe, maybe not.

I end with a passage from David Hume:

> We are placed in this world, as in a great theatre, where the true springs and causes of every action are entirely concealed from us; nor have we either sufficient wisdom to foresee, or power to prevent those ills, with which we are continually threatened.[8]

I believe that the subject of this essay would find much in these words to please him: not least the simile.

(1990)

CHAPTER 5

Two Concepts of Secularism
Leon Wieseltier

Sage jeder, was ihm Wahrheit dünkt, und die Wahrheit selbst sei Gott empfohlen

Lessing

I

It is the rare political philosopher who really believes in the limits of politics. The political philosopher has more often been characterized by a kind of architect's arrogance, by the feeling that it has fallen to him to assign each of the ends of life to its station, to put this sentiment here and that interest there, the market here and the church there, to dispatch each 'good' to its 'sphere' and vigilantly mark the boundaries. From the trivial observation that all of human life is social life, that there are no human purposes that are pursued by individuals who do not live in association with other individuals, the conclusion is frequently drawn (and not only by cozy communitarians) that social life is all of human life. Politics, according to this tradition, is 'pervasive,' even 'all-pervasive.'

The confidence of the political philosopher is mocked, however, by the unruliness of human affairs. For, before the philosopher comes to circumscribe the reach of economic behavior, or to judge the claims of religion upon social life, people are already buying and believing, selling and unbelieving. They have not waited for the philosopher to put their thoughts and their actions in order, nor have they lived all their inner and outer lives with a view of the political implications. Politics usually comes last, especially where people are free. The charge of the political philosopher is not to design the human world, but to keep up with it.

The givenness of the human world, its antecedence to every attempt to grasp it theoretically or practically, has been most stridently championed, of course, by conservatives. They have often castigated liberals with their lively feeling for facticity. But they have just as often found in the fact of the world's priority to thought a reason to put a limit to thinking, to let prejudices stand for ideas and contingent arrangements stand for hallowed traditions. They experience the limits of politics as the limits of political philosophy. But they are the victims of an irony. The turgid, untamed realities of society and culture shrink the political philosopher, but they do not shrink his load; if they leave him a lesser worker, they also leave him a harder one. The smaller the tractability of the world to thought, the greater the need for the thinker. It is not enough simply to proclaim the limits of politics and leave the field. For those limits are rarely respected. The passions and the interests do not stay put; the parcels of human life run into each other; the frontiers are porous.

In a free society, in other words, politics is the practice, and political philosophy is the theory, of separations. (In an unfree society, separations are precisely what is lacking, and politics really are pervasive.) It is perhaps not completely obvious to say that an open society is characterized by spaces between individuals and between institutions, that is, by regions of emptiness. For that reason, life in an open society is confusing, even damaging, for some of its citizens: it is not easy to live in an order for which emptiness is a positive value. And yet democracy adores a vacuum.

So does liberalism. I take this to be one of Isaiah Berlin's most important teachings, expressed most famously in his ideal of 'negative liberty' – 'a maximum degree of non-interference compatible with the minimum demands of social life'. His account of the free individual in the free society, to be sure, tells more about pleasures than pains; but then Berlin's work has been a voluptuous, analytical song of praise to the intensity and the variety of human development. Berlin loves the human world in the way that philosophers of another age loved the natural world. He is like the serendipitous scholar that the second century Rabbi Jacob ben Korshai warned against, the one who interrupts his study to remark upon the beauty that surrounds him: 'How beautiful is that tree! How beautiful is that newly broken ground!' Berlin, too, is cheerfully interrupted by the sight of newly broken ground. In his case, though, the distraction is not a tree or a field, it is a philosophical idea or a literary form or a musical phrase; and it is not a distraction from study, it is an object of study; and serendipity is a method, born of a conviction that one of the instruments of knowledge in a various world is the experience of surprise.

A philosophy of emptiness is not always an empty philosophy. Berlin's 'negative liberty' is not negative, as its critics, and the critics of the liberalism of Constant and Mill to which Berlin has fallen heir, have angrily contended. It is the name for an opportunity, for an absence of impediments to human powers, for the promise of the possibility, the permanent possibility, of a beginning in the search for meaning. Berlin believes not only in the beginning, moreover, but also in the middle (though he is skeptical about the end). He did not do with the empty field that he took from Mill's theory of politics what Sartre did with the empty field that he took from Husserl's theory of consciousness, that is, romanticize it, refuse to advance beyond it, promote it into a positive ideal, welcome it as an occasion for suffering, exalt it into a form of heroism. Freedom is where Sartre's individual stops, but it is where Berlin's individual starts. Berlin's individual searches for meaning no less stubbornly than Sartre's; but Berlin's individual finds it, loses it, finds it again. He holds out the possibility, indeed the likelihood, of what he calls, in one of his most cherished phrases, 'the ends of life.' Negative liberty exists for the ends of life: these are the essential poles of Berlin's thought. He is not a purely formal, or a purely procedural, liberal; and the radical freedom which he recommends does not flirt with nihilism, it pre-empts nihilism. Without negative liberty, the ends of life could not be pursued. Without the ends of life, negative liberty would be, well, negative, an experience of nothing – emptiness in the bad sense, if you will.

But the ends of life are positive things; and as these positive things begin to occupy the empty field that has been furnished by negative liberty, as the individual in a free society makes use of the privacy that such a society has secured for him, as he makes his unobstructed choice among the possibilities that the open society has presented to his freedom, as he becomes philosophically, culturally, and politically specific, and chooses one particular identity over other particular identities, an anxiety is introduced into the liberal world. Freedom must confront the consequences of its own exercise. Do positive ends affect negative liberty? Do they furnish freedom with different, and more exclusive, foundations? Is the freedom that enabled the search for meaning insulated against the meaning that is found? Is negative liberty a self-cancelling condition, or is it itself one of the ends of life?

Berlin's thought is itself not immune to this tension. In his criticism of 'positive liberty,' for example, he writes eloquently against doctrines of self-realization, according to which the individual fulfills himself by conforming to an ideal, even a rational ideal, whose objectivity compels obedience. And yet at the same time he believes that 'the grand leading principle' (to use Humboldt's words, from the sentence that served Mill as the epigraph to *On Liberty*) 'is the absolute and essential importance of human development in all its diversity.' What is the difference, however, between self-realization and human development in all its diversity? What is wrong with the former and right with the latter? If conformity to an objective ideal is excluded from the legitimate sphere of human fulfilment, then the faith in diversity is seriously compromised, and an altogether new and unexamined criterion for human development – a criterion of subjectivity – is smuggled into the discussion.

Berlin's liberalism is suspicious even of Kant. He worries that the Kantian notion of obedience to law as a form of freedom resembles, however unwittingly, the rhetorical and ontological tricks of theocratic and totalitarian persuasions. There is no denying, to be sure, the eschatological pages in Kant, particularly in his late writings, or their slightly chilling interest in perfection. And yet Kant's critics to the right have more ground for complaint, I think, than Kant's critics to the left. The Kantian notion of participation in the ideal is a benign one; and the ideal is moral, not metaphysical. As the ultras of all faiths have known for more than a century, obedience that is freely chosen is, in the most fundamental sense, no longer obedience. It is, rather, an outer limit of voluntarism, an especially austere self-limitation of a perfectly free will. In any event, slavery is something much greater, or rather something much lesser, than the sense that one is living for a principle or a being larger and more certain than oneself. Indeed, if nothing is more certain to one than oneself, if the only proper ground for the realization of the will is the will itself, then one has anyway abandoned Kant for Nietzsche, or worse.

Berlin, of course, is aware of the problem. Sometimes he writes as if the free individual, 'a being capable of choice, one who is most himself in choosing and not being chosen for,' lives not to choose, but to celebrate choice, as if one of the ends of life, perhaps the highest of the ends of life, is to contemplate, in their multiplicity, the ends of life themselves. But since 'the ends of men are many, and not all of them are in principle compatible with each other,' the individual is condemned, by such an account, to conflict, or tragedy, or aestheticism, or (this is the apotheosis of Richard Rorty's liberalism) irony – to anything but a single, unembarrassed, freely elected, philosophically considered view of the world. It is almost as if the irreconcilability of the various views of the world is proof against them all, as if the existence of many alternatives abolishes the need for choice.

'Diversity,' 'versatility,' 'fullness of life,' 'variety,' 'colour' – these are possible only in a pluralist order, to be sure, but they are only experiences of pluralism. (And they are all aesthetic categories, which are premised on detachment even as they commend participation.) Surely the experience of its own openness is not all that an open society may allow. It is no wonder that Berlin makes two important qualifications to his strict construction of negative liberty, two concessions to the inevitable impact of the pursuit of positive ends upon the condition of negative freedom. The first is, loosely speaking, a liberal accreditation of nationalism, of the willing sacrifice of a part of the individual's liberty for the sake of the liberty of the group. 'Although I may not get "negative liberty" at the hands of the members of my own society, yet they are members of my own group; they understand me, as I understand them; and this understanding creates within me the sense of being somebody in the world.' There is no warrant for such a 'hybrid form of freedom' in the theory of negative liberty. The theory, rather, has wisely accommodated itself to a fact.

Berlin's second exception is still more repercussive. I quote it at length:

> I must establish a society in which there must be some frontiers of freedom which nobody should be permitted to cross. Different names or natures may be given to the rules that determine those frontiers: they may be called natural rights, or the word of God, or Natural Law, or the demands of utility or of the 'permanent interests of man'; I may believe them to be valid *a priori*, or assert them to be my own ultimate ends, or the ends of my society or culture. What these rules or commandments will have in common is that they are accepted so widely, and are grounded so deeply in the actual nature of men as they have developed through history, as to be, by now, an essential part of what we mean by a normal human being. Genuine belief in the inviolability of a minimum extent of individual liberty entails some such absolute stand.

A 'normal human being,' an 'absolute stand': for the purpose of pre-empting the tyranny of the majority, that degradation of democracy that robbed Tocqueville and Mill of sleep, a fine gaping hole has been opened in the theory of negative liberty. And through this hole we have slid back into the rude world. There the ends of life do not wait on negative liberty. There negative liberty catches up to the ends of life.

It may not matter to the political philosopher, who has a practical objective, and seeks the most effective protection of the rights of the individual, whether that protection has a religious name or a secular name, whether the appeal be made to God's providence or man's design. We may be sure, however, that it will matter to the believers and the unbelievers in a society. Certainly the believers will construe the 'absolute stand' as a form of absolutism. There are societies, remember, the United States most notable among them, in which democracy was founded by religious men and women. And the unbeliever will have the delicate task of demonstrating that this 'absolute stand' is not a form of absolutism, that the open society is not finally based on some positive propositions, if only about the nature of man. It is a peculiarly constituted creature, after all, who demands emptiness as a condition of its fulfillment. An appeal to metaphysics may not be required for the explanation of such a constitution, but it is hard to see how the explanation can avoid an appeal to some kind of philosophical anthropology – by which point the empty field is filling up, and liberalism has been entangled with precisely the sorts of values that were deemed a danger.

And so we are returned to the porousness of human existence, and to the problem of separations. Or, to put it differently, we are faced with the question of the relationship of democracy to truth. To a certain kind of truth, of course, democracy cannot be indifferent. To factual truth, for example: democracy is the antithesis of all political systems based upon lies, or myths, or any theory of legitimate deceit. It proposed to subject the ideas and the images of power to a public test of reason. But is the rationalism at the basis of democracy hostile not only to lies, but also to errors? Are there propositions, not factual, but philosophical, that must be true for the intellectual foundations of democracy to be secure? And are there others which, for the same end, must be false?

II

There is probably no more difficult and dramatic case of the infiltration of democracy by truth, of negative liberty by the ends of life, than the case of religion. It is often thought that the democratic ideal of life emerged in early modern Europe as a rejection of the religious ideal of life. Democracy could not have reared its lovely head, certainly, until the theocratic tradition in European political thought and political practice had been successfully breached, until the public sphere had been rid of received religious notions of authority and legitimacy. Still, it is too coarse to construe the history of modern liberalism as a war between freedom and faith. This is, for a start, a historical simplification. Freedom and faith have lived together as much as they have lived apart: the first philosophers of a secular, liberal order were, all of them, men of faith, God-interested or God-intoxicated; and the American story of democracy, again, stands as a different model for the relationship of religion to democracy. Worse, it is a philosophical simplification, which has the consequence, as we shall see, of impoverishing the ends of life to which the citizen of an open society may aspire.

The significant fact about the process that we call 'secularization' is that it was, philosophically and socially, never completed. Many Western political cultures – not least the tormented political culture of Israel, so dear to Berlin's heart – are paying a high price in confusion and reaction for believing the opposite, for assenting to the shrill fantasy of the radical Enlightenment, according to which democracy demands not the limitation, but the elimination, of religion. (This demand has appeared again in Rorty's insistence that liberalism requires the abolition of metaphysics.)

There are different ways, in other words, to police the boundaries, different grounds for secularism and its separations. I suggest that secularism comes in two forms, which I will call hard secularism and soft secularism. Hard secularism is the separation of religion from politics that is based on the truth or the falsity of religion. Soft secularism is the separation of religion from politics that is based on indifference to the truth or the falsity of religion. These concepts of secularism do not differ in their outcome. Both prescribe a strict separation, a ruthlessly neutral space for politics. Still, they issue in very different accounts of the public and private life of the individual in an open society.

86

Hard secularism comes in two forms, the view that religion should be banished from politics because religion is true, and the view that religion should be banished from politics because it is false. Their obvious difference notwithstanding, these views have more in common than their advocates have admitted. The former view seems surprising, even paradoxical; it is a call for a really radical inhibition. And yet this unexpected willingness to expel truth may be called the classical view, the original seventeenth-century and eighteenth-century ground for the dream of a democratic order.

The argument is, broadly, that an involvement of truth with power is forbidden by the nature of truth. Truth is established by the mind, even if it originates (according to some thinkers) in experience, and it recognizes only the authority of the mind, only the force of rational demonstration. Strictly speaking, a man cannot be compelled to believe something; he can be compelled only to appear to believe something, or to be silent about what he believes. A man who believes something because he was instructed to believe it, or because he inherited the belief, is what Milton called a 'heretic in the truth,' that is, somebody who holds a true belief for a false reason. (He once defined heresy as 'a religion taken up and believed from the traditions of men.') Milton, Locke ('no Religion, which I believe not to be true, can be either true, or profitable unto me. In vain therefore do Princes compel their Subjects to come into the Church-communion, under pretense of saving their souls. If they believe, they will come of their own accord; if they believe not, their coming will avail them nothing'), Jefferson ('Reason and free inquiry are the only effectual agents against error. Give a loose to them, they will support the true religion, by bringing every false one to their tribunal, to the test of their investigation . . . It is error alone which needs the support of government. Truth can stand by itself'), Mendelssohn ('I recognize no eternal truths other than those that are not merely comprehensible to human reason but can also be demonstrated and verified by human powers . . . Propositions and prescriptions of the [legislative] kind were revealed to [the Jews] in a miraculous and supernatural manner, but no doctrinal opinions, no saving truths, no universal propositions of reason. These the Eternal reveals to us and to all other men . . .'): the view that religion has no place in public affairs for the reason that it is true is one of the foundations of liberalism, though many liberals may be discomfited by the discovery.

The repression of truth: it is difficult, at this late hour in the history of godlessness, and in the enjoyment of our pluralist polities, to appreciate the courage that was required for such a position. Democracy is not commonly experienced as a renunciation anymore. Perhaps the unbeliever cannot finally understand the magnitude of the sacrifice that these hard secularists asked of the believer. For the thinkers who pioneered this position, all their philosophical differences notwithstanding, still lived largely in a cultural consensus, in a world in which falsehood, not truth, was the threat, and in which the repression of falsehood seemed perfectly just. Examples of the voluntary limitation of unlimited truth, of theological self-containment for the sake of social peace, were rare, though Mendelssohn, in his reply to Lavater, offered his own creed as such an example, when he pointed apologetically to the absence of a powerful impulse toward proselytisation in Judaism. As Jacob Katz has written, 'from Mendelssohn's controversy with Lavater one almost receives the impression that what Mendelssohn valued above all in Judaism was not its objective truth, but its desire to keep the truth to itself.' But truth does not naturally keep to itself, surely not eternal truth. The secularization of politics, then, was an intellectual perversion, an intervention in the natural life of truth, a brake upon it, a dam to alter the course of the mighty waters.

But none of these thinkers mistook a prescription for a description. Truth may be one, but it is not uniform; it may be discovered, but its discovery is slow. Truth may be eternal, but falsehood is constant. Locke in particular was exquisitely sensitive to the progress of knowledge; his epistemology was launched with an attack on innate ideas and metaphysical presuppositions. Against the force of reason, there is the friction of reality. And against the one truth of Christianity, more specifically, there was the multiplicity of Christian confessions. In Locke's patient hands, this multiplicity became a powerful argument for tolerance:

> There is only one of these which is the true way to Eternal Happiness. But in this great variety of ways that men follow, it is still doubted which is this right one. Now neither the care of the Commonwealth, nor the right of enacting Laws, does discover this way that leads to Heaven more certainly to the Magistrate, than every private mans Search and Study discovers it unto himself. I have a weak Body, sunk under a languishing Disease, for which (I suppose) there is one only Remedy, but that

unknown. Does it therefore belong unto the Magistrate to prescribe me a Remedy, because there is but one, and because it is unknown? Because there is but one way for me to escape Death, will it therefore be safe for me to do whatsoever the Magistrate ordains? Those things that every man ought sincerely to enquire into himself, and by Meditation, Study, Search, and his own Endeavours, attain the Knowledge of, cannot be looked upon as the Peculiar Possession of any one sort of Men. Princes indeed are born Superior unto other men in Power, but in Nature equal. Neither the Right, nor the Art of Ruling, does necessarily carry along with it the certain Knowledge of other things; and least of all of the true Religion. For if it were so, how could it come to pass that the Lords of the Earth should differ so vastly as they do in Religious Matters?

Religion must not be established in power, then, not only because it is true, but also because it is diverse; because truth comes in many forms.

And yet it is still *the* truth. For all its fortitude, this secularism had its own dogmatic limits. The diversity of Locke is emphatically not the diversity of Mill. Locke's tolerance does not protect atheists ('those are not at all to be tolerated who deny the Being of a God') and Muslims, who represent, for Locke, the case of a religion whose political form amounts to 'the service of another Prince' makes the assimilation of its members into society impossible (a charge usually levelled against the Jews, though not by Locke, who was forthright in his support of their civil rights), and all holders of 'Opinions contrary to human Society, or to those moral Rules which are necessary to the preservation of Civil Society.' There were not many Muslims in Locke's England, but the terms of his exclusion would apply neatly to Catholics. To modern ears, moreover, those last words must sound a little sinister, a little like an alibi for tyrants. For we know, perhaps too well for our own good, that the rules that are necessary to the preservation of civil society change over time, that social norms are historically determined.

This is not, in other words, an acceptance of diversity for its own sake, and it is not a plea for perfect tolerance. It is, instead, an acceptance of more or less Christian diversity, of more or less rational diversity; and it is a plea for what might be called second-order tolerance, the tolerance of dissent within Christianity, not against Christianity. Atheists are disqualified by Locke – as they are by Mendelssohn, whose attack upon coercion in matters of religion exempted the use of a ban against 'atheism and Epicureanism' – for what seems to be a practical reason, which is that their oaths cannot be trusted, since they are not taken sincerely in God's name; but this practical reason is itself the expression of an orthodoxy, itself an endorsement of unanimity about first principles. This tolerance is premised, in other words, upon a philosophical sameness in religious difference. It extends its protection to variations on an absolute.

Locke explains his intolerance of atheism in this way: 'Those that by their Atheism undermine and destroy all Religion, can have no pretence of Religion whereupon to challenge the Privilege of a Toleration.' This is a remarkably revealing sentence. It captures the strengths and the weaknesses of Lockean secularism: not only must religion be tolerated, but only religion must be tolerated. The offense to this kind of liberalism was not religious intolerance, but intolerance of religion. Locke expanded the range of freedom, then, by expanding the range of faith. He pushed back the boundaries of religion, and admitted its concrete and conflicting forms as valid reflections of its eternal essence, and so he pushed back the boundaries of politics, too; but boundaries remained. This theory of separation is largely a theory of identification. The limits of democracy are still identified with the limits of truth, except that those limits are momentously more distant. Truth opens up the political system and truth shuts it down.

This kind of hard secularism, this banishment of religion from politics because it is true, was the consequence of a particular conception of religion: the dispensation made sense only for rational religion. Even rational religion, however, leaves room for intolerance, as we have observed. Reason tolerates the varieties of reason, rational religion tolerates the varieties of rational religion. Nor is that the only manner in which liberalism may find rational religion wanting. There is also the question of its social scope. Rational religion is not the religion of ordinary men and women, not common religion; it is, in fact, its proud antithesis. Rational religion consisted in the philosophical purification of popular beliefs, and so itself served as one of the most powerful instruments of the criticism of religion. For this reason, it was almost always portrayed by its Christian, Jewish, and Muslim proponents as the achievement of a spiritual and intellectual elite. Its teaching could not be apprehended by the easily manipulated imagination of the *demos*.

Rational religion is not, then, a secure foundation for democracy, because it is itself undemocratic, intellectually and sociologically. In the American case, certainly, too much has been made of the religion of the Founding Fathers in its connection to American constitutionalism. For deism, from the standpoint of democracy, was a freakish bit of good fortune; it is not impossible to build a religious foundation for a political system of non-interference on the notion of a God who Himself chooses not to interfere. And there is also the cautionary case of revolutionary France: the failure of its Cult of the Supreme Being, and the alacrity with which re-Christianization followed upon the recognition that the God of reason could not be addressed, could not offer protection, could not be imagined, is another warning to the political theorist that religion exists prior to the theory of its proper role, and that it is the task of political theory to come to grips with the religion that exists. For *that* religion, real religion, irrational religion, ordinary religion, institutional religion, religion construed emotionally or symbolically or historically, is the source of the pressure on democracy. There are no deists anymore. Reason may be universal, but rationalism is not; and liberalism is a thin reed if it rests upon the expectation of a rational world.

It was a small step, though it was not a necessary step, from the rational criticism of popular religion to the rational criticism of all religion. As faith became more and more accommodated to the requirements of the human mind, it came to look more and more like a requirement of the human mind. From the end of the eighteenth century, there developed a second tradition of hard secularism, according to which religion should be banished from politics because religion is false. The historical patience that characterized the first form of hard secularism becomes historical impatience in the second; becomes a historical analysis of religion, for which religion is an illusion of human origin in the service of power – not true, but useful.

The greatest hard secularist, of course, was Marx. 'We do not turn secular questions into theological questions; we turn theological questions into secular ones,' he boasted in his 'Essay on the Jewish Question,' which is one of the most violent arguments ever made for the expulsion of religion from politics. 'History has for long enough been resolved into superstition; but we now resolve superstition into history.' The grounds for separation, in other words, were no longer to be sought in religion, or more generally in the realm of ideas (except insofar as 'scientific' criticism remained in that realm). For Marx, the materialist analysis of history removed the question of religion's truth and put in its place the question of religion's meaning; and the meaning of religion was not religious. Religions, rather, were 'nothing more than stages in the development of the human mind – snake skins which have been cast off by history, and man [is] the snake who clothed himself in them.'

The Marxist view of religion as ideology is well known, and it does not need to be rehearsed here. But some of its implications should be noted. The first is that its separation of religion from politics is premised upon a reduction of religion to politics. The establishment of religion in the state is not described by the hard secularist with mixed feelings, as a union of opposites, as an unnatural arrangement, as a situation of tension, as religion's surrender to the state or the state's surrender to religion; it is, rather, a dark union of the same, a distinction only between means of control. To speak about separating religion from power is absurd, since religion's relationship to power belongs to its essence. There is no distinction between its falsity and its utility. There is a precedent for this style of secularism in Machiavelli, who wrote that rulers 'must favor and encourage all those things which arise in favor of religion, even if they judge them to be false,' since this will make it 'easy for them to keep their republics religious and, as a consequence, good and united.' (His notion of religion as a unifying force within a state, as an immunity to conflict, as one of 'the arts of peace,' as he calls it elsewhere, is odd, for the fifteenth century no less than the twentieth century.)

If religion is false, furthermore, it should be banished not only from public life, but also from private life. According to this sort of secularism, religion must be abolished, not abridged. Marx was particularly strident on the subject:

> The state may have emancipated itself from religion, even though the immense majority of people continue to be religious. And the immense majority do not cease to be religious by virtue of being religious in private . . . The infinite fragmentation of religion in North America, for example, already gives it the external form of a strictly private affair. It has been relegated among the numerous private interests and exiled from the life of the community as such. But one should have no illusions about the scope of political emancipation. The division of man into the public person and the private person, the displacement of religion from the state to civil society – all this is not a stage in political emancipation but its consummation. Thus political emancipation does not abolish, and does not even strive to abolish, man's real religiosity.

Of course, Marx was right: the political agitation of the bourgeoisie in the nineteenth century was indeed designed to secure the distinction between the public and the private, to expel religion from politics and then let it alone. He was right, too, that such a vision of the state allowed for what he called 'a double existence,' which amounted to a 'decomposition of man.' Marx was troubled by the detachment of the individual from the community that such an arrangement comfortably left in place. It is an anxiety that contemporary communitarians share.

The anxiety is owed, in Marx and in the communitarians, to an unexamined love of wholeness, and to a Romantic nostalgia for unity. But when was human life, individual or social, unified? And why is a single life more admirable than a double life? An undiversified existence may be dull and dangerous, whereas an existence that does not add up may be a tribute to the difficulty of the questions of life, and to the seriousness of the pursuit of the answers. Alienation, moreover, may not be the pejorative thing, the lapsarian condition, that our post-Hegelian culture has called it. It may also be a form of autonomy, and a recognition of the deep truth of individuation (which was not, incidentally, one of the evils of modernity). Social criticism, certainly would be impossible without it. Anyway, we have some data about the critics of detachment, some acquaintance with the consequences of Romanticism in politics: those who denounce alienation from their own people are usually those who demand alienation from other people.

There are greater crimes than contradiction. Liberalism must not flinch from the discontinuities that arise as a result of the division into the public and the private. And the reason is not only political, not only the gain in social peace. It is also that the division into the public and the private is not primarily an ideological construction of a particular period of Western history. Before it was a political fact, individualism was a spiritual fact. There has always been a solitariness for which no solidarity can compensate (and religion, so praised and so pilloried for its service to the group, is, as Whitehead said, what the individual does with his solitariness). Liberalism, the theory of individual rights, will always have this advantage: it honors loneliness. Indeed, it is the only way we know to take account of loneliness in politics without letting it kill.

A religious liberal, a democrat with a rich metaphysical life: such a person cannot exist according to the hard secularist stipulation. This secularism, in other words, is finally not a theory of separation at all. It is a theory of abolition. It does not separate between the things, it erases the one and enthrones the other. And this erasure has not been only theoretical. The view that religion should be banished from politics because religion is false issued in the anti-clerical savagery of Year II (it was the Thermidorian Convention that grudgingly declared a separation of church and state) and the contemptible Yevsektsiia (which, on Rosh Hashana 1921, 'tried' and 'convicted' Judaism, and issued 'a sentence of death for the Jewish religion,' in the same courtroom in Kiev in which Mendel Beilis had been tried less than a decade earlier).

III

The appeal to the criterion of truth or falsity as a foundation for a secular democratic politics, in sum, is a failure. To use Berlin's language, this introduction of the ends of life into the field of negative liberty results in the severe curtailment of negative liberty. The interest in absolute truth is an absolutist interest. (Even in the gentle empiricist Locke and in the noble rationalist Mendelssohn, there are eschatological echoes; and in the wrathful Marx there are eschatological plans.) Both forms of hard secularism, as we have seen, lead to varieties of intolerance. One is a theory of identification, the other is a theory of abolition. Neither, in other words, is truly a theory of separation. For such a theory we must turn to what we will call soft secularism, to the view that religion should be separated from politics not *because* it is true or false, but *whether* it is true or false.

Such a view might be described as the application of philosophical skepticism to politics. It hangs on a distinction between the status of certainty in the world of politics and its status in the world of religion. It argues that the principles of politics do not require the sort of certainty that is required by the principles of religion. Politics is conducted, instead, in an empirical spirit, in an experimental spirit; in the expectation of slow and steady improvement, not in the contemplation of an absolute, sacred or profane, with respect to which all political action, except the most extreme, will be found wanting. The principles of political thought and political action do not have to be true; they may turn out, indeed, to have been false; but they will have been valid to the extent to which they account for more of the complexity of the phenomenon to which they are applied. The appetite for complexity, the sense of the irreducibility of certain differences, is a

94

democratizing tendency. (Procrustes was not only a simplifier, he was also a torturer.)

It is in the greatest skeptic of all that I have found the clearest statement of what I am calling soft secularism. 'Pyrrhonism is dangerous in relation to this divine science [theology],' wrote Bayle,

> but it hardly seems so with regard to the natural sciences or the state. It does not matter much if one says that the mind of man is too limited to discover anything concerning natural truths, concerning the causes producing heat, cold, the tides, and the like. It is enough for us that we employ ourselves in looking for plausible hypotheses and collecting data. I am quite sure that there are very few good scientists of this century who are not convinced that nature is an impenetrable abyss and that its springs are known only to Him who made and directs them. Thus, all these philosophers are Academics and Pyrrhonists in this regard. Society has no reason to be afraid of skepticism; for skeptics do not deny that one should conform to the customs of one's country, practice one's moral duties, and act upon matters on the basis of probabilities without waiting for certainty. They could suspend judgement on the question of whether such and such an obligation is naturally and absolutely legitimate; but they did not suspend judgement on the question of whether it ought to be fulfilled on such and such occasions. It is therefore only religion that has anything to fear from Pyrrhonism. Religion ought to be based on certainty. Its aim, its effects, its usages collapse as soon as the firm conviction of its truth is erased from the mind.

Bayle was a believing man, whose skepticism was designed as a bolster of faith. 'A man is happily disposed toward faith,' he wrote elsewhere in his *Dictionary*, 'when he knows how defective reason is.' He was not an early democrat. Still, in his suggestion that politics can proceed merely 'on the basis of probabilities' – that the certainties of religion need not be either extended or abolished, but merely suspended, in their relationship to the state and society – he pointed to a way out of the perplexities in which the hard secularist construction of democracy is trapped.

Suspension is true separation, since what is suspended is intact, even if it is circumscribed. And not cruelly circumscribed, either: if certainty in politics and certainty in religion are different kinds, then religion has not been banished from home, it has been returned to it. It has been isolated, and thereby rescued from its dispersal in the world of power, which has usually debased it. In its proper realm, metaphysical inquiry – the study of, and the search for, spiritual experience, may flourish. For man abides in more than one realm; he shuttles between heaven and earth, between the angels and the animals, a creature of the incommensurate. It is a measure of the politicization of religion in our time that its confinement to the private realm may be suspected of diminishing it. For the most strenuous spiritual tasks fall far from the sight of society. The religious man advances when he moves with his back to the social world.

The Romantic simplification of existence is a grosser distortion of it than the liberal complication. And the true separation of religion from politics acknowledges the essential privacy of religious experience. The establishment of religion in the state, by contrast, and the hard secularist alternatives to such an establishment, preferred to dwell on the public character of religion, on its institutional and communal aspects. Thus the problem came to be defined as the relationship of 'church and state,' of 'synagogue and state,' as if all of religious life was contained in the church and the synagogue. In fact, the church that was to be separated from the state had a great deal in comon with it. For that reason, many of the philosophers of tolerance, Locke and Mendelssohn especially, attacked the coercion of its own members by the church in the same breath in which they attacked the coercion of the church by the state, though they stopped short of certain conclusions about the obstacles that organized religion places in the way of spiritual life. The interests of the soul, after all, are not always the same as the interests of religion. The soul, unlike religion, can survive without institutions. Between the state and the soul there exist the dense mediations of the institutions, the not-quite-public but not-quite-private structures of community and tradition, without which the soul could not, at least at the beginning of its way, be fed; but it is not precisely for the survival of religious institutions, or for the ratification of a community or a tradition, that the soul hungers.

Soft secularism does the believer the democratic courtesy of respecting his beliefs; and for that reason it is a restriction that the believer may accept. It asks not that the believer abandon or disguise his belief, only that he contain it. Still, it is important to grasp that the believer in a free society will experience its freedom partially as a restriction. Democracy is vexing for a member of an open society who sincerely believes that he is in the exclusive possession of the truth. There is no revealed religion, after all, that does not insist upon the exclusiveness of its revelation. (Other religions may share to some extent in the truth, but they are not the true religion, they are a condition or a consequence of it.) And this feeling of exclusiveness is the undemocratic feeling par excellence.

But it is, as I say, also the monotheistic feeling par excellence. The frustrations of a believer in a democratic society may therefore be likened to the predicament of a monotheist in a polytheistic universe. Hume was shrewd to remark upon 'the tolerating spirit of idolaters,' and to observe, however mischievously, that 'the intolerance of almost all religions, which have maintained the unity of God, is as remarkable as the contrary principle of polytheists.' There is a natural progression from unity to unanimity, from one God to one life. It was the achievement of liberalism to disrupt that progression.

The believer is less puzzled to be told that his belief is false than he is to be told that his belief is beside the point. Hard secularism met the believer on his own ground; it shared, even in its opposition to metaphysics, a metaphysical urgency; and it agreed that the relationship of faith to power should be decided by a consideration of its truth. In the hard secularist world, the believer who lost the struggle for the identity of the society could feel martyred, physically or symbolically, and await the day when his account of the world is finally accepted. In the soft secularist world, by contrast, in a world of perfect tolerance, the urgency of ultimate issues has vanished from the public sphere of life, and the discussion has been curiously relaxed. There is no martyrdom, there is only marginality. Religious arguments about the public sphere of life will be neither accepted nor rejected, since all the arguments of all the religions about the public sphere of life have lost interest, have been discarded as an indifferent subject for political conversation. Absolutes are not destroyed by democracy. They are disarmed by it. They may swell within the souls of individuals, and within the fellowship of individuals, who prefer not to live thoughtlessly, who have given over to the protections of secularism their public lives, not their private lives; but beyond a particular point the storm must subside, the agitation must abate.

When a rich man travels through a kingdom in which money does not matter, he is not rich; but neither is he poor, because he will cross the frontier again, and return to the place where his riches have value.

The believer in a democracy experiences the same sort of neutraliz-ation, the same partial but permanent shift in value. What has disarmed religion in the soft secularist society, in other words, is not a change of thought, but a change of context. And the change in context may be described in this way: truth has been transformed into opinion.

The transformation of truth into opinion has been a favorite theme of the critics of democracy, from Plato, who deplored the *doxa* that reigned in the marketplace, to Ortega and others, who denounced the massification of thinking in modernity and its relativistic result. From the standpoint of secularization, however, this transformation is a strength, not a weakness, of democracy. It means that political argu-ments will be measured by their merits, not by their provenance – more specifically, that the origin of a particular social or political idea in a religious experience or a religious tradition no longer pertains to the debate about it. The public sphere is the sphere of immanence. The religious citizens of an open society may vigorously propound their views on the questions of the day, but they must understand that in this sphere some of their reasons will fail to persaude – that their most compelling reason for their views, God's will, will not commonly compel. They will have to argue for their views on other grounds. That is, they will have the exasperating experience of having others treat as opinion what they treat as truth.

Their exasperation, of course, will be a small price to pay for their freedom and their security. For the urgency that believers enjoy in religious discussion is not unrelated to the urgency that is expressed in religious conflict. Surely the threat of assimilation is preferable to the threat of persecution: better to be lost in an open society than to be killed in a closed society. And politics will damage religion just as surely as religion will damage politics. When politics is sacralized, the sacred is politicized. The interest in separation, therefore, should be mutual. If religion does not wish to be reduced to politics, it should stay away from politics. 'By mixing religion and politics,' wrote Constant, 'you will eventually lead the people to religious indifference.' The converse is no less the case: by unmixing them, you will lead the people to . . . no, not to political indifference, but to the apprehension of the limits of politics, to the understanding that the most cherished ends of life are not the political ones.

who say that we should not look to liberalism for spiritual satisfaction are right. And yet liberalism's gift to the spirit has been immeasurable.

By unburdening the soul of politics, liberalism gives it back its wings, and watches benevolently, if not quite knowingly, as it flies higher than politics could ever take it, while the just overtakes the unjust in the mottled world below.

(1990)

CHAPTER 6

Two Concepts of Liberty
Ronald Dworkin

When Isaiah Berlin delivered his famous Inaugural Lecture as Chichele Professor of Social and Political Theory at Oxford, in 1958, he felt it necessary to acknowledge that politics did not attract the professional attention of most serious philosophers in Britain and America. They thought philosophy had no place in politics and *vice versa*; that political philosophy could be nothing more than a parade of the theorist's own preferences and allegiances with no supporting arguments of any rigour or respectability. That gloomy picture is unrecognisable now. Political philosophy thrives as a mature industry; it dominates many distinguished philosophy departments and attracts a large share of the best graduate students almost everywhere.

Berlin's lecture, 'Two Concepts of Liberty', played an important and distinctive role in this renaissance. It provoked immediate, continuing, heated and mainly illuminating controversy. It became, almost at once, a staple of graduate and undergraduate reading lists, as it still is. Its scope and erudition, its historical sweep and evident contemporary force, its sheer interest, made political ideas suddenly seem exciting and fun. Its main polemical message – that it is fatally dangerous for philosophers to ignore either the complexity or the power of those ideas – was both compelling and overdue. But chiefly, or so I think, its importance lay in the force of its central argument. For though Berlin began by conceding to the disdaining philosophers that political philosophy could not match logic or the philosophy of language as a theatre for 'radical discoveries' in which 'talent for minute analyses is likely to be rewarded', he continued by analysing subtle distinctions that, as it happens, are even more important now, in the Western democracies at least, than when he first called our attention to them.

I must try to describe two central features of his argument, though in this short note I shall have to leave out much that is important to them. The first is the celebrated distinction described in the lecture's title:

between two (closely allied) senses of liberty. Negative liberty (as Berlin came later to restate it) means not being obstructed by others in doing whatever one might wish to do. We count some negative liberties – like the freedom to speak our mind without censorship – as very important, and others – like driving at very fast speeds – as trivial. But they are both instances of negative freedom, and though a state may be justified in imposing speed limits, for example, on grounds of safety and convenience, that is nevertheless an instance of restricting negative liberty. Positive liberty, on the other hand, is the power to control or participate in public decisions, including the decision how far to curtail negative liberty. In an ideal democracy, whatever that is, the people govern themselves. Each is master to the same degree, and positive liberty is secured for all.

In the Inaugural Lecture Berlin described the historical corruption of the idea of positive liberty, a corruption that began in the idea that someone's true liberty lies in control by his rational self rather than his empirical self, that is, in control that aims at securing goals other than those the person himself recognises. Freedom, on that conception, is possible only when people are governed, ruthlessly if necessary, by rulers who know their true, metaphysical, will. Only then are people truly free, albeit against their will. That deeply confused and dangerous, but nevertheless potent, chain of argument had in many parts of the world turned positive liberty into the most terrible tyranny. Of course, Berlin did not mean, by calling attention to this corruption of positive liberty, that negative liberty was an unalloyed blessing, and should be protected in all its forms in all circumstances at all costs. He said, later, that on the contrary the vices of excessive and indiscriminate negative liberty were so evident, particularly in the form of savage economic inequality, that he had not thought it necessary much to describe them.

The second feature of Berlin's argument I have in mind is a theme repeated throughout his writing on political topics. He insists on the complexity of political value, and the fallacy of supposing that all the political virtues that are attractive in themselves can be realised in a single political structure. The ancient Platonic ideal, of some master accommodation of all attractive virtues and goals, combined in institutions satisfying each in the right proportion and sacrificing none, is in Berlin's view, for all its imaginative power and historical influence, only a seductive myth.

One freedom may abort another; [he said, summing up later] one freedom may obstruct or fail to create conditions which make other freedoms, or a larger degree of freedom, or freedom for more persons, possible; positive and negative freedom may collide; the freedom of the individual or the group may not be fully compatible with a full degree of participation in a common life, with its demands for cooperation, solidarity, fraternity. But beyond all these there is an acuter issue: the paramount need to satisfy the claims of other, no less ultimate, values: justice, happiness, love, the realisation of capacities to create new things and experiences and ideas, the discovery of the truth. Nothing is gained by identifying freedom proper, in either of its senses, with these values, or with the conditions of freedom, or by confounding types of freedom with one another.[1]

Berlin's warnings about conflating positive and negative liberty, and liberty itself with other values, seemed to students of political philosophy in the great Western democracies in the 1950s to provide important lessons about authoritarian regimes in other times and places. Though cherished liberties were very much under attack in both America and Britain in that decade, the attack was not grounded in or defended through either form of confusion. The enemies of negative liberty were powerful, but they were also crude and undisguised. Joseph McCarthy and his allies did not rely on any Kantian or Hegelian or Marxist concept of metaphysical selves to justify censorship or blacklists. They distinguished liberty not from itself, but from security; they claimed that too much free speech made us vulnerable to spies and intellectual saboteurs and ultimately to conquest. In both Britain and America, in spite of limited reforms, the state still sought to enforce conventional sexual morality about pornography, contraception, prostitution and homosexuality. Conservatives who defended these invasions of negative liberty appealed not to some higher or different sense of freedom, however, but to values that were plainly distinct from and in conflict with freedom: religion, true morality, and traditional and proper family values. The wars over liberty were fought, or so it seemed, by clearly divided armies. Liberals were for liberty, except for the negative liberty of economic entrepreneurs. Conservatives were for that liberty, but against other forms when these collided with security or their view of decency and morality.

But now the political maps have radically changed and some forms of negative liberty have acquired new opponents. Both in America and Britain, though in different ways, racial and gender conflicts have transformed old alliances and divisions. Speech that expresses racial hatred, or a degrading attitude toward women, or that threatens environmental destruction has come to seem intolerable to many people whose convictions are otherwise traditionally liberal. It is hardly surprising that they should try to reduce the conflict between their old liberal ideals and their new acceptance of censorship by some re-definition of what liberty, properly understood, really is. It is hardly surprising, but the result is dangerous confusion, and Berlin's warn-ings, framed with different problems in mind, are directly in point.

I shall try to illustrate that point with a single example: a lawsuit arising out of the attempt by certain feminist groups in America to outlaw what they consider a particularly objectionable form of por-nography. I select this example not because pornography is more important or dangerous or objectionable than racist invective or other highly distasteful kinds of speech, but because the debate over por-nography has been the subject of the fullest and most comprehensive scholarly discussion.

Through the efforts of Catherine MacKinnon and other prominent feminists, Indianapolis in Indiana enacted an anti-pornography ordi-nance. The ordinance defined pornography as 'the graphic sexually explicit subordination of women, whether in pictures or words . . .', and it specified, as among pornographic materials falling within that definition, those that present women as enjoying pain or humiliation or rape, or as degraded or tortured or filthy, bruised or bleeding, or in postures of servility or submission or display. It included no exception for literary or artistic value, and opponents claimed that applied literally it would outlaw James Joyce's *Ulysses*, John Cleland's *Memoirs*, various works of D. H. Lawrence, and even Yeats's *Leda and the Swan*. But the groups who sponsored the ordinance were anxious to establish that their objection was not to obscenity or indecency, as such, but to the consequences of a particular kind of pornography, and they presum-ably thought that an exception for artistic value would undermine that claim.

Publishers and members of the public who claimed a desire to read the banned material arranged a prompt constitutional challenge. The federal district court held that the ordinance was unconstitutional because it violated the First Amendment to the United States Constitution, which guarantees the negative liberty of free speech.[2] The Circuit Court for the Seventh Circuit upheld the district court's decision,[3] and the Supreme Court of the United States declined to review that holding. The Circuit Court's decision, in an opinion by Judge Easterbrook, noticed that the ordinance did not outlaw obscene or indecent material generally but only material reflecting the opinion that women are submissive, or enjoy being dominated, or should be treated as if they did. Easterbrook said that the central point of the First Amendment was exactly to protect speech from content-based regulation of that sort. Censorship may on some occasions be permitted if it aims to prohibit directly dangerous speech – crying fire in a crowded theatre or inciting a crowd to violence, for example – or speech particularly and unnecessarily inconvenient – broadcasting from sound trucks patrolling residential streets at night, for instance. But nothing must be censored because the message it seeks to deliver is a bad one, because it expresses ideas that should not be heard at all.

It is by no means universally agreed that censorship should never be based on content. The British Race Relations Act, for example, forbids speech of racial hatred, not only when it is likely to lead to violence, but generally, on the grounds that members of minority races should be protected from racial insults. In America, however, it is a fixed principle of constitutional law that regulation is unconstitutional unless some compelling necessity, not just official or majority disapproval of the message, requires it. Pornography is often grotesquely offensive; it is insulting, not only to women but to men as well. But we cannot consider that a sufficient reason for banning it without destroying the principle that the speech we hate is as much entitled to protection as any other. The essence of negative liberty is freedom to offend, and that applies to the tawdry as well as the heroic.

Lawyers who defend the Indianapolis ordinance argue that society does have a further justification for outlawing pornography: that it causes great harm as well as offence to women. But their arguments mix together claims about different types or kinds of harm, and it is necessary to distinguish these. They argue, first, that some forms of pornography significantly increase the danger that women will be raped or physically assaulted. If that were true, and the danger were clear and present, then it would indeed justify censorship of those forms, unless less stringent methods of control, such as restricting pornography's audience, would be feasible, appropriate and effective. In fact, however, though there is some evidence that exposure to pornography weakens people's critical attitudes toward sexual violence, there is no persuasive evidence that it causes more actual incidents of assault. The Seventh Circuit cited a variety of studies (including that of the Williams Commission in Britain in 1979) all of which concluded, the Court said, 'that it is not possible to demonstrate a direct link between obscenity and rape . . .'[4] A recent and guarded report on a year's research in Britain said: 'The evidence does not point to pornography as a cause of deviant sexual orientation in offenders. Rather, it seems to be used as part of that deviant sexual orientation.'[5]

Some feminist groups argue, however, that pornography causes not just physical violence but a more general and endemic subordination of women. In that way, they say, pornography makes for inequality. But even if it could be shown, as a matter of causal connection, that pornography is in part responsible for the economic structure in which few women attain top jobs or equal pay for the same work, that would not justify censorship under the Constitution. It would plainly be unconstitutional to ban speech directly *advocating* that women occupy inferior roles, or none at all, in commerce and the professions, even if that speech fell on willing male ears and achieved its goals. So it cannot be a reason for banning pornography that it contributes to an unequal economic or social structure, even if we think that it does.

But the most imaginative feminist literature for censorship makes a further and different argument: that negative liberty for pornographers conflicts not just with equality but with positive liberty as well, because pornography leads to women's *political* as well as economic or social subordination. Of course pornography does not take the vote from women, or somehow make their votes count less. But it produces a climate, according to this argument, in which women cannot have genuine political power or authority because they are perceived and understood unauthentically, made over by male fantasy into people very different, and of much less consequence, than the people they really are. Consider, for example, these remarks from the work of the principal sponsor of the Indianapolis ordinance. '[Pornography] institutionalizes the sexuality of male supremacy, fusing the eroticization of dominance and submission with the social construction of male and female . . . Men treat women as who they see women as being.

Pornography constructs who that is. Men's power over women means that the way men see women defines who women can be.'

Pornography, on this view, denies the positive liberty of women; it denies them the right to be their own masters by recreating them, for politics and society, in the shapes of male fantasy. That is a powerful argument, even in constitutional terms, because it asserts a conflict not just between liberty and equality but within liberty itself, that is, a conflict that cannot be resolved simply on the ground that liberty must be sovereign. What shall we make of the argument understood that way? We must notice, first, that it remains a causal argument. It claims not that pornography is a consequence or symptom or symbol of how the identity of women has been reconstructed by men, but an important cause or vehicle of that reconstruction.

That seems strikingly implausible. Sadistic pornography is revolting, but it is not in any general circulation, except for its milder, soft-porn manifestations. It seems unlikely that it has remotely the influence over how women's sexuality or character or talents are conceived by men, and indeed by women, that commercial advertising and soap operas have. Television and other parts of popular culture use sex to sell everything, and they show women as experts in domestic detail and unreasoned intuition and nothing else. The images they create are subtle and ubiquitous, and it would not be surprising to learn, through whatever research might establish this, that they do indeed do great damage to the way women are understood and allowed to be influential in politics. Sadistic pornography, though much more offensive and disturbing, is greatly overshadowed by these dismal cultural influences as a causal force.

Judge Easterbrook's opinion for the Seventh Circuit assumed *arguendo*, however, that pornography did have the consequences the defenders of the ordinance claimed. He said that nevertheless the argument failed because the point of free speech is precisely to allow ideas to have what ever consequences follows from their dissemination, including undesirable consequences for positive liberty. 'Under the First Amendment,' he said, 'the government must leave to the people the evaluation of ideas. Bald or subtle, an idea is as powerful as the audience allows it to be . . . [The assumed result] simply demonstrates the power of pornography as speech. All of these unhappy effects depend on mental intermediation.'

That is right as a matter of American constitutional law. The Ku

Klux Klan and the American Nazi Party are allowed to propagate their ideas in America, and the British Race Relations Act, so far as it forbids abstract speech of racial hatred, would be unconstitutional there. But does the American attitude represent the kind of Platonic absolutism Berlin warned against? No, because there is an important difference between the idea he thinks absurd, that all ideals attractive in themselves can be perfectly reconciled within a single utopian political order, and the different idea he thought essential, that we must, as individuals and nations, choose among possible combinations of ideals a coherent, even though inevitably and regrettably limited, set of these to define our own individual or national way of life. Freedom of speech, conceived and protected as a fundamental negative liberty, is the core of the choice modern democracies have made, a choice we must now honour in finding our own ways to combat the shaming inequalities women still suffer.

This reply depends, however, on seeing the alleged conflict within liberty as a conflict between the negative and positive senses of that virtue. We must consider yet another argument which, if successful, could not be met in the same way, because it claims that pornography presents a conflict within the negative liberty of speech itself. Berlin said that the character, at least, of negative liberty was reasonably clear, that although excessive claims of negative liberty were dangerous, they could at least always be seen for what they were. But the argument I have in mind, which has been offered, among others, by Frank Michelman of the Harvard Law School, expands the idea of the negative liberty in an unanticipated way. He argues that some speech, including pornography, may be itself 'silencing', so that its effect is to prevent other people from exercising their negative freedom to speak.

Of course it is fully recognised in First Amendment jurisprudence that some speech is silencing in that way. Government must indeed balance negative liberties when it prevents heckling or other demonstrative speech designed to stop others from speaking or being heard. But Michelman has something different in mind. He says that a woman's speech may be silenced not just by noise intended to drown her out but also by argument and image that change her audience's perceptions of her character, needs, desires and standing, and also, perhaps, change her own sense of who she is and what she wants. Speech with that consequence silences her, Michelman supposes, by making it impossible for her effectively to contribute to the process

Judge Easterbrook said the First Amendment protected, the process through which ideas battle for the public's favour. '[I]t is a highly plausible claim', Michelman writes, '. . . [that] pornography [is] a cause of women's subordination and silencing . . . It is a fair and obvious question why our society's openness to challenge does not need protection against repressive private as well as public action.'[6]

He argues that if our commitment to negative freedom of speech is consequentialist – if we want free speech in order to have a society in which no idea is barred from entry – then we must censor some ideas in order to make entry possible for other ones. He protests that the distinction American constitutional law makes, between the suppression of ideas by the effect of public criminal law and by the consequences of private speech, is arbitrary, and that a sound concern for openness would be equally concerned about both forms of control. But the distinction the law makes is not between public and private power, as such, but between negative liberty and other virtues, including positive liberty. It would indeed be contradictory for a constitution to prohibit official censorship but also to protect the right of private citizens physically to prevent other citizens from publishing or broadcasting specified ideas. That would allow private citizens to violate the negative liberty of other citizens by preventing them from saying what they wish. But there is no contradiction in insisting that every idea must be allowed to be heard, even those whose consequence is that other ideas will be misunderstood, or given little consideration, or even not be spoken at all because those who might speak them are not in control of their own public identities and therefore cannot be understood as they wish to be. These are very bad consequences, and they must be resisted by whatever means our constitution permits. But they are not the same thing as depriving others of their negative liberty to speak, and the distinction, as Berlin insisted, is very far from arbitrary or inconsequential.

It is of course understandable why Michelman and others should want to expand the idea of negative liberty in the way they try to do. Only by characterising certain ideas as themselves 'silencing' ideas, only by supposing that censoring pornography is the same thing as stopping people from drowning out other speakers, can they hope to justify censorship within the constitutional scheme that assigns a preeminent place to free speech. But the assimilation is nevertheless a confusion, exactly the kind of confusion Berlin warned against in his original lecture, because it obscures the true political choice that must be made. I return to Berlin's lecture, which put the point with that striking combination of clarity and sweep I have been celebrating. 'I should be guilt-stricken, and rightly so, if I were not, in some circumstances, ready to make [some] sacrifice [of freedom]. But a sacrifice is not an increase in what is being sacrificed, namely freedom, however great the moral need or the compensation for it. Everything is what it is: liberty is liberty, not equality or fairness or justice or culture, or human happiness or a quiet conscience.'

CHAPTER 7

Isaiah's Marx, and Mine
G. A. Cohen

I

Isaiah says that nothing is historically inevitable. Maybe he is wrong to think that nothing is, but it is surely true that many things are not. If, for example, I had not happened to attend – I was not required to be there – the seminar on 'Identity and Individuation' given by David Wiggins and Michael Woods in New College, Oxford, on 9 October 1961, then I might never have come to know Isaiah Berlin. Although he was not at the seminar himself, my presence there was the first link in a loose causal chain that led to our friendship.

I had arrived in Oxford on 14 September of that year, having boarded ship eight days earlier in my native Montreal, in fresh possession of a McGill University Bachelor of Arts degree in Philosophy and Political Science. At McGill I was educated well in the history of European political theory, and in parts of the history of European philosophy, but I had not learned how to handle philosophical issues in their own right. I could expound, quite effectively, what Descartes and Hobbes and Hume said, but I was not well placed to comment on whether what they said was true. I was, moreover, almost entirely untouched by the philosophy then current in Oxford, a philosophy which my McGill teacher Raymond Klibansky had described, without derision, as 'talk about talk'. I was not arrogant. Although I had satisfied my teachers at McGill, I did not expect to shine at Oxford, nor did I feel any need to do so. But I was also not terrified at the prospect of having to master something quite new. I expected to get by, and to come away with a B.Phil. The seminar meeting on 'Identity and Individuation' dissolved that expectation.

At the time, I hardly knew what identity and individuation were, and I was going to the seminar to learn about them, and also to learn about Oxford seminars, since this was to be my first one, on the first day of my first Oxford term. At the head of the table sat Wiggins and Woods, and

Woods proceeded to read a paper to the meeting. He began by saying that he would call a criterion of identity a 'CI' and a principle of individuation a 'PI'. He then said that his purpose was to investigate how CIs and PIs were related to one another.

This was not a good beginning, as far as I was concerned. Since I did not really know what identity and individuation were, reflection about the relationship between the criterion of the first and the principle of the second was, for me, premature. I did not understand what Woods went on to say. I could not construe particular sentences, nor did I get the general drift. Woods was and is a lucid expositor, but he reasonably took himself to be addressing graduates who were accustomed to high-powered argument, and that did not include me.

In the discussion following Woods's paper, things got worse. A young man began to examine Woods's claims, using (what I would learn was) the touchstone of Oxford philosophy, a particular example. The young man was Willie Charlton, who went on to become a professional philosopher. The particular example concerned a charac-ter called a 'pursuivant'. The word sounded French, and, for a Montrealer, that was, initially, reassuring. I thought it must mean *something that follows*, and, although I had not followed Woods's paper, I had noticed that whether or not this followed from that seemed in these parts to be an important issue. But if we had words in Montreal which sounded like 'pursuivant' (such as the word '*poursuivant*'), we did not, in my recollection, have any pursuivants there, and before long I realised that I was, once again, lost. I could not achieve control over Willie Charlton's example.

I left the seminar in a state of apprehension. The big frog from the small pond was at sea, and likely to sink without trace. As I have said, I did not need to excel at Oxford, but I did need to get the B.Phil. degree: for self-esteem, for the sake of making a living, for the old folks at home. And now I was confident that I could not master this difficult thing, Oxford philosophy, in the two years available to me. Or, if that statement is a misremembering overdramatisation of the sense I then had of my plight, what is certainly true is that I was not confident that I would be able to pass the B.Phil. examination. Feeling threatened, I sought a risk-reducing strategy, a way of meeting the B.Phil. require-ments which was consonant with my unpromising undergraduate preparation.

Those requirements, then as now, were a thesis of 30,000 words and three written examinations: two on selected branches of philosophy, and one on a great dead philosopher or great superseded school of philosophy, a list of these being provided. With respect to the branches, almost all B.Phil. candidates chose at least one of Epistemology and Metaphysics and Logic and Scientific Method, since those subjects were thought to constitute the centre of philosophy, and they were, moreover, ones in which Oxford was pre-eminent. They were also, and not only as far as I was concerned, the hardest options, and the Wiggins/Woods seminar had convinced me that they were too hard for me. Moral Philosophy and Political Philosophy were also available, and they were less redoubtable, but few chose more than one of them, and almost no one chose Political Philosophy. That was partly because Oxford then participated in the neglect of political philosophy which characterised the Anglophone philosophical scene generally. In 1961, the 'sixties', which were to put many political topics on the philosophical agenda, had not yet occurred, and there was no commanding work in political philosophy[1] to inspire the student: John Rawls's *Theory of Justice* had begun to germinate in the fifties, but it did not appear until 1971. Moral philosophy was in better shape, locally, with Richard Hare and Philippa Foot locked in fierce illuminating controversy, and Alan Montefiore looking on nearby and ruminating wisely. But moral philosophy was nevertheless thought to be relatively easy to master, a softish option; and political philosophy was thought soft to the point of viscidity, held in contempt (not entirely unfairly, considering the quality of most of the very little that was then produced within the field) if not by the paid professionals then certainly by most of my B.Phil. cohort. It was regarded, at best, as a byway or curio. As for the dead thinkers and schools, they were Plato, Aristotle, Kant, the Rationalists, the Empiricists, Medieval Philosophers, and the Original Authorities for the rise of Mathematical Logic. But candidates could also choose alternative philosophers, provided that they had 'special permission'.

My first decision, which I thought cowardly but to which I was resolved to stick, was to do Moral Philosophy and Political Philosophy: the combination was, after all, allowed, even if it was not encouraged. The problem of the historical paper was thornier. Of medieval philosophers I had only a smattering of Aquinas; as for the Rationalists and the Empiricists, there were, in each case, too many of them for either paper to be a prudent option; Kant was also out because, although I had read his *Groundwork* and *Prolegomena*, his formidable *Critiques* were unexplored territory; I knew quite a bit of Plato and Aristotle, but I also knew that, to study them seriously in Oxford, I would need to know (what I did not) Greek; and, since I had not done even unmathematical logic, the Rise of Mathematical Logic could not be contemplated.

I decided that I would be well advised to sue for 'special permission' to do something else. Yet I could not think of a philosopher whom Oxford would regard as appropriately major and whom I thought I might master in an Oxford way in the available time. Marx might be regarded as major, but certainly not as a philosopher. Hegel might be regarded as major, and even (albeit with some reluctance) as a philosopher, but I had not read much Hegel and I did not think that two years would be enough time for me to be able to absorb his forbidding texts, let alone for me to be able to present and criticise their content at the required level of competence.

Anxiously examining the *Regulations*, I noticed that there existed a B.Phil. (later to be renamed 'M.Phil.', so that Americans might realise that it was a higher degree) in Politics, and that one of its papers was the Political (and so, presumably, not the other) Theories of Hegel and Marx. Those theories I felt pretty sure I could manage.

In the wake of these reflections, I approached my supervisor, Gilbert Ryle, and I asked him whether I could do Moral Philosophy, Political Philosophy, and, in place of a historical paper in Philosophy, the Politics paper on Hegel and Marx, and a thesis on some aspect of Marxism. 'Yes', he said, 'as long as you keep your ears open for other noises.' I made (and kept) a promise to do so. The frog from the small pond was now treading water.

II

Halfway into that first Michaelmas Term Ryle decided that it was time for me to address the Hegel and Marx side of my programme. He announced that he would arrange a meeting with Isaiah Berlin. I gulped, and looked forward to the occasion.

It was, however, deferred. I received one of Ryle's little notes, famous for their brevity, often saying just 'yes' or 'no' to would-be contributors to his journal, *Mind*. The note I got was a bit longer, and more mischievous. It read: 'There will be a delay, since Isaiah is in India, helping to celebrate – as who would not? – the death of

Rabindranath Tagore.' (Tagore was born in 1861 and he died in 1941. So probably it was the centennial of his birth, rather than the vigesimal of his death, that Isaiah was helping to celebrate.)

For me, at that time, Isaiah was the author of three works which I had admired as an undergraduate: *Karl Marx*, *Historical Inevitability* and *The Hedgehog and the Fox*. I had no quarrel with the last of these, but I was hostile to the message of each of the others. I believed in Marx, and in the historical inevitability in which he believed. Isaiah was negative both about my hero's personality and about his doctrine. My attitude to Isaiah's negativity was not, like that of some other young leftists, contemptuous. I thought of his books as weighty challenges.

Eventually, the Tagore engagement over, Isaiah summoned me, and I turned up at his comfortable All Souls room with its super-large armchairs and sofa. There ensued our first interview, and it was rather a trial, as far as I was concerned. For Isaiah was tough, even severe; the only time, indeed, that I have known him to be so, whether towards me or about anybody else, across twenty-nine years of an otherwise consistently giving attitude towards people and their projects. I do not know why he presented himself sternly on that first occasion.

I said that I wanted to do a thesis on Marx. Isaiah said that that was a bad idea, that so much had been written about Marx that there was little interesting left to say. With some trepidation I said that, even so, I wanted to work on Marx. Isaiah yielded. He then said that if I wanted to work on Marx, I would have to start with Hegel, and that Baillie's translation of the *Phenomenology* was abominable. Next, he asked a question: 'Do you read German?'

The frog from the small pond was at sea again, for I did not. 'No,' I croaked. A moment's silence, then, 'Well, do you read French?' 'Yes,' said the drowning frog, grasping the *bouée de sauvetage*, and feeling suddenly grateful to the pond from whence he came. 'Very well: then, read Hyppolite's translation of the *Phenomenology*. It's not at all bad.' 'Yes,' I said, 'I will.'

That afternoon my friend Marshall Berman and I went to Parker's bookstore and I bought Hyppolite's two-volume translation of Hegel, and, for good measure, his two-volume commentary, *Genèse et Structure de la Phénoménologie de l'Esprit*. I am afraid that I have not yet cut the pages of any of those four volumes, and that I never read *The Phenomenology*, in any language, while at Oxford: it was not required for the Hegel and Marx paper, and I did not, in the end, do a thesis on

Marx anyway. (Some years later, I read vast stretches of *The Phenomenology*, though not, thank God, the whole thing, in A. V. Miller's translation, which is not easier, even if it is, as they claim, more faithful, than Baillie's.)

III

At my second meeting with Isaiah, we talked not about Marx but about a character invented by Isaiah to make a point about morality. This character enjoys sticking pins into people. When you ask what the pleasure of that is, he says that it is the way the skin first resists and then gives way: it is the puncturing of the skin that supplies the fun. When you ask whether he can get the same pleasure in any other way, he says that he can, by sticking pins into tennis balls: they are just as good. When you then ask why he does not concentrate on tennis balls and leave people alone, he looks puzzled. Tennis balls are not *more* enjoyable than people are, he explains.

The pin-pusher knows that he causes pain, and he knows what pain is, but he fails to see in the fact that people suffer pain, and tennis balls (which are easy to get) do not, a reason for leaving people alone. The pin-pusher is blind to its being a reason against doing something that it causes a person pain. And, since he is not mistaken about any pertinent facts, his blindness shows that there is such a thing as a specifically moral perception (which he lacks).

I was fascinated by Isaiah's construction, and persuaded of its point, and, for our third meeting, I prepared a short essay called 'Brave New World and the Pin Pusher'. I do not remember how I used Isaiah's fable. In any case, Isaiah listened attentively to my effort and he responded to something I said by reflecting that, although he thought that Jews should either assimilate or go to Israel, he could do neither himself. He began to talk about being Jewish, about Weizmann and Namier and Disraeli and other Jews, about Marx *as* a Jew, about the Holocaust, about great rabbis, about the Zionist movement, and about the Bund in Russia, whose attitude to 'the Jewish question' was comparable to the one I had been taught growing up in a communist Jewish community in Montreal. He went on and on and I found it riveting and hugely instructive. Our common Jewishness, and not a shared interest in Marx, connected us in that third session of supervision.

According to Isaiah, 'all Jews who are at all conscious of their identity as Jews are steeped in history.'[2] I was very conscious of my Jewish identity, from an upbringing which gave me near fluency in Yiddish and a certain familiarity with its literature, even while I was taught to reject Jewish (and all other) religion and also, after Israel's initial honeymoon with the Soviet Union, the claims of Zionism. But I was not 'steeped in history', if that implies knowing a lot about it, and here I was, getting steeped (or, at least, dipped) in it by Isaiah, in so engaging a way.

That afternoon, so I felt, and I basked in the thought of it, Isaiah accepted me. I saw him frequently as a student at Oxford, and he told me about many things, and we talked very little about Marx. One thing which we did talk about was Oxford philosophy, about whose claims I had developed some doubts, partly as a result of an unsettling reading of Ernest Gellner's *Words and Things*, which said that Oxford philosophy was terrible. Isaiah helped me to negotiate and contain the Gellner challenge. He defended a posture towards Oxford philosophy which was, characteristically, neither fanatically pro nor obstructively anti.

One doctrine then still sovereign in Oxford was the *Wienerkreis* tenet, brought to Britain by A. J. Ayer, that all *a priori* truths (ones that can be known by thinking about their content, without empirical research) are analytic (true by virtue of the meanings of the terms used to express them). I could see that synthetic *a priori* truths would be peculiar things, but, so it then seemed to me, the true sentence 'nothing can be red and green all over' was undoubtedly synthetic, and yet not something we know to be true just because we have not found a counter-instance to it. Isaiah said that I might be right, but joked that in the reigning climate one should perhaps not *call* the thing 'synthetic *a priori*'. That might be too provocative, and some sort of Marrano[3] strategy was wiser.

I have continued to see Isaiah regularly over the ensuing years, and I learn from him on every single occasion. As is widely recognised, his erudition is deep, and it covers an immense range. Less well known are the ingenuity and resourcefulness with which he is able to justify his claims, for they become evident only in his responses to the relentless questioning which not everyone will have had the opportunity of directing at him.

But I am supposed to be saying something about Marx, and I must make my way back to that.

IV

In June of 1963 I left Oxford, B.Phil. in hand, to lecture in philosophy at University College London. In my first couple of years at UCL I worked little on Marx, being more occupied with trying to reduce my persisting ignorance of central areas of contemporary philosophy. But in the autumn of 1965 I went back to Marx, having sailed to Montreal to teach for a term at McGill University. There I taught a lot of Marxism, and, as a result, I conceived the idea of writing a defence of Marx's theory of history. On my return in January to UCL, I set to work.

My meetings with Isaiah continued, in London cafés and clubs, but, despite my new preoccupation, they were not burdened by extensive discussion of Marx. For I judged that Isaiah would not be interested in the theoretical problems of historical materialism which were exercising me: what are relations of production? how, exactly, are they explained by productive forces? what belongs in the superstructure, and what falls outside it? and so on. For Isaiah, Marx was a brilliant but dislocated personality, whose theory was an expression of both of those properties. It was a theory destined to produce great fruit for social science and disastrous results for humanity. Isaiah has never belittled Marx's achievement. He describes historical materialism as 'without parallel' in its 'clarity . . . rigour . . . and [intellectual] power', and Marx as 'the true father of modern economic history, and, indeed, of modern sociology'.[4] But for all its fertility for future intellectual developments, it was, in its consuming ambition, fundamentally misconceived; and, since I knew that Isaiah thought that, I could not expect him to share my interest in making it precise.

While I worked on *Karl Marx's Theory of History*, Isaiah took a warm and supportive interest, but not a close one, in what I was doing, and we did not argue about it very much. His confidence meant a great deal to me, and I could bear the lack of criticism. Occasionally, of course, a dispute erupted, and often I felt that I was fighting a rearguard battle. I would protest that Marx was not anti-democratic, and I would furnish forth chapter and verse. I would protest, also with documentation, that he was not a fanatical Utopian. Isaiah would acknowledge the scriptural premiss but reject the interpretive conclusion, and he would offer me a wry smile which said that in my heart I could not accept it either. We disagreed profoundly about historical materialism, but, while now and then briefly airing our disagreement, we did not pursue it with vigour, not because we feared conflict, but because we wanted to avoid predictable grooves.

V

Isaiah's antipathy to Marxist theory reflects more than his belief that it has had baneful political effects and his disagreement with its distinctive claims. For there is in Isaiah a certain empiricist resistance to the project of grand theory as such, a conviction that it is bound to be one-sided. He is wary of the desire for formula and system, and of the need, by which some are seized, to find a dramatic, roundly plotted 'libretto'[5] in history. Isaiah's opposition is excited by any sign of a propensity to the regimentation of fact by self-driving reason.

Though sceptical about general theories of society, Isaiah is not their philistine opponent. He did much to secure a place for sociology in Oxford studies, and no one has done more to promote an interest in the history of large conceptions of humanity and politics. Isaiah is attracted to the theatre of theory, but he cannot help remembering what is concealed backstage, all the spoiling qualifications and complications which grand theorists conceal from themselves. So he writes, tellingly, that Marx found 'moorings' for himself 'only at the price of ignoring a good deal of reality seen by less agonized, more ordinary, but saner men'.[6] Yet Isaiah would surely agree that if people like Marx did not press forward with unsober zeal, then saner people would be possessed of less that is worth reckoning with.

The reckoning in Isaiah's *Karl Marx* must be judged a remarkable achievement, particularly when one reflects that its author was not yet thirty when he completed it, and that it rests on an enormous knowledge of nineteenth-century European history. The book manifests what Peter Strawson has called Isaiah's power to 'breathe life into the history of ideas'[7] and, too, his capacity to show how ideas grow out of circumstances: for a compelling illustration, see his ravishing characterisation of the politics of Paris at the mid-century.[8] There are also splendidly vivid and subtle expositions of central Marxist ideas, such as the claim that social being determines consciousness.[9] And, beginning with the third (1963) edition, there is Isaiah's agile response to the then recent extensive discussion of Marx on alienation. His rendering of the connection between the alienation problematic and historical materialism proper, though lightly carried off, would be difficult to surpass.[10]

Yet it is not, in the first instance, a theory that Isaiah expounds, but a thinker, a human being, a mental temper displayed not only in a theory but in a life.[11] Isaiah goes for what animates the person, for his governing passion and consequent bent. But what makes a person tick, what drives him, is not a sure guide to the structure of his theory, for theories are abstract objects, sets of sentences subject to logical laws, which impose themselves on the theorist and consequently force his theory to take unexpected turns which may not be noticed when the existential meaning of the theory for the thinker is always in prime focus. For my part, I can only admire and not emulate the work of figuring forth the phenomenology of a great thinker's experience. Propositions, not people, are my academic material, and for me Karl Marx is more a set of writings than he is a man.

That generates a difference between Isaiah and me which, unlike some other ones, is not rooted in discrepant political attitudes. And this difference of approach made it difficult for me to discharge the commission which the editors of this volume laid on me, which was to write about 'Isaiah's Marx'. My difficulty is that I am not equipped to comment shrewdly on Isaiah's portrait of Marx the man, and although I might be able to take apart some things he says about Marx's theory, it would show lack of proportion to bang on unduly on that particular drum. But, having said that, I shall now express some disagreements with Isaiah. I shall start with a few dissenting observations about Marx's personality (section VI), and I shall then criticise Isaiah's contentions (a) that Marx did not condemn capitalism at the bar of moral principle (sections VI, VIII); (b) that he thought that communism would realise, completely, all worthwhile values (section VII); (c) that his commitment to the working class was a by-product of his inevitabilitarian view of history (section VIII); and (d) that, more generally, he regarded the course of history, and not moral principles, as the right guide to political choice (section VIII).

VI

To respond fully to Isaiah's vision of Marx I would have to measure it against my own, but I have never formed a clear image of Marx's character. I lack what Isaiah has: a feeling for the nature of the man, a strong sense of what he was like, of a sort that I can have of people only if I have actually met them, or if they have revealed themselves in diaries or in letters. (There is no Marx journal, and he does not expose himself, as opposed to his theoretical and political views, in his letters.)

I do, of course, have some idea of Marx's character, and it does overlap with Isaiah's, unflattering though the latter is. I do not think that Marx was a man on whom one could rely for genial companionship. I agree that he could be precipitately aggressive, that he was richly endowed with spleen, that he was sometimes ungenerously impatient with what he thought were mediocre minds, and I do not think that can all be put down to the rigour of his circumstances. I also have to say that I am ashamed of Marx's anti-Semitic strain, which Isaiah documents unanswerably.[12]

My sense of Marx is that on a good day he would be expansive, side-splittingly funny, happy to acknowledge his own limitations, even, for part of the time, courteously attentive to what one had to say oneself, and full of incisive questions. On a bad day, he would be intolerable: dogmatic, bitter, scornful and dismissive. I cannot put a probability on the proposition that a random Marx day would be a good one, so, if I wanted relaxed company, rather than spectacle, my preference would be to spend the day with the gracious and gallant Engels. One thing we could do is talk about Marx, in the safety of his absence.

That said, it strikes me that Isaiah forsakes nuance and balance and goes overboard when he takes Marx's spleen as emblematic of his entire (including political) personality and describes him as 'a grim and poverty-stricken subversive pamphleteer, a bitter, lonely and fanatical exile [etc.],'[13] 'an isolated and bitterly hostile figure'.[14] 'Pamphleteer' is hardly a fair summary of Marx's literary achievement, and 'isolated' leaves out of account his reassuring awareness of a large and growing international socialist movement which looked to him for inspiration. There is too much denigration in the quoted phrases, and it gets worse in the allegation that there is in Marx 'an unmistakable note of sardonic, gloating joy in the very thought of . . . the coming holocaust of all the innocents and the fools and the contemptible philistines, so little aware of their terrible fate'[15] and a 'savage exultation' at the 'approaching cataclysm'.[16] These characterisations are not documented, and they are not, in my view, sustainable. They imply that Marx felt disappointment when he concluded that in Britain and the Netherlands there might be a peaceful parliamentary dissolution of capitalism,[17] whereas I think that he was unambivalently satisfied with that conclusion. I also think that he was expressing heavy regret and no exultation at all when he sombrely reflected that pre-socialist history (to which, of course, the socialist revolution itself belongs) resembles 'that hideous pagan idol, who would not drink the nectar but from the skulls of the slain'.[18]

If Isaiah overplays Marx's savagery and vindictiveness, he also, and curiously – because then the picture begins to look self-contradictory – overstates his imperturbability. I do not agree with Isaiah that, despite the outer adversity and (partly consequent) inner turmoil of Marx's life, 'it is a singularly unbroken, positive and self-confident figure that faces us during forty years of illness, poverty and unceasing warfare.'[19] Were that so, Marx's bitterness (for I do not question the bitterness, as opposed to its unremitting pervasiveness) would be inexplicable. It is inconceivable to me that Marx's 'inner life' was 'uncomplicated and secure'.[20] The only evidence for that is that he did not express insecurity (as such), but that is not strong evidence, since it is readily counter-explained by his towering pride.

I believe that Marx must often have been broken and depressed and that he deserves, among other reactions, a measure of compassion. Had he possessed the confidence and control attributed to him in Isaiah's depiction, he would surely have done more towards finishing *Capital*, the jungle-like condition of which shocked Engels when he confronted Marx's *Nachlass*. Anyone who has ploughed through, or even just peered at, the fragmented and neurotically repetitive voluminous writing which Marx spidered out in the late 1850s and the 1860s will recognise a personality more vulnerable and more self-flagellating than Isaiah's description suggests. (How, anyway, is Isaiah's attribution to Marx of unbroken self-confidence consistent with his recording elsewhere that he was 'haunted by a perpetual feeling of insecurity?'[21])

The sheer mass and detail of what Marx wrote about the capitalist and other economies prompts a further disagreement with Isaiah. I cannot accept that the supposed absence from *Capital* of 'appeals to conscience or to principle' and of 'detailed prediction' of the socialist future 'follow[s] from the concentration of attention on the practical problems of action',[22] for such concentration would be incompatible with the presence in the *Capital* manuscripts of thousands of pages of abstract theory[23] and (what is from a practical point of view even less urgent) of the history of abstract theory. I would, moreover, deny that *Capital* lacks 'appeals to . . . principle': there is an extensive, even if usually only implied, appeal to principle in the hundreds of pages of description of the exploitation and misery of the working class. When

Marx exclaims that 'capitalist justice is truly to be wondered at!',[24] when he calls the capitalist a 'robber'[25] and an 'embezzler'[26] he must be understood to be voicing a (fully justified) moral condemnation.

VII

It is unacceptably paradoxical to represent Marx as unconcerned with values. To do so is to take too seriously those *macho* moments when he disparaged them in the name of class militancy. Isaiah has, of course, offered us persuasive reflections on the structure of value, and it is appropriate to test Marx against the truths about values which Isaiah has stressed.

A number of Enlightenment thinkers claimed that all human values would be realised, once reason was at the helm of society. Isaiah regards that as a dangerous delusion, and he has indefatigably insisted that the values which have in fact and with good reason attracted human beings are incapable of full joint realisation, in some cases for reasons of logic, and in others because of general truths of human nature and social organisation. There are different things to admire in different forms of society, and not all the admirable things can be had together. Accordingly, we must reject the 'ancient faith . . . that all the positive values in which men have believed must, in the end, be compatible, and perhaps even entail one another.'[27] The chief problem, in politics as in personal life, is a sound choice of sacrifices, and there is damage to both thought and practice when people imagine that sacrifice is avoidable.

Isaiah construes Marx as an apostle of the myth 'of a final harmony in which all riddles are solved, all contradictions reconciled'.[28] He thinks Marx believed that communism would deliver everything that is worthwhile in a perfect synthesis, and that such a belief underlay his supposed willingness to countenance any kind of savagery in the service of achieving that communism.

Now Marx did not, of course, expressly deny that fundamental human values are compatible. Few have: Isaiah's affirmation of value incompatibility is a strikingly original contribution. But I do not think that Marx offended against the truth about values as much as Isaiah supposes, partly because Marx's canvas displayed not human life as a whole but only the part of it that (more or less) immediately reflects social division. The historical materialist prediction of an end to specifically *class* conflict is not a forecast of heaven on earth. There remains, after all, 'individual [non-class] antagonism',[29] and consequent room for the persistence of 'human misery'[30] and even 'tragedy'.[31]

Although I agree with Isaiah that significant values are seriously incompatible,[32] I think that the particular disvalues which Marx hated most, to wit, social injustice and socially generated restriction on the development of the faculties of the individual, can both be defeated, and, moreover, that each is likely to be defeated only when and because the other has been. (In saying that Marx hated injustice, I am mindful of the fact that he sometimes disparaged justice as a value. But that is because he was confused about justice, and he mistakenly thought that he did not believe that capitalism was unjust.[33])

I also cannot endorse Isaiah's statement that there is an incompatibility between 'unlimited personal liberty' and 'social equality',[34] not because I believe that social equality is compatible with unlimited personal liberty, but because I think that unlimited personal liberty for all is itself impossible. I think, moreover, that social equality, if truly achieved,[35] would greatly increase the liberty of those individuals who have little of it, even if it reduces (in some ways drastically) the liberty of very rich people. So while there is indeed a conflict between social equality and the liberty of some people, that is no reason for moderating the pursuit of social equality, since a humane concern for liberty must first of all direct itself to the condition of those who enjoy hardly any of it.

I should add that Isaiah does not himself believe that unlimited personal liberty is possible: he denies, in effect, that it is possible in the very sentence in which he asserts its incompatibility with social equality. Nor does he assign to liberty absolute priority over equality. He thinks that liberty may, to a degree, yield to equality: hence his commendation of Roosevelt's New Deal as 'the most constructive compromise between individual liberty and economic security which our own time has witnessed'.[36]

VIII

In my judgment, nothing was more fundamental to Marx's motivation than his perception of the misery which the capitalism of his day imposed upon the working class. I therefore strongly disagree with Isaiah's view of the relationship in Marx's thought between the march of history and the cause of the proletariat.

In Isaiah's presentation, Marx held that 'those men alone are rational who identify themselves with the . . . ascendant class in their society . . . Accordingly Marx, having identified the rising class in the struggles of his own time with the proletariat, devoted the rest of his own life to planning victory for those at whose head he had decided to place himself.'[37] Setting aside the separate question of whether Marx indeed conceived quite so leading a role for himself, my principal objection to the foregoing representation is that Marx's condemnation of the exploitation and alienation of the proletariat preceded his invention of historical materialism and thoroughly sufficed to determine his commitment to the proletariat's cause. In tracing that commitment to a special view about rational life-choices – one which, in any case, I do not think Marx held – Isaiah makes Marx out to be less soundly motivated than he was in fact.

This induces me to express a reservation about an aspect of Isaiah's arresting comparison between the psychologies of Karl Marx and Benjamin Disraeli. Each, he says, was a precariously marginal Jew who moved towards the centre of things by allying himself with a social class distant from his own origins: in Disraeli's case, the British aristocracy, in Marx's, the proletariat.[38] But the proletariat were a fitter object of solidarity than were the Tory nobility, and an outsider's sympathy for them need not be explained by peculiarities of his psychology. In fact, Marx cared greatly in an ordinary human way about the workers' suffering, whatever other motives that care might have mingled with, and whatever other attitudes, including the contempt Isaiah would allege and emphasise, he might also have had.

In my view, Isaiah sharply exaggerates the strength of vindictive personal motivation in Marx's embrace of the proletarian cause. I cannot agree that, when Marx 'speaks of the proletariat', he speaks less 'of real workers' and more 'of his own indignant self', that 'the insults he is avenging and the enemies he is pulverising are, as often as not, his own', and that '*this* it is that lends passion and reality to his words'.[39] The accusation that Marx dealt only with an abstract 'humanity in general'[40] and lacked strong concern for real people is, I believe, refuted by (to take just one example) his masterful and compassionate use of the British government Blue Books' description of the plight of very particular worker human beings, a use which, elsewhere,[41] Isaiah respectfully commends.

Nor do I think that 'Marx denounces the existing order by appealing not to ideals but to history:.' What follows the colon in that sentence of Isaiah's is hard to reconcile with what precedes it: ': he denounces [the existing order] . . . as being the effect of laws of social development which make it inevitable that at a certain stage of history one class . . . should dispossess and exploit another, and so lead to the repression and crippling of men.'[42] To say that there was no appeal to ideals in Marx is to say, incredibly, that dispossession, exploitation, repression and crippling played no part in generating Marx's condemnation of the system.

To be sure, Marx did not think, and he was right not to, that *simply* denouncing the system for its manifest injustice would suffice to spirit it away. And it is also true that, for Marx, there is a task which capitalism must perform before it will be either possible or desirable to overturn it. For capitalism serves to develop 'the productive forces of social labour': that is its 'historic mission and justification'.[43] Only when that development has been accomplished, is its 'historical destiny . . . fulfilled',[44] and then it is time for it to go. Capitalism is tolerable while it is carrying out its progressive task, but humane ideals declare that there is not a shred of justification for it once it has done so.

It scarcely follows that, for Marx, 'the only sense in which it is possible to show that something is good or bad, right or wrong, is by demonstrating that it accords or discords with the historical process.'[45] Not a single text of Marx demands that strange restriction on the scope of social criticism.[46] A famous sentence in the *Critique of the Gotha Programme* which is frequently cited in substantiation of some such attribution to him in fact subverts it. The sentence is preceded by a morally informed critique of the norm of distributive justice ('to each according to his contribution') which Marx thought would perforce govern the initial, immediately post-capitalist, stage of communism. Having displayed the 'defects' of that norm, Marx says that they are unsurprising, since 'right can never be higher than the economic structure of society and its cultural development conditioned thereby.'[47] The sentence presupposes – it is amazing that in the vast realms of Marxology this is never, to my knowledge, remarked – an anti-relativist contrast between lower and higher forms of right or justice. One page before Isaiah writes what I quoted at the top of this paragraph he says, in similar vein, that, for Marx, 'the only real rights are those conferred by history, the right to act the part which is historically imposed on one's class.'[48] That statement, and the one quoted above, appear to me to be contradicted by Isaiah's recognition, nearby, that, in Marx's view, the proletariat's 'destitution causes it to represent human beings as such – what it is entitled to is the minimum to which all men are entitled.'[49]

Far from dismissing ideals as mere instruments of history, Marx saw the realisation of an ideal of freedom from subordination as history's highest purpose, and he measured historical epochs according to their contribution to the achievement of that ideal. I think it fitting to close this counter-case with the following pregnant quotation:

> The recognition [by labour] of the products as its own, and the judgment that its separation from the conditions of its realization is unjust – forcibly imposed – is an enormous awareness, itself the product of the mode of production resting on capital, and as much the knell to its doom as, with the slave's awareness that he *cannot be the property of another*, with his consciousness of himself as a person, the existence of slavery becomes a merely artificial, vegetative existence and ceases to be able to prevail as the basis of production.[50,51]

(1990)

CHAPTER 8

Nationalism
Stuart Hampshire

In 1918, in the preface to *Eminent Victorians*, Lytton Strachey wrote: 'We have never had, like the French, a great biographical tradition; we have had no Fontenelles and Condorcets, with their incomparable éloges, compressing into a few shining pages the manifold existences of men.' This is a reproach that collapses in the face of Isaiah Berlin's series of éloges which precisely 'compress . . . the manifold existences of men' with a vivid particularity and which resume the French tradition of celebration and insight, making the *oraison funèbre* almost a philosophical form. He explores 'the manifold existences of men', stressing the 'manifoldness' and the irreducible variety of individual temperaments and virtues. Weitzmann, Namier, Edmund Wilson, J. L. Austin, Pasternak, Akhmatova, Moses Hess, Belinsky, Herzen, Turgenev and many others become physical presences, so sharply are they envisaged; but at the same time they embody peculiar attitudes to experience, peculiar gifts and dispositions. The celebration of them is, in each case, a celebration of particularity. They are praised and commemorated because their lives and their words conveyed an individual essence not previously known and never to be repeated. The éloges, taken together, present the irreducible variety of human lives, thoughts and impulses. They each rescue and record a largely unwilled 'experiment in living', in Mill's phrase.

This delight in individuality, and in the unplanned jungle of individual differences, has formed Isaiah Berlin's complex attitudes to nationalism: both his positive and his negative attitudes. Stepping backwards in time, he places himself in the centre of nineteenth-century liberalism, alongside Mill and Constant, in claiming that men and women can only be free, and can only feel free, if they feel themselves to be at home and secure in the social setting that is naturally theirs. In a setting that is alien to them they will be inhibited and constrained, unable to express themselves freely and spontaneously. Their individual natures and peculiarities will never be realised. Feeling themselves to be strangers, they will conform, with some effort of self-control, to a model which is unrelated to their inborn inpulses. They will be tempted to make themselves as nearly as possible like their neighbours, and therefore their value as persons and as individuals will be lost, or at least will be greatly diminished. J. S. Mill had associated the value of freedom in a liberal society with the diversity of experience and attitude which a liberal society will permit. But Berlin has gone beyond Mill in examining the conditions under which spontaneity and experiments in nonconformity can be expected to exist. Under what conditions do people, typically and for the most part, feel 'at home', unconstrained, and free to express themselves? This is the point at which the idea of nationalism needs to be introduced as a necessary part of any liberal philosophy of politics.

Berlin has argued with great force that Enlightenment thinkers who looked forward to men and women becoming citizens of an undivided world were deceived. Herder, Hamann and Hume were, in their different ways, right to represent persons as governed in their thoughts and sentiments by the habits and the customs in which they were nurtured, and not by rational principles demanding universal agreement. Vico was right to assert against Descartes that natural languages, and civilisation itself in its many forms, are the products of imagination and of poetic invention and of metaphor, and not of abstract reasoning and of clear and distinct ideas. Clear and distinct ideas are accessible to all humanity; the idioms of a natural language are not.

In his essays on the great figures of the Counter-Enlightenment, Berlin is constantly insisting on the natural roots of national sentiment and contrasting this naturalness with the artificiality of appeals to universal and timeless standards of rationality, which are appropriate to mathematical reasoning, but not to moral reflection. The moral sentiments of men and women do not altogether transcend their origins in a customary way of life, and this way of life, whatever it may be, forms and limits both their sentimental interests and their moral concerns. Apart from Herder, most thinkers of the Enlightenment, both in France and in Germany, disastrously under-estimated the ineradicable strength of these attachments in normal men and women, having drawn their models of human nature from the exceptional case of the free-thinking intellectual. It is often difficult to distinguish in Berlin's writing about the Enlightenment, a vivid description of human nature, as history reveals it in individual cases, from a normative assessment of what he considers most valuable in human nature. It is not an accident that there is this difficulty of interpretation. He reasons from historical constancies to moral conclusions.

In all Berlin's thinking and writing one is aware of the ample, generous, humorous and seductive figure of David Hume smiling in the background. Hume's philosophy encourages the smooth transition from the mere description of normal human sentiments to the approval of such sentiments as Nature's provision for human welfare. We ought to follow Nature's guidance, and we make a serious mistake if we try to act against the natural and normal sentiments implanted in us. That is the way that leads to fanaticism, to false feeling and to dissimulation, and to a loss of self-assurance and of a clear sense of identity. So Hume, and after him, Berlin.

I think it is important to stress that Berlin's attitude to nationalism has both a philosophical and a historical foundation. The attitude is not just an attitude; it is part of, and follows from, a coherent moral philosophy, which in turn rests on a Humean epistemology. Philosophers who design some rational order for society are entangled in a web of illusion and mere conceit, appealing, as they inevitably do, to some *a priori* notions of ideal freedom, ideal harmony and ideal felicity. Always following Hume and Mill, Berlin has consistently and at all times argued that there can be no place for pure *a priori* reasoning in ethics and politics. In spite of his extraordinary ability to expound convincingly Kant, Hegel and the German Romantics, he treats them as interesting aberrations, and as instructive examples of powerful illusions and of false grandeur. Hegel and the German Romantics, like Russian ultra-nationalists and religious Zionists of the extreme right, are part of the pathology of politics. Their doctrines begin as a kind of poetry and end as a kind of disease. A sane nationalism does not project itself beyond historically justified frontiers, and does not think of itself as a mission to humanity. In the last analysis, a sane nationalism is to be justified by a utilitarian argument – that most men and women are happy only when their way of life prolongs customs and habits which are familiar to them.

Berlin and the present author had a seminar together in political philosophy at Oxford in the late 1950s; its title was 'The Origins of Liberalism', and the authors we considered were Condorcet, Kant,

Mill and G. E. Moore. I tried on some occasions to defend the idea that we have some *a priori* notions of justice and fairness in the distribution of good things, and that justice is intuitively recognised as an independent value – independent, that is, of the consequences for human well-being. Evidently this was the most direct attack that is possible both on Hume's and Berlin's philosophy and it was uncompromisingly rejected. Each of our four liberal thinkers were exposed to Hume's scepticism, and Berlin criticised each of them for making *a priori* assumptions or *a priori* claims, and for not sufficiently respecting the observable facts of human feeling, observable by historians and also in current and contemporary politics. He repeatedly argued that each of these liberal thinkers, with their cosmopolitan ideals, had drastically tidied up human nature for the sake of their projects of rational reform. Both in private and in political morality, reason is, and ought always to be, the slave of the passions. The passions associated with loyalty and with pride are formed in a particular locality and among friends and family relations, and they are expressed and reinforced in a cherished language, which is one language among many others. Sympathy can be extended over the horizon by reflection and by rational considerations; but always within limits and not without some loss of intensity and immediacy.

The more one reflects upon it, the more clearly one perceives that Berlin's political thought is all of one piece and remarkably consistent across the whole wide range of his writings: in the lectures on freedom and on historical determinism, in the studies of individual thinkers and in the essays on Russian subjects. The power of national and ethnic loyalties and of historical memory is at the centre of his thought. Even in his study of Karl Marx he draws attention to Marx's instinctive national and ethnic prejudices. Berlin has always believed that the rational designs of socialists would not anywhere be realised in our century except where they are reinforced by nationalist feelings or by ethnic or by tribal loyalties. He has never shared the optimism of those nineteenth-century liberals who expected steady progress in the erosion of national and racial prejudices. Berlin's lack of optimism – almost pessimism – was particularly evident towards the end of the British mandate in Palestine, when various power-sharing and bi-national schemes were being proposed for that country. He did not believe that historical memories of conflict and bitter feeling could be overcome by any reasonable appeals to common – and particularly to common economic – interests. Reason, in the form of enlightened self-interest, was likely to be powerless in the matter. It would be an error in political understanding to expect an ethnic or religious minority, passionately clinging to its own threatened way of life, to accept compromises for the sake of economic advantage. Condorcet and the Encylopaedists had projected into the future a gradual expansion of human sympathies together with an overcoming of ancient super-stitions and supernatural enthusiasms. They had a concept of belief which corresponded to nothing in the real world except mathematics and natural science. Moral and religious beliefs are generally formed by custom and participation in a shared way of life, not by solitary deductions. Contemporary events in Israel, Northern Ireland, Cyprus, Ceylon, Lebanon, Soviet Armenia fit into a repeating pattern which was not anticipated by most of us in the 1930s, when Berlin had already arrived at his Humean scepticism and at his understanding of the powers of modern nationalism. These contemporary conflicts are the inflamed and feverish forms of normal attachments and loyalties, and it is the work of statesmanship to foresee and to avert the situations which produce the fevers.

Within a political philosophy that recognises and encourages a plurality of ways of life and a plurality of moral values, each with their distinct history, Zionism is still a special case. It cannot be understood simply as a form of nationalism, because the Zionist pro-gramme was to create a nation from scattered elements having very different forms of life and different languages, elements held together only by the vestiges of a shared and peculiar religion. The idea of the nation had to be constructed on the basis, first, of a shared inheritance of religious observances and, secondly, of a shared history of persecu-tion. Once the new nation was successfully formed, familiar forms of nationalism in fact asserted themselves in the internal politics of Israeli democracy. Throughout his active life, Berlin has thought with inten-sive concentration and care about the claims of Zionism and about their ultimate moral justification. Zionism itself was originally a side-effect of the agitation of ultra-nationalist parties and groups in Europe, particularly as this agitation was associated with pogroms in Russia and with anti-Semitic movements elsewhere, as in Vienna around the turn of the century and in France during *l'affaire Dreyfus*. Anti-Semitism was a natural, even a rational, concomitant, of the ultra-nationalism which was coming to life in Europe towards the end of the last century, and, later, in former colonial territories in Africa and in the Middle East. The plan for a national home for Jews in Palestine was a natural and rational response to persisting anti-semitism. Not only in his inaugural lecture, 'Two Concepts of Liberty', but throughout his writing, Berlin has proclaimed his allegiance to J. S. Mill's picture of a free society, in which diversity in forms of life – 'experiments in living' – are to be protected and encouraged. Therefore, ultra-nationalism, and the integralist ideas of T. S. Eliot's *Towards a Definition of Culture*, are repugnant, being the negative of any acceptable liberal tradition of tolerance and diversity. Ultra-nationalism occurs at two ends of the development of Zionism: first, as a factor in the desperation that led to the Zionist movement as the only escape from persecution and from exclusion for Jews in many parts of the world: secondly, and later, as a feature of Israeli politics and popular feeling under the pressure of the hostility of the surrounding Arab states and of displaced Palestinians. Berlin's liberal principles lead him to reject and to deplore the role of ultra-nationalism at both ends of the history of Zionism, first in Europe and North Africa, and then in Israel itself.

It is important to stress that Berlin's sympathy with nationalism is sympathy with the nationalism of the Risorgimento and with the European revolutionaries of 1848; it is sympathy with the nationalism of Verdi and Clemenceau, not with the nationalism of Treitschke and Barrès. He never strays far from his twin philosophical foundations, exemplified in the often contrasting thoughts of David Hume and John Stuart Mill. He accepts from Hume the doctrine that the ultimate test of institutions and policies is to be found in human feelings as they are actually experienced and observed. He agrees with Mill that individuality and spontaneity are supreme moral values, being at once the essence and the outcome of life as a free person. A Jew may choose, for himself and for his children, to be assimilated to the nation and to the gentile culture which surrounds him, and he may be quite uninterested in the way of life of his grandparents and in contemporary Israel. A just society will leave the options open for the individual's unconstrained choice: unconstrained, that is, by any form of social pressure. No one has a duty to feel himself more intimately part of the history of the Jews than of the history of Britain, or vice versa. The irreducible differences of natural feeling in this sphere must be respected. Different sentimental loyalties have subtle natural causes and such sentiments, deeply rooted, are not to be commanded.

There is one defect, or at least oddness, in Berlin's Humean liberalism, otherwise so consistent, which I think is worth noting. As a student of Marx and Marxism, and of Communism in Russia, Berlin has seen the evils of a centrally planned unification of culture which tries to stamp out all national differences and sentimental attachments. From these evils he infers that political planning for the sake of a cause dear to the planners is always to be distrusted. Lenin and the Bolsheviks were a small minority of fanatics who imposed an *a priori* plan, a theoretical blueprint, on a vast and diverse population and thereby created a hideous tyranny. But it would be unsafe to infer that all plans conceived *a priori*, and in advance of obvious and widespread sentiment, will lead to tyranny or will simply fail in practice. I do not recall that Berlin anywhere, in fact, commits himself to this inference. But the rhetoric in some of his writing on the Enlightenment may cause readers to leap to this unsound conclusion. The Zionist movement, and the foundation of the state of Israel, are examples of a theoretical construction, a rational plan conceived by a small group of thinkers, well in advance of a popular sentiment, which came to fruition without the imposition of a tyranny. Whenever someone asserts that theoreticians and intellectuals are always helpless in politics, the Zionist movement may be quoted as one counter-example. As Condorcet's rational plans for French education were realised in the Napoleonic lycées, so Herzl's and Weitzmann's plans for a national home were realised in Ben-Gurion's state of Israel.

Neither Hume nor Berlin has been so unreasonable as to claim that his own theories of politics admit of no exceptions to the generalisations implied. Berlin has repeatedly argued that there is no reason to expect exceptionless universal truths in politics. We have no knowledge of natural laws governing human behaviour and human sentiment, and we have no clear picture of what it would be like to possess such knowledge. The individual case, and the emotional tone of a particular government or a particular society, are always of more importance in his estimation than some general principle or abstract criterion of democracy. He felt more at home with the New Deal, and with the liberal democrats who surrounded Roosevelt, than with any other powerful men whom he had known at first hand. He responds always to a fiery temperament and to generous high spirits as in

Churchill, Salvemini, Clemenceau, Roosevelt himself, Pasternak: all men who had a sense of glory in politics and who from time to time exhibited some of the qualities of a heroic march by Verdi or Bellini.

CHAPTER 9

*Understanding Fascism?**
Michael Ignatieff

Isaiah Berlin has always displayed a remarkable capacity for interpreting the presuppositions of personalities and philosophies antithetical to his own. No one could be further removed for example, from Berlin's personal temperament than Karl Marx, yet Berlin's biographical study of that prodigious hater manages to convey to any reader what it would be like to see the world through Marx's eyes.[1] In the most recent collection of Berlin's essays. *The Crooked Timber of Humanity*, there is a remarkable study of another great hater, Joseph de Maistre, the Sardinian diplomat and essayist, whom Berlin interprets as an important theoretical precursor of modern fascism. In his essay on de Maistre, Berlin demonstrates that a Jewish liberal can manage to view the world, though with horror, through fascist, or proto-fascist eyes.

What is required in such exercises in understanding is something more than comprehending the logic of alien argument. What is called for is an intuitive grasp of 'the particular vision of the universe which lies at the heart of [a writer's] thought'.[2] Approaching this core vision means reconstituting the context of their times and the intended audience of their writing. To these standard procedures of intellectual history Berlin has added a quite special emphasis on the psychological colouring of belief, on the imprint of personality upon ideas. For Berlin, historians can claim to have understood the past only when they have 're-enact[ed] within themselves the states of mind of men tormented by questions to which [their] theories claim to be solutions.'[3]

Such empathy, needless to say, is most difficult when temperaments and ideas are opposed. Berlin's ability to understand opposites is more than a personal quality he brings to the history of ideas. Empathy plays an important role in his account of how conflicting views are reconciled in liberal society. Compromises between competing values would be impossible if individuals were unable to enter into the views of those with whom they are in disagreement. Were such understandings impossible, political argument would have little point; attempts at persuasion would be in vain; and force or the tyranny of majority rule would decide all political outcomes. In practice, liberal societies cohere because of agreement; because individuals, even when firmly gripped by conviction, remain capable of seeing the world as others might see it, of removing their own ideological and moral blinkers and imagining how their own position must appear when viewed from the outside. Empathy and its twin, self-detachment, are what make liberal compromise possible.

Some of Berlin's most interesting political writing deals with the problems which arise around the project of understanding moral and political difference. How does a person make sense of views radically different from his own? Supposing such understanding is possible, what right does he have to judge other views in terms of his own values? The two questions, though distinct, have the same answer for Berlin. He argues that human beings are capable of understanding each other because we share common passions, interests and needs which enable us to discern an ultimate identity of human concern transcending our shorter term differences. It is in the light of this limited but common humanity that we manage both to see ourselves as others see us and also to judge, both others and ourselves, according to the criteria of shared moral sentiments. Empathy enables us to disagree in good faith, i.e., to accept the ethical plausibility of each other's intentions.

Much of Berlin's political theory has been written to rebut the conservative charge that liberals do not believe in the existence of such shared moral sentiments. On this caricatural view, liberalism is the politics of moral relativism. Liberals put liberty first, not because they believe in its intrinsic moral priority, but simply because no other political arrangement is capable of ordering human debate about ultimate ends. This debate is between incommensurables. In the absence of a shared moral universe, liberals give priority to individual liberty simply because this priority enables everyone to pursue incommensurable ends within a legal framework of procedural rules. To the degree that liberalism encourages mutual understanding, conservatives charge, it is of a relativist kind: *tout comprendre, c'est tout pardonner.* For a liberal, to understand is to forgive; to explain is to explain away. Liberal 'understanding' is, on a conservative account, a kind of social emollient, at best smoothing the edges off conflicts, at worst, tolerating the intolerable.

Berlin's liberal doctrine insists, on the contrary, that we can understand antithetical points of view because we share an understanding of how human beings ought to be treated. Because we do share these attachments, we can call each other to account when what we do or say fails to accord with these understandings.

For Berlin, there is more of such common moral ground than the visible contentiousness of liberal society might lead us to believe. 'We must not,' he writes, 'dramatise the incompatibility of values – there is a great deal of broad agreement among people in different societies over long stretches of time about what is right and wrong, good and evil.'[4] When Berlin speaks of universal values, he means European ones. When he speaks of the rules of 'our' conduct, he means 'the habits and outlook of the western world . . . the common notions of good and evil, which reunite us to our Greek and Hebrew and Christian and humanist past.'[5] In specifying that these are the values that distinguish the civilised from the barbarian, he makes it clear that he does not mean a set of human universals tested against ethnographic evidence from non-Western societies. Indeed, the question of whether Westerners have the right to judge and condemn the practices of other civilisations is not central to Berlin. All of his thinking has been about the traditions of the West. His problem with relativism is not ethnographic; his primary concern has been whether there remains sufficient continuity of moral outlook in the western tradition for us to understand the world view of our own past. Berlin believes that these continuities exist and make the historical comprehension of the world view of our ancestors possible.

These continuities are something more than traditions, to which we give atavistic or unreflecting allegiance. For Berlin, our common understandings about ethics are rationally held beliefs about the minimum standards of decency appropriate to the treatment of human beings. They continue to order moral behaviour, not because they are traditional, but because they continue to convince: they are the thought-experiments we all conduct to answer the question: what forms of behaviour must we require for ours to be a minimally humane existence?

Because the answers given to this question display a long-run continuity in human experience and because ordinary men and women continue to feel persuaded by these continuities, moral conflict in

Western society tends to occur on common ground. People disagree in society, Berlin argues, not because each is enclosed in a subjective web of relativistic conviction impervious to argument; in fact, they are able to break out of this subjective web and enter into the moral worlds of those with whom they are in conflict. The disagreement occurs because the goods that men contend about – for example, equality versus liberty, justice versus order – are themselves difficult to reconcile in practice. Berlin stresses that we disagree not primarily because we fail to understand each other, but because we seek goals that are in conflict or because, while we agree about ultimate goals, we disagree about how to achieve them in practice. As Bernard Williams has pointed out, Berlin's liberalism is one in which loss is central, in which tragic choice – achieving one good, but sacrificing another – is inescapable.[6]

It has been said that Berlin's view of political choice actually implies a version of utilitarianism as the common scale to use in adjudicating between competing moral values. If Berlin's admiring essay on John Stuart Mill is anything to go by, it is not. 'Only a competent social psychologist,' Berlin says ironically, 'can tell what will make a given society happiest.' There are societies, he says, where human sacrifice itself might have been seen, even by those sacrificed, as contributing to the happiness of the majority. This, for Berlin, is the *reductio ad absurdum* to which utilitarianism is led if not held in check by a higher principle of individual inviolability. Utility, Berlin says, was not Mill's ultimate moral criterion, and neither is it his.[7] Utility is too historically relative, too dependent, within any given society, on the tyrannous ethical certainties of the majority, to provide a moral scale capable of protecting essential human interests. The common human scale for Berlin is a set of basic propositions about human nature: above all, our capacity to choose between good and evil, hence our capacity to take responsibility for our actions. These facts define each individual as a moral agent and as an object of moral concern.

Because these suppositions about human nature are evident to most people, in liberal society, Berlin argues, most conflict can be reconciled. In the face of practical choices, most of us are capable of squaring competing values through trade-offs. 'The concrete situation is almost everything. There is no escape. We must decide as we decide; moral risk cannot, at times, be avoided.'[8] In other words, values that are incompatible in theory may remain so: but in practice, a clear understanding of practical constraints will make choice possible.

In the political arena, values may be incompatible, yet practical exigency itself requires that they be reconciled. In other areas of life, Berlin argues, values may come in conflict which are truly incommensurable. The claims of the spiritual versus the material life cannot be squared by trade-offs, and their relative merits certainly cannot be computed. In such cases of incommensurability, a liberal society encourages each side to tolerate the other. Indeed, Berlin argues that it is in the romantic era itself that the West began not merely to be aware of, but to appreciate and give respect to the incommensurability of competing idealisms.[9]

Because values can be both incompatible, and upon certain occasions, incommensurable, it follows for Berlin that political society ought to value liberty above all else it values. He believes that liberal society is the political arrangement best suited to the fact that human beings disagree about ends, and that there are many plausibly good ends that they can choose to serve. A crucial additional fact about human beings is that they know this to be so: they can enter into the universe of moral premises they do not happen to share and can understand, in Bernard Williams's words, 'that these different values do each have a real and intelligible human significance, and are not just errors, misdirections or poor expressions of human nature.'[10]

In Berlin's thought, moral disagreement occurs mainly in conflicts between positive human goods – liberty versus equality, justice versus efficiency. The common ground of moral agreement for Berlin seems to consist chiefly of definitions, not of good, but of bad human conduct. There do remain, in the end, he argues, a small number of acts which all sane individuals can agree are inhuman, indecent, beyond the pale, hence punishable. Thus any society can generate sufficient agreement about what is human in order to punish what is inhuman; a liberal society is distinctive in limiting its shared moral ground to its periphery, to the circle which defines what is beyond the pale. Within that circle, there are so many competing human goods individuals can legitimately seek that a society has no warrant for intensive regulation of private conduct. To use the terms of Berlin's two concepts of liberty, the facts of human nature permit sufficient agreement to guarantee the conditions of negative liberty: freedom from; but not sufficient agreement to justify collective pursuit of some ideal: freedom to.

In *The Crooked Timber*, Berlin makes it clear how much this account of liberalism owes to his historical studies. Indeed, it is on the basis of believing that it is possible to enter into the world view of thinkers in societies historically remote from our own, that he believes we can all enter into the presuppositions of people with whom we disagree in our own society.[11] It was from Vico that Berlin grasped the significance of imaginative insight into otherness, which Vico calls *entrare*.[12] To the relativist doctrine that each epoch's centre of gravity is so different that succeeding generations cannot hope to understand it, Vico famously replied, in his New Science, that what has been made or thought by human beings can be understood by them.[13] It was Vico who pointed Berlin's way to a reconciliation between the Enlightenment's faith in the universality of human nature and the Romantic movement's insistence on the historicity of human culture.

Berlin's liberalism has charted a middle course between Romantic and Enlightenment poles. On the one hand, he has pointed out the dangers that flowed from the Enlightenment's overconfidence in rationalism in politics, and its accompanying conviction that there must be one single political solution to human ills; on the other, he has sought to salvage the Enlightenment's faith in a politics and morality based in a universal anthropology of human nature from the Romantic movement's veneration of the national, the particular and the personal.

On the one hand, Berlin has accepted the romantic emphasis on the plurality of human goods that men can plausibly serve and embrace; while on the other, he has pointed out that the Romantic insistence on utter devotion to personal ideals was translated into a doctrine of radical will that led to the politics of fascism.

Berlin's account of fascism raises two difficulties. First, a fascist or proto-fascist ideology explicitly questions the status of those human values liberalism takes as universal; how, therefore, does Berlin defend his commitment to the universal from the fascist critique? Secondly, fascist behaviour is a practical test case of Berlin's belief that it is possible to enter into and understand world views repugnant to one's own. He believes that we can understand what we abhor because we share a common humanity even with the abhorrent. There is no conflict, on this view, between understanding and judging, and between comprehending and condemning. Indeed, Berlin would maintain that one can judge only what one has fully understood, and that the phrase *tout comprendre c'est tout pardonner* reverses the actual psychological relation between understanding and judging. The more we

140

understand, he would say, the easier it is to judge, and the more incumbent on us it is to do so. He has little patience with the claim that the more one understands the historical, social or psychological conditions of an odious action, the less odious it can be made to seem.[14]

The relation between understanding and judging should also be investigated from the other way round. It is obvious that there are cases where judging impedes understanding, where strong moral repulsions make one reluctant to undertake that voyage of empathy which Berlin regards as a prelude to comprehension. Fascist behaviour towards the Jews might be an example of something so inhuman that while we have no trouble abhorring it, we have considerable difficulty understanding it.

Berlin's most sustained attempt to think about fascism occurs, in a mediated and indirect form, in his essay on a fascist precursor, Joseph de Maistre, ultra-conservative essayist of the European counter-revolution in the early nineteeth century. In Berlin's analysis, de Maistre deserves to be called a fascist precursor, not because twentieth-century fascists claimed him as such, but because his thought prefigures fascist belief: its distrust of human reason, celebration of violence and irrationality in human conduct, insistence on the necessity of social subordination, its apotheosis of leadership and radical will in politics; its impatience with any restraining framework of human rights, constitutional impediments or countervailing institutions to the exercise of a leader's power. De Maistre moved the conservative counter-revolution against the French Enlightenment well beyond the Burkean defence of tradition and history, into the terrain of absolute authoritarianism.

De Maistre is a disturbing figure for liberals, Berlin argues, because he set out to demolish faith in any trans-historical moral scale based on an anthropology of human nature. De Maistre insisted that there was no such thing as Man; only men, only Frenchmen, Italians, Russians, in all their self-referential particularity. As Berlin shows, de Maistre argued in contradictory ways: first he denied the very possibility of a universalist definition of man on Enlightenment lines, and then went on to argue for a dark definition of human nature every bit as universalist as the one he was criticising. De Maistre maintained that, to the degree that cross-cultural and trans-historical generalisations about human conduct are possible at all, they go to show that aggression and love of violence are as much facts of human nature as sociability and co-operation. In Berlin's paraphrase of de Maistre's essential premiss: 'men's desire to immolate themselves is as fundamental as their desire for self-preservation or happiness.'[15] War is the eternal law of human kind. The violence which is natural to the human species is part of the essential violence of the natural world: 'The whole earth, perpetually steeped in blood, is nothing but a vast altar upon which all that is living must be sacrificed without end, without measure, without pause, until the consummation of things, until evil is extinct, until the death of death.'[16]

From this vision of animal life and human psychology, an authoritarian political order is easily derived. Berlin does not spell out the different kinds of authoritarianism that might follow from de Maistrean premisses. Avishai Margalit has observed that the deeply religious content of de Maistre's thought points more obviously to Franquist fascism than to the thoroughly secular fascism of Hitler; certainly de Maistre's arguments seem to lead most obviously to Catholic conservative authoritarianism, which would seek to use political authority to repress or suppress the natural violence and aggression of its subjects. Hitler, by contrast, sought to channel such aggression along a path of violent conquest and warfare.

Berlin clearly believes that de Maistre's vision of human nature exaggerated human malignity, yet could it not be said that Berlin himself exaggerates the commonality of moral outlook and co-operation? Equally, how does he face up to the de Maistrean view that any anthropology of human passions and interests is too highly generalised to be of any use in adjudicating practical human disputes?

Berlin does not deal with these challenges to his position directly. Yet there is one essay in *The Crooked Timber*, 'European Unity and its Vicissitudes', which can be read as an indirect response to the challenge which the experience of European fascism posed to liberal tenets. Again, he emphasises that fascism is an extreme form of romantic nationalism. It denied the very idea of a common human nature and insisted that human kind was divided, by the facts of race and nationhood, into human and sub-human types. Fascism, therefore, carried the doctrine of moral relativism to its ultimate extreme. When this nationalist relativism was married to the romantic ideal of sincerity – of absolute devotion to one's own ideal, however conceived – the roots of fascist politics were laid.

One important implication of this analysis is that it seeks to recover fascism as an authentic product of some of the best and most central European traditions. Some critics, like Perry Anderson, have argued that Berlin is inconsistent because he derives both fascism and anti-fascist resistance from the same matrix of Romantic values. But it is not inconsistent for a historian to claim that 'the same doctrines' exercise 'diametrically opposite effects'; surely that is what doctrines do: the same Marxian texts have been glossed in antithetical ways by their heirs, and it is unsurprising that the same Romantic doctrine of self-hood might inspire Hitler and von Stauffenberg.

More interestingly, if the same doctrine could inspire both evil deeds and noble resistance, the implication must clearly be that fascism is not the eruption of primordial or instinctual evil, but the perverse elaboration of romantic doctrines of sincerity, integrity and national pride which, in other contexts, could have noble consequences. In this manner, Berlin insists that fascism is a historical rather than a de-moniacal or psychologically aberrant phenomenon. Such an interpretation provides the basis for his argument that fascism is humanly comprehensible, that we can understand what we abhor, because in this case, the ideology at least is human only too human.

Accordingly, Berlin argues, we should think of fascism as a faithful working out in politics of some of our most cherished European values: the reverence for individual will, human creativity, and personal sincerity:

> The moving figure of Beethoven in his garret creating immortal works in poverty and suffering duly yields to that of Napoleon, whose art is the making of states and peoples. If self-realisation is aimed at as the ultimate goal, then might it not be that the transformation of the world by violence and skill is itself a kind of sublime aesthetic act?[17]

From this vision of politics as the aesthetic manipulation of men and societies to 'extreme nationalism and fascism' is, Berlin writes, 'but a short step'.

It is here, I think, that Berlin's account, important and suggestive as it is, may require further elaboration. For the step from Romantic theories of the aesthetic to the real historical practices of the SS is anything but small. An important chain of causation linking the Romantic ideology to fascist practice remains to be specified. It is one thing to demonstrate the specifically anti-human content of fascist

Romanticism, and quite another to explain how people could have believed it to be true, for example, that Jews did not belong to the same human family. What needs developing in Berlin's account of fascism is why anti-humanist belief remained entirely impervious to the demonstrable fact that Jews were human and why this belief seemed so plausible that individuals could murder in its name.

This piece of the argument is important because Berlin's liberalism is premissed on the belief that most people do happen to perceive the common humanity of other human beings. How then does Berlin sustain his own belief in the idea of common humanity, given that many fascists so evidently did not?

He accepts that the fascist experience administered a terrible rebuke to human pride, but rejects the argument that the Holocaust destroyed the possibility of believing in the common goodness of humanity or in the idea of a common human nature. Berlin's own reaction makes it clear that he will not be party to this form of despair. By 'trampling on certain values', Berlin argues, fascism has paradoxically demonstrated their importance as the starting point for any politics of decency. There has been in Europe, he writes, a 'kind of return to the ancient notion of natural law', in our discovery that 'no court, no authority . . . could . . . allow men to bear false witness, or torture freely or slaughter fellow men for pleasure.'[18]

Instead of defining what human beings have in common in terms of various human capabilities and attributes, Berlin defines our common humanity in negatives, in terms of those derogations of human dignity and human personhood that all can agree are unacceptable. Thus, in place of an optimistic Enlightenment view that all men share the attributes of reason, we have instead a pessimistic view that what men share is their capacity to suffer.

Such a definition of common human interests appears to set the limits of liberal tolerance for Berlin. 'If,' he writes, 'we meet someone who cannot see why . . . he should not destroy the world in order to relieve a pain in his little finger, or someone who genuinely sees no harm in condemning innocent men, or betraying friends, or torturing children, then we find that we cannot argue with such people, not so much because we are horrified as because we think them in some way inhuman – we call them moral idiots.'[19]

The important phrase 'moral idiots' clearly implies an agent who, while ostensibly rational in instrumental ways, does not appear either to understand or to attach any significance to Berlin's idea of a common humanity. Such a description applies perfectly to the fascist or, more accurately, to the type of fascist Berlin particularly wishes to understand, not the brute who acts under the compulsion of orders or his own sadistic instincts, but individuals like Albert Speer, whose 'high degree of scientific knowledge and skill, and indeed of general culture' did not prevent them from committing or abetting moral abomination.[20]

The problem with the phrase 'moral idiots', when applied to such people is that it appears to accept that their moral choices are beyond the possibility of genuine understanding. The ideal of moral idiocy appears to take back what the earlier historical analysis of fascist ideology seemed to grant: namely that they were acting upon a perverted, yet none the less understandable interpretation of post-Romantic European values. A 'moral idiot' cannot be held to act on any consistently understandable premises whatever. He can only be resisted and, when apprehended, locked up.

On this reading, therefore, Berlin can give us plausible grounds for judging, condemning, even locking up fascists. Fascist politics indeed offers historical vindication of the abject human consequences of a politics which denies the existence of trans-historical, trans-cultural, trans-national human interests. Berlin's liberalism here reveals how far indeed it is from all-forgiving relativism. The real problem is that the practices of empathetic understanding, central to liberal politics, break down in the case of fascists. Or at least a wide gap remains between understanding the Romantic preconditions of fascist belief and understanding why these could produce practices of murder and extermination.

The dilemma Berlin's analysis presents us with is this: either you maintain that fascists are human only too human, and you therefore absorb into your account of human nature some measure of the de Maistrean vision of human beings as innately and naturally violent; or you maintain that all human beings know what inhumanity consists in, in which case fascists cease to qualify as normal human beings. Berlin wants to maintain both that all human beings know what it is to be human, and that fascists were human only too human. It is not clear how he can. That appears to be the dilemma left unresolved in his account of fascism. If it is left unresolved in his account, it is left unresolved in most others as well.

CHAPTER 10

Whose History? What Ideas?[1]
Yael Tamir

The first time I saw Berlin he was standing at the far end of All Souls' lawn. In his three-piece dark blue suit, the golden chain of his watch hanging over his vest, he seemed to fit the Oxford background as much as the library tower behind him. For me, as for many others, he looked entirely the part of the Oxford don. But when I once referred to the symbolic role he had come to play in British academic life, he paused for a moment and replied: 'Well, this may be the way others think of me, but I know that I am still a Russian Jew from Riga, and all my years in England cannot change this. I love England, it has become my home, I have been very well treated here and I cherish many features of English life, but I am a Russian Jew; that is how I was born and that is who I will be to the end of my life.'

We often talked about matters of personal identity, and this paper continues those discussions. I find it worthwhile to pursue some of these arguments because I find Berlin's reflections on his own identity, and on Jewish identity in general, central to the understanding of his philosophy. Furthermore, I think that, paradoxically, Berlin's awareness of the singularity of Jewish fate led him to an understanding of a more general issue lying at the heart of much of the contemporary philosophical and political debate – the longing for status.

When I congratulated Isaiah after he was awarded the Agnelli prize for 'an unusual contribution to the values of post-industrial society', he amusingly remarked that he had never used the term 'post-industrial society' nor could he recall any contribution he had ever made to the values of such a society. However, in this paper I shall argue that a characteristic feature of this society – the struggle of ethnic minorities and women with issues of recognition and status – can find support in Berlin's approach to these questions, as well as in his general views on the nature of philosophy.

Berlin would almost certainly be dismayed to find himself in such unexpected company, but his dread is unfounded. Women and members of ethnic groups put forward claims that have found clear and convincing support in his own writings. They have adopted and developed themes which are central to his philosophy: a criticism of the Enlightenment; a historicist point of view which claims that social norms and values, as well as the categories in which we think of them, have no metaphysical *a priori* justifications but only historical explanations; the notion that learning about the values central to our society is a matter of historical inquiry, which will reveal that individuals have adopted different forms of life, distinct languages, categories of thinking and 'evaluative horizons' (to borrow Taylor's concept) that cannot be reconciled either in theory or in practice; and that the only possible way to respect individuals and their autonomy is by advocating pluralism – of values, cultures and discourse, as well as of practical and moral solutions.

Blacks, women and members of minority groups demand that their society be open-minded and acknowledge the different cultural traditions found within it. They warn against the destructive and oppressive results of intellectual vanity, of assuming one group possesses a privileged source of knowledge or special insights into wisdom and truth. They share Berlin's concern that 'too much enthusiasm for common norms can lead to intolerance and disregard for the inner life of man' (*FEoL*, p. lviii).* And, most importantly, they adopt Berlin's view that pluralism is the public virtue most necessary for the just and stable existence of modern, heterogeneous societies.

The Search for Status

A Jew, Berlin once told me, is someone whom others normally take to be a Jew. Much of the complexity of modern ethnic identity is encompassed by this definition. It is only in the modern world, where matters of identity are both crucial and debatable, that Jewishness can be reasonably defined in social rather than religious categories, in terms of the ways in which one is described by others.

Doubts concerning the definition of ethnic identity emerge only when the walls of the closed, primordial community crack and individual members find themselves confronted with the external world. This

* The following abbreviations of Berlin's works will be used: *A C* = *Against the Current*, Hogarth Press, 1980. *C C* = *Concepts and Categories*, Hogarth Press, 1978. *F E o L* = *Four Essays on Liberty*, Oxford University Press, 1969.

confrontation shatters the old, self-evident sense of communal identity, evokes confusion and frustrates the individual's sense of belonging.

As long as Jews were confined to their ghettos, living separate and intense communal lives and practicing their religion and culture, their distinct identity was evident both to them and to the surrounding society. Questions of identity became problematic only after Emancipation, when Jews confronted new opportunities and dilemmas. Some chose to remain within their traditional, familiar surroundings, while others assimilated and became what Berlin calls marginal Jews – Jews who are in the process of leaving the community. But some, although feeling incapable of assimilation, nevertheless wanted to become part of the surrounding society. These individuals are often the most tormented, wandering in a no-man's-land; they have detached themselves, at least partly, from their community of origin, yet cannot find their place in the new society. Their perplexed relation to their own background, oscillating between self-contempt and aggressive arrogance, is associated with a deep desire to be accepted by members of the surrounding society and an even deeper fear that they will turn into 'objects of scorn or antipathy to those very members of the new society by whom they most wished to be recognized and respected' (A C, p. 255).

In their intense desire to be accepted by the new society, they might be willing to disguise their particularistic features and be 'a Jew at home, and a man in the street', but this strategy often leads to a torn, schizophrenic, existence. Individuals wish to avoid the pain caused by the adoption of a split identity and desire to express their particularities in public, to retain their identity and yet be recognised as full members of society. Rather than assimilate, they wish to integrate within their new society. When denied this possibility, when forced to choose between assimilation and withdrawal, individuals face the unsolvable dilemma typical of 'an age of nationalism in which self-identification with the dominant group becomes supremely important, but, for some individuals, abnormally difficult' (A C, p. 255).

The emergence of nation-states which demand ultimate allegiance and encourage social and cultural homogeneity, coupled with growing waves of immigration, created a situation in which growing numbers of individuals found themselves living in alien societies and facing the need to give up their ethnic identity in return for membership.

Members of such minority groups stake a claim for recognition and status. They wish to be able to identify openly with their community of origin without feeling ashamed, patronised or despised. They revolt against those who either ignore or question the uniqueness and worthiness of their group.

This desire for status is best described by Berlin in his celebrated 'Two Concepts of Liberty'. What members of oppressed classes and nationalities demand, argues Berlin, is

> neither simply unhampered liberty of action for their members, nor, above everything, equality of social and economic opportunities, still less assignment of a place in a frictionless, organic state devised by rational law givers. What they want, as often as not, is simply recognition (of their class, or nation, or colour, or race) as an independent source of human activity, as an entity with a will of its own, intending to act in accordance with it (whether it is good or legitimate, or not), and not to be ruled, educated, guided, with however light a hand, as being not quite fully human, and therefore not quite fully free (*FEoL*, p. 157).

Individuals desire their group to be respected and recognised because their personal identity is intertwined with that of the group and because what they are, feel and think, the ways in which they act and the way in which others perceive them, is deeply influenced by the community of which they are part. Affronts to their community are thus perceived as a personal offence, and the rejection of their community's values and traditions as a debasement of their own beliefs and norms of behaviour.

Being forced to reject one's past and communal affiliations can result in personal tensions and identity crises. Those who are able to come to terms with their roots are, therefore, better off than those who suppress or ignore them. Hess and Weizmann are Jews who proudly, though not arrogantly, accepted their national roots. They understood national affiliations to be a real, influential force in human life and argued that those who deny their nationality forfeit everyone's respect. It seems that this is the source of Berlin's sympathy for these two figures of early Zionism. Like Hess and Weizmann, Berlin always respected his origins. Though he integrated in English society and adopted some of its features – the correctness of English life, its moderation, the civilised contempt for extremes and the whole tone of its public life (indeed, he became the modern prophet of these values) –

he proudly retained his Jewish-Russian identity. The attempt to manifestly adopt the features of the surrounding society, the permanent self-conscious quest for identity, the additional effort demanded from those who are never confident of their acceptance, these are the features that characterise, for Berlin, Jewish life in the Diaspora.

Zionism was meant to relieve these pressures, to create a society where Jews could lead a normal, uncomplicated life and where, to borrow Hess's words, 'the existence of Jewish self-identity will neither need to be demonstrated nor to be demonstrated away' (*A C*, p. 238). To the extent that Zionism has succeeded in doing this, it has achieved its goal. Zionism illustrates what I consider to be the first strategy through which individuals may acquire status – the separatist strategy. This strategy, adopted by most national movements in the twentieth century, suggests that groups can acquire status and redeem their members from a permanent feeling of alienation only by creating a nation-state.

Several advantages can be claimed for the nation-state from the perspective of the struggle for status. It provides a political framework with which individuals can identify, which expresses their values, endorses their way of life and tells their history. Living in such a framework reinforces the feeling that these beliefs and norms have value, and can act as a source of personal dignity. It also promotes feelings of solidarity, fraternity, mutual understanding and a shared fate, and thus grants individuals comfort and security. Moreover, nation-states are a source of status and recognition because international institutions (like the United Nations) accept only states as members, thus implying that only those groups that have established a nation-state can gain international recognition as distinct and worthy.

The separatist stage of the struggle for status is not yet over, as is clearly evident from the re-emergence of demands for the establishment of nation-states in Eastern Europe. Ukrainians, Moldavians, Serbs, Slovaks, all take to the streets waving their flags, singing their hymns, and unearthing national heroes buried deep in the shadows during the long years of Communism. These popular uprisings reflect a belief two centuries old, that status and recognition can be achieved only with the establishment of a nation-state.

Yet the second half of this century has also witnessed a different struggle for status. I shall define this type of struggle as a struggle for integrative status, motivated by the desire to join the surrounding society rather than to separate from it. Americans of Greek, Italian and Hispanic origin, British citizens of Pakistani or Indian origin, French citizens of Algerian origin, as well as Blacks in America and women all over the world neither wish to nor can establish independent political frameworks. However, they desire the society in which they live and the state of which they are citizens to recognise and appreciate their distinct values, traditions and histories. They demand more than equal rights and opportunities and the ability to experience full formal political participation. They wish to participate in a deeper way, to partake in the creation of the less formal, though no less important, aspects of society. They hope to bring into the public sphere their specific historical memories, local traditions, language, values and norms, which have so far been ignored or marginalised, and thus bestow upon them social legitimation and respect. Members of such groups thus challenge the closure of the existing culture, the hegemony of one historical narrative over others, the artificial homogeneity of the central norms and values adopted by the society. In short, they call for a recognition of the heterogeneous nature of society.

In this endeavour for integrative status, women play an important role. Though their claims are continuous with those of other social, racial and national groups, they have greater force. Women are not a minority, they do not have a homeland to which they can return, they neither wish to nor can create a separate social framework. The feminist claim can thus serve best to explain the logic of the integrative stage which the struggle for status has entered.

Entering Sarastro's Temple – the Feminist Creed
'Feminism' is a term Berlin would probably never be caught using. Yet his concern with issues of identity, his defence of the struggle for status and his firm condemnation of theories of 'self-realisation' provide excellent tools for analysing the sources of the subjection of women.

Like Jews, Blacks and members of other 'hyphenated' groups, as Berlin calls them, Greek-, Hispanic-, Italian- or Black-Americans, British-Pakistanis, French-Algerians, Canadian-Indians, women re-alise that attaining formal rights and equal opportunities is just scraping the tip of the iceberg. Women still feel downgraded, because they are regarded as inherently weak, both mentally and physically, and unable to play significant roles in the social, moral or public realms. Individuals, Berlin tells us, can feel unfree if they are members of 'an unrecognized or insufficiently respected group' (*FEoL*, p. 157). They may therefore strive not only for their own liberation but for the emancipation of an entire class, community, race and, in our case, a whole gender. There is no better description of the motivation for involvement in the women's movement.

Women want to be recognised as a source of autonomous human activity and reject the notion that their physical constitution makes them naturally emotional and incapable of rational skills. They state their refusal to be 'ruled, educated, guided with however light a hand, as not being quite fully human, and therefore not quite fully free.' Women claim that they are capable of self-rule, and that qualities such as rationality, objectivity, logical thinking and matter-of-factness are not necessarily masculine.

The craving for recognition, argues Berlin, can lead individuals to escape the weakness and humiliation of their social group by identifying with another group that is free from the defects of their original condition. In the attempt to acquire a new personality they adopt 'a new set of clothing, a new set of values, habits, new armour which does not press upon the old wounds, on the old scars left by the chains one wore as a slave' (*AC*, p. 259). Hundreds of businesswomen in their executive suits and briefcases have followed this strategy. They claim to be able to play according to men's rules, or even tell men: 'Anything you can do I can do better.'

Yet this strategy can turn into a trap. It suggests that, in order to participate, women must turn against their gender, denounce their femininity and be like men, only more so. Realising the inherent deficiencies of this strategy, women sought alternatives. Some were drawn to adopt the exact counterpart of the first: they started to glorify their femininity, invented heroines as models for identification and claimed that a world ruled by women would be a better world. They attempted to describe themselves as raised above men, adopting slogans like the rear-window stickers on many feminists' cars: 'When God created man, what did She mean', to retell human history and reconstruct its moral. Eve, feminists claimed, tempted Adam not into sin but into acquiring knowledge; without women, men would still be going around naked and eating acorns in the woods.

Clearly, neither approach could really bring women the status they hoped for. Like others struggling for status, women soon found that they have to put forward a more complex, yet more sincere, claim. On the one hand, they must state that they possess the attributes required in order to act in the public sphere of their societies; on the other, they must claim that they have been socialised to develop and exhibit particular characteristics which are of general value. Women thus claim they can be as rational, objective and logical as any man and also that values like caring, sharing, devoting oneself to the welfare of others and expressing warmth and attentiveness, which have all been categorised as female virtues, should be fostered by society at large. They suggest it is unjust and unwise to force women into giving up these qualities in order to become active members in the public sphere.

Women rule out the image of themselves as lighthearted, frivolous and helpless creatures, as well as its implication, namely, that women need men in order to save them from outer threats as well as from their own irrational selves. Above all, women reject the notion that they should gladly and gratefully subject themselves to men, who are naturally rational, responsible and trustworthy, and that only this subjection will allow them to be free and discover their real, true selves.

Berlin warns against the awesome consequences of the illusion that we can attain 'true freedom' or that we may discover our 'real', 'higher' self through subjection to a 'self' identified with reason. Theories of 'self-realisation', as Berlin pointed out, have generally been used in the service of severe oppression. Feminists suggest that such theories have been particularly devastating for women. Women are led to believe that they must face a painful dilemma, since they can achieve self-realisation either by subjection to men or by adopting 'manly qualities'; in other words, by renouncing either their freedom or their femininity.

However hard women have tried to fit into the masculine world, they have found that they are still kept out of the public realm, blocked by what feminists describe as a 'glass ceiling' which can be neither seen nor passed. Even today, for most women, the answer to the question: 'Who governs me?' is 'A man', and 'How can I succeed?' is 'Adopt "manly" qualities.' This reflects the informal yet very real subjection women are exposed to. It may explain why, even in liberal democratic societies where women enjoy the full scale of rights and benefits on a par with men, they feel uncomfortable and constrained.[2]

Berlin, though never concerned with the oppression of women as such, rightly identifies the strategy adopted by many women in their attempt to evade oppression as a retreat into an inner citadel. Women have turned inward, into the private sphere where they feel safe, and have convinced themselves that their man, the head of the family, will surely protect their best, true interests and desires.

Feminists have pointed to an inevitable process by which women, from this 'voluntary' withdrawal into the private sphere, slid into a forced one which has locked them within the warmth of the homely jail. They call attention to the fact that the dichotomy between public and private, originally meant to secure for each person a range of negative liberties, has become an oppressive device in the case of women, who are often forced to remain in the protected private sphere and be excluded from public life.

In the first stages of their struggle for status and respect, women demanded to be allowed to take their place within the public sphere. However, today they have further demands. They desire the public sphere to be transformed. Feminists thus reject the ideal of a harmonious, neutral and rational public sphere. Such a public sphere is necessarily oppressive, since unity and coherence are achieved by ignoring the so-called 'feminine virtues', by overlooking the relevance of race and culture and by denying the importance of membership in any association but the state. An emancipatory conception of public life will, on the other hand, explicitly promote heterogeneity by allowing members to 'bring their specific *histories* into the public'.[3]

Women, non-whites and members of national minorities no longer agree to play the role of the passionate savage in need of guidance and restraint; they want to enter the public realm as full members, without losing their particularity. Struggling to enter Sarastro's temple, Tamino and Papageno are warned by the priest against the treachery of women, who have deceived many wise men. In Sarastro's temple, so they learn, the rules of manly brotherhood prevail and duplicity has no place. Those outside, however, wish to enter this temple of wisdom as equals, without being suspected of treachery or of possessing mythical satanic powers. They wish to be initiated as full members, able to share in the bonds of human friendship without relinquishing their membership in their own particular groups or disguising their particularistic features.

Women, Blacks, and members of national minorities wish to change the nature of Sarastro's temple and play a new music within its walls. Their claims are important because they refute a common liberal view, namely, that the public sphere should and could be culturally neutral.

Whose History? Which Ideas?

It is always those who are at the fringes of society who appreciate the extent to which the public sphere expresses the values, traditions and the conception of history of the ruling group (or groups). It is they who feel most alienated from the public sphere, but yet do not wish to withdraw and create their own political entity, and would rather integrate to become full members. However, they will feel accepted as members only if the political institutions officially recognise their language, respect their holidays and embrace their heroes – teach about them in schools, name streets after them, put their portraits on stamps and bills – in short, incorporate, at least symbolically, some elements of their culture and history.

Blacks and American-Indians, Sephardic-Israelis, Aboriginal-Australians, as well as women, claim that they will be able to see themselves as full members if, and only if, their historical narratives, their particularistic features and their contribution to society attain their proper place. They therefore call for a critical and reflective attitude toward the 'shared', as it were, history, culture, language and values.

These claims imply that society should be ready to reflect on the foundations of its social makeup, on the way it defines its origins, on its terms of membership and on its code of behaviour. Such reflections cut through two spheres: the first has to do with the way in which society sees its history and the second with the way in which it defines its present culture, values and traditions.

Members of 'hyphenated' groups claim that society should be ready to retell its history to include events that have so far been marginalised or ignored, either because they were a source of moral embarrassment or because they were significant only to groups which had no social or political power. For us in Israel, this means we should critically reflect upon uncomfortable moments in our history such as how the pre-state establishment dealt with the Holocaust, how the newly established state absorbed immigrants from Oriental countries, how the Israeli-Palestinian conflict has developed since the end of the nineteenth century, and so on. In America, this attitude might imply that the story of the injustice done to native Indians and that of Black slavery should be retold. A similar reconstruction of history is called for in places such as Australia, Canada and many South American states. Moreover, in almost every society the place of women should be reconsidered.

Retelling history could, at least in some cases, be a liberating experience, as it is nowadays in many Eastern European countries. Yet it is a painful process. It opens old wounds and forces people to confront the notion that the stories they have been told so far were biased in favour of those groups holding social power. Moreover, it forces all to come to terms with the idea that fellow citizens have been wronged and mistreated. Still, its value is enormous. It seems that individuals prefer to cope with the idea that they were once part of a poorly treated, even enslaved, group, subscribing to values they themselves, in their present position, can no longer endorse, rather than being ignored and considered 'human dust' to be rescued from their past, re-educated and guided by members of the ruling group. The collective must therefore encompass the moments of glory of every one of its group, as well as the moments of humiliation.

However, the struggle for status embodies a second claim, which relates to an altogether different sphere. It questions the present values and norms considered central to society. This criticism is shared by those founding members of society who have so far been marginalised, as well as by those who are relative newcomers. Such claims are raised, for instance, by members of the growing Moslem community in the United States, by American-Hispanics, by Pakistanis in England and by Algerians in France, who all complain of prejudices against them and of the marginalisation of their religion, language and traditions. Being equal members, they claim, means that they should at least be able to express their values and traditions, as well as speak their language in the public sphere.[4]

Those advocating these challenges might well adopt, as their starting point, Berlin's views on philosophy and morality. They must contest the idea that there are eternally true answers to normative issues, to be found by either *a priori* deduction, empirical inquiry or formal analysis. They must express disbelief in the notion that all essential philosophical questions could simply be eliminated by proving they are founded on intellectual error, verbal muddles or ignorance of facts. They must accept Berlin's historicism, suggesting that the only way to define the values central to our society is to look back at our shared history. They must also accept that these historical investigations will not teach us ultimate truths, but will inform us which values and norms have turned out to be necessary components of our society.

Those who claim that society cannot define its shared values if it is not attentive to the plurality of its normative roots must agree with Berlin that questions concerning basic human features or values have only quasi-empirical answers: 'This is to say, it seems to be a question for the answer of which we must go to historians, anthropologists, philosophers of culture, social scientists of various kinds, scholars who study the central notions and central ways of behaviour of entire societies, revealed in monuments, forms of life, social activity, as well as more overt expressions of belief such as faiths, philosophies, literature' (*FEoL*, p. liii).

While accepting Berlin's method, women and members of minority groups suggest that our view of the areas where we have looked for the roots of our society has so far been too narrow and, consequently, we have a distorted view of our central values and traditions. They suggest we search for answers in new territories.

The idea that society should respect or incorporate at least some of the values, norms and traditions upheld by members of minority groups, as well as by women, need not be seen as an invitation to total relativism and moral havoc. We should remember that our discussion takes place in a particular context, that the justification for the process of social reflection is the liberal democratic ideal of equality, entitling all to equal concern and respect, both as individuals and as members of particular groups. When members of particular groups demand that society, in the name of equal treatment, adopt values or norms that curtail this basic idea, they undercut their own claim. This is a thin, though rigid, safeguard from the slide into moral relativism, and it is as far as we can go to secure ourselves without oppressing those members of our society who do not share the liberal point of view.

Some may claim that this position represents the worst of all possible worlds. It gives priority to a very thin layer of liberal values, yet undercuts those cultures or religions that cannot accept the liberal axiom that individuals should be treated with equal concern and respect. I would suggest that this is the unavoidable result of the uneasy relations between liberal pluralism, which endorses the right of cultural groups to preserve their own lifestyles, and the contents of such lifestyles which, when preserved, may at times foster illiberal values. The alternative, however, is to assume the arbiter's role and decide which groups will be allowed to display their values in the public sphere, entailing a paternalistic, oppressive position, which contradicts many basic liberal beliefs. Liberals, aware of the incommensurability and incompatibility of their own values, must therefore strike an uneasy compromise, and they are best advised to follow Berlin's warning that the imposition of absolute solutions too often leads to blood, and driving principles to their limits tends to create grave and unnecessary suffering. When faced with two colliding worthwhile principles, to accept one and reject the other entirely leads to unwelcome results, and what we could at most look for are decent compromises and untidy solutions. Tidiness, argues Berlin, is not a proper ideal for any country, particularly not for heterogeneous ones.

The integrative struggle for status can succeed only in societies which see pluralism rather than tidiness as the most important feature of the state. Pluralism recognises that there are many human goals, not all of them commensurable and often at odds with each other, that different cultures foster values and norms which are not necessarily compatible, and that our intellectual history is one of competing trends of thought, none of which can prove to supersede all previous ones.

Pluralism, argues Berlin, is human because it does not deprive human beings of much that they have found to be indispensable to their life. 'In the end men choose between ultimate values; they choose as they do, because their life and thought are determined by fundamental moral categories and concepts that are, at any rate over large stretches of time and space, a part of their being and thought and sense of their own identity; part of what makes them human' (*FEoL*, p. 172). To demand that they abandon their values, commitment and language is to question their humanity and their freedom.

Genuine pluralism, namely, pluralism not based on tolerating ways of life we think are wrong or inferior to ours but fostering real respect for other ways of thinking and for beliefs different and even contrary to our own, might lead to social and moral confusion. But it is the only honest way to respect the freedom and autonomy of individuals and to grant them the status and recognition they desire to achieve.

This line of argument evokes justified theoretical and practical concerns: How are we to make normative decisions if our starting point is that only history can provide us with an answer? How are we to justify our acceptance of the filter of 'equal concern and respect'? Barring any other way, should such decisions be taken democratically, and should we accept the right of society to do a 'democratic wrong' as long as it is ready to reflect on it and, when necessary, revise its decisions? What if we cannot reach an agreement, if our society is composed of too many subcultures which find it hard to define any shared values? These are honest, if frightening, dilemmas, but the alternative to contending with them is to endorse oppressive homogeneity.

What Berlin teaches us is that liberal societies must learn to accommodate conflicting cultures, views, values and life plans. They must learn to face the limits of their philosophy and the ambiguities and uncertainties that accompany it. They must be deeply pluralistic in the sense that they must conceive of their public life as a continuous struggle for the realisation of freedom rather than as a search for one eternal, universal moral truth. They will therefore carry on the tradition of philosophical debate which can best be fostered in a 'world where ends collide' (CC, p. 149).

CHAPTER 11

Six Variations
(Thoughts for Isaiah Berlin, arising from reading Pepys' Journal)
Stephen Spender

So busy: Pepys at Cambridge, 1660

February 26: 'With my father –
Walked in the fields behind King's College
Chapel yard . . . Met Mr Fairbrother
Who took us both to Botolphe's Church
Where Mr Nicholas of Queens preached: text –
*   "For thy commandments are broad."*

. . . Thence to dine with Mr Widdrington
Who had with him two fellow commoners
And a Fellow of the college, Mr Pepper . . .
Later, to Magdalen to obtain
The certificate of my brother's entrance –
After which Mr Pechell joined us
And we all sat in the Rose Tavern
Drinking the King's health until dark . . .
Back to our lodging next, then once more
To the Tavern again with Mr Blayton
And Mr Merle with a quart of wine.'

I

Such talking drinking life – three hundred
And thirty years ago! Reading, I don't think:
'Where are they now, those chatterers? – Thrust
'In graveyards? Less than dust – salt sown

'In ship-wrecked oceans? Blood-red rust
'Of battlefields that crops
'Green out of? Left, some relics
'Rotting in attics – sword-hilt, snuff box,
'Silver or ivory – skeletons
'Cased in provincial museums?'

II
No, when I read Pepys now, he and his cronies
Burn from their days and through my veins –
Their acts and passions one with those
Moving through mine! As though
To live meant to be tenant of
This temporary flesh through which
Continually the one life flows
Out of the past – through us, and to
Those generations yet unborn.

III
What do I speak but dead men's words?
What are my thoughts but dead men's minds?

IV
Well, there's the being conscious. *Now!* –
Each separate life, an 'I' (a world,
To his own self) within which meet
All that's outside: the multitudes
That make this time – and the dead past
Buried within the present – and,
Light-years away, that furthest star
Proved, yet unseen; all pulsing through
My living world to make the future.

V
What haunts us now are not those ghosts –
From the cased past, but from the future:
Ghosts of the unborn – avatars,
Maddened with greed that was our time's – ,
Powered with the means that our times made –

To end all life on Earth, and leave
This planet a charred shell within

VI

The elemental Universe
Of minerals, fire, and ice, and air,
That know not Time nor Space – where are
Nor eyes to see nor ears to hear
The roaring and the silences
The never-meeting distances
– Nor consciousness, nor Mind, wherein
The shaping atoms recognize
Their world within a word, the name,
Joined on the tongue, those points of flame.

CHAPTER 12

A Puzzle about Italian Art
Francis Haskell

Isaiah Berlin's range of enthusiasms is so wide that it would be difficult to pick out any one country as holding a quite special place in his affection and interests. But as soon as one makes the effort – an effort akin to those party games which he much enjoys playing (who are the ten most famous Portuguese? The five best twentieth-century composers? and so on) – one sees that Italy must count as a very strong candidate. This may come as a surprise to those who are familiar above all with his studies of Russian poets and thinkers or of the Jewish contribution to intellectual life or of German responses to the Enlightenment. And yet there is much evidence to support the claim. The study of Machiavelli and Vico has been immeasurably enriched by his essays on these most complex of writers; his love of minor Italian operas of the nineteenth century will take him, in a hot summer, on the longest and most tiresome of train journeys to enjoy the revival of some unfamiliar work; and, above all, he spends some two months every year in a house perched high above the Ligurian coast which can be reached only on foot by a precipitous mountain path – from here he will emerge for a long walk and a short bathe and to purchase ice cream and the newspapers. A plentiful supply of 'Prego, Prego' in reply to even the most importunate requests will testify to the enjoyment with which he engages in all these activities. To them must be added the fact that having been awarded a very substantial prize by the Agnelli Foundation in Turin, he has generously donated most of it to the furtherance of Italian studies in Oxford, to which therefore his name will in future always be linked.

Northerners have been coming to Italy for many centuries, and for most of them the main attractions have been the great buildings, paintings and sculptures which have long since been codified by guide books and tourists. Isaiah's Italy, which is not codified, is a different one, and I suspect that he has been fascinated by her monuments more because of the importance they have held for others than for any direct appeal they have made to him. In the context of a volume devoted to Isaiah, it may therefore be worthwhile discussing a few earlier writers for whom art posed significant problems rather than presented instantaneous delight – problems that they felt to be of immediate relevance to their own and problems that they felt could be tackled seriously only by the historian or the philosopher. The temptation to touch on the attitudes of these men to art is all the greater in this case because some of the most important among them were to very varying degrees associated with Giambattista Vico – though Vico himself seems to have shown no interest whatsoever in the visual arts.

The problem that caused greater concern than any other was the following: why had art declined during the later Roman Empire – for (unlike today) there was, from the sixteenth century onwards, universal agreement that it *had* declined. It could be argued that the problem was not strictly historical: civilisations were, like biological organisms, subject to decay and death, and no contingent factors were therefore needed to explain what had happened. But although many claimed to subscribe to such views in principle, few could actually resist trying to be more precise when it came to the point. It need hardly be said that discussion of this problem, far from being confined to Italians, has occupied a place near the centre of European historiography as a whole for many centuries. But it is equally obvious that its significance was greater for Italians than for anyone else, for (as they very well appreciated) the cultural as well as the political standing of Italy, and not just of Rome, was always closely related to the fortunes of the Empire and the Church. For this reason the present essay will confine itself to those particular aspects of a very wide-ranging debate which were raised above all in Italy itself.

The first people to consider the problem at all were themselves artists, and it was fall rather than decline that aroused their interest. For during the fifteenth century no one seems to have expressed the view that in antiquity itself artistic styles had changed for better or for worse: at some point art had merely come to an end. At some point – but most embarrassingly that point had coincided (chronologically) with the establishment of Christianity as the favoured religion of the Empire. Coincidence or cause? That was the main controversy that dominated early discussion of the issue. It could be – and often was – claimed that the real damage had been done by the barbarian invasions:

the destruction of pagan idols had been deeply regrettable, but it had been as nothing compared to the savage incursions of the Huns and Vandals, the Goths and the Lombards who had not only destroyed all good art but had also introduced appalling styles of their own.

Early in the sixteenth century Raphael had lifted the argument on to a new footing by implying that what was truly surprising was that the excellence of ancient architecture had survived so long, for 'literature, sculpture, painting and nearly all the other arts went into a long period of decline, getting worse and worse by the time of the last Emperors.' It was simply not true, said Raphael in words whose tenor strongly suggests that he was challenging the birth of a new theory (of whose existence at this date we would otherwise know nothing), that 'among ancient buildings, those that were less old were less beautiful, or less well composed or designed in some other style'. In other words, there had been no decline in the quality of architecture before the arrival of the Goths, because although many earlier buildings had been restored or even replaced by the Romans themselves, the work had always been carried out in traditional styles. To demonstrate how long and successfully the standards of Roman architecture had been maintained, Raphael singled out one of the last great monuments in the city, the Arch of Constantine, which 'was well composed and well made'. However, the sculptured decorations on the surface told a very different story. Immediately above the two smaller arches on both the main façades and, at the same level, on the sides of the monument were six narrow rectangular friezes which Raphael evidently recognised as being contemporary with the arch: they were 'quite ridiculous, without art or any sense of good design'. However, just above these were roundels, and in the passageway and on the attic there were some far more elegant friezes which, noted Raphael, had been removed from monuments dedicated to Trajan and Antoninus Pius (who had lived two centuries earlier), and these were 'absolutely excellent and of the most perfect style'.

Although earlier artists seem to have been well aware of the change which had occurred between the earlier and the later decorations – for among surviving drawings made of various parts of the Arch there are none of the Constantinian reliefs – Raphael was the first to comment in writing on the evidently drastic decline in sculptural quality which had taken place between the second and the fourth centuries, and he may even have been able to anticipate most of the conclusions which were reached by archaeologists only three or four hundred years after his researches, though this cannot be proved. In any case, the implications of Raphael's observations were clear enough: the 'end of art' had not been a uniform process as hitherto suggested, and – as regards sculpture and painting – it had not been brought about by either of the causes proposed: barbarian invasions or Christian iconoclasm. Indeed, he seems to have felt that Christianity had had no part in the process at all, for the two examples of sculptural decoration which he picks out for special contempt are those produced for the persecuting Emperor Diocletian and for Constantine – both of whom are however credited with having inspired fine architecture. The slow decline of the figurative arts was virtually complete by the time of Constantine – the much admired equestrian monument once said to represent that Emperor was now believed by scholars to portray Marcus Aurelius or one of the other Antonines – and although Raphael gave no specific explanation for this decline, it is clear that he (and those later writers who shared his analysis of late Roman art) would have thought of it as a natural consequence of the decline of the Empire itself.

Finally in 1550, and then more elaborately in 1568, Vasari took over all the factors that had hitherto been raised – biological determinism, barbarian and Christian iconoclasm, political weakness of the Empire – and welded them into a (fairly coherent) whole backed up by evidence drawn not only from the Arch of Constantine, which had been indicated by Raphael, but from a large number of other works of art which he had looked at all over Italy.

With Vasari the contribution made to the discussion by artists themselves came to an end, and it was through his great and enormously influential book on Italian artists that it entered general historical consciousness.

It had long been distressing to cultivated Catholics that, even though the decline of art was widely agreed to have been a gradual process, the actual sculptures which were particularly singled out as examples of degenerate art were the reliefs on the Arch built to commemorate the triumphs of the Emperor Constantine who had brought about the peace of the Church. In 1594 it was just this problem that was directly faced by Cardinal Baronius, the greatest Catholic historian of his time, and himself a man of wide culture. When discussing the Arch in the third volume of his *Annales Ecclesiastici*, he produced a completely new explanation to account for the incorporation into it ('which it is easy for even the novice to see') of excellent sculpture taken from buildings which had been erected by Marcus Aurelius and other earlier Emperors, and he implicitly rejected Vasari's suggestion that this had been made necessary by the feeble state of the arts in the time of Constantine. The presence of these fine reliefs, he claimed, demonstrated the marvellous and quite incredible enthusiasm for Constantine displayed by the Senate which, in order to honour him, had not demurred from demolishing the works of those previous Emperors whom it held most dear. And Constantine had welcomed this step, even though he too greatly respected Marcus Aurelius, because it made clear 'how far the majesty of a Christian Emperor towered over the most renowned [pagan] Emperors since those images of pagan superstition that had been placed there [on the Arch] would show that that same superstition had been conquered as if they were spoils of victory, since it was the custom that conquered enemies were displayed on triumphal monuments to do them honour.' In reaching this impressive insight, Baronius was surely stimulated by the policy of Pope Sixtus V, being put into effect just as this section of the *Annales* was being written, of surmounting famous pagan monuments, such as Trajan's column, with statues of the Apostles. However, when Baronius tried to account for what he was forced to acknowledge was 'the crude, rough and unpolished' style of the reliefs dating from Constantine's lifetime, he came up with a solution of the most extravagant and perverse ingenuity: all the outstanding Christian artists had, he suggested, been swept away in the great persecution (of Diocletian) so that sculpture seems to have come to a complete end. The implication that it had been the Christians, rather than the pagans, who had maintained traditional standards of artistic quality as the Roman Empire declined proved so totally unacceptable that no credence was given to Baronius's theory even by his close followers – indeed it was later to be wholly reversed and, in general, silence seems to have constituted the most prudent course in this respect both as regards the Arch of Constantine and – still more – the paintings which in 1578 had been discovered in the catacombs.

The problem aroused by these was very similar to that aroused by the Arch of Constantine with which they were more or less contemporary. To educated taste they were hideous. Of course the evidence they provided about early Christian practices was enthralling, and as a weapon with which to fight Protestant reformers, who were keen to play down the cult of images in the early Christian church, they were invaluable. But while it was possible to account for artistic feebleness when it was to be seen in the works of the late pagans, it was much harder to do so when the artists had been devout adherents of the true faith. And so as far as possible the topic was avoided by those who studied them, and the few comments that have come down to us from men of artistic sensibility (such as Rubens) are short and evasive. In 1716, however, an antiquarian, whose name alone provides some guarantee on this score, came up with a solution which, whether directly or indirectly, has proved to be one of the most influential ever proposed to a problem of this kind.

Filippo Buonarroti, the great-nephew of Michelangelo the Younger, who was himself the great nephew of the artist, was born in 1661 and at the age of twenty left his native Florence to go to Rome, where he spent the next eighteen years or so and where he devoted himself largely to antiquarian studies. He filled notebook after notebook with sketches, both rapid and very careful, and some of them of real quality, of coins, medals and small artefacts, and he quickly earned the reputation of being one of the greatest authorities in the field – 'profound, weighty and reflective; taciturn in company though open enough in genial company; a lover of natural philosophy . . . very cautious and reserved and never one to pursue extravagant or chimerical fantasies', as he was to be described by Scipione Maffei, one of his particular admirers. Through his membership of Queen Christina's circle and later of the 'Arcadian' Academy, he met many of the leading figures of the intellectual community and became closely involved in some of the most important scholarly enterprises of the time, above all the editing (towards the end of his life) of Thomas Dempster's *De Etruria Regali*, which had been written a hundred years earlier.

In 1698 Buonarroti published his first book, which was devoted to medals belonging to Cardinal Carpegna, his principal patron. This follows the conventional pattern of identifying subjects and symbols, but – as might be expected from an author coming from such a cultivated background – he shows a greater feeling for quality than was usual among numismatists, and he refuses to accept without question the notion of inevitable decline. Thus the excellence of design and sheer beauty of a medallion of the short-lived Emperor Trebonianus Gallus of the mid-third century strikes him as being at least as good as anything made by the Greeks themselves, and this proves to him that a good artist can rise above the standard of his times; and he looks with equal freshness on other coins.

Soon afterwards Buonarroti returned to Florence, and there in 1716 he published his *Observations on some Fragments of Ancient Glass Vases Decorated with Figures Found in the Cemeteries of Rome*. He had visited the catacombs in the company of other scholars interested in Christian archaeology, and he had also acquired an impressive familiarity with ivories, mosaics and wall paintings. To a man of his taste most of these appeared repulsive, a depressing contrast to the medals of Hadrian which had so appealed to him in the Carpegna collection. Like his earlier book this one also was dedicated to the cultivated but extremely bigoted Grand Duke Cosimo III of Tuscany, and Buonarroti goes to extravagant lengths to demonstrate the extent of his piety. It was just this combination of genuine (or perhaps contrived) religious devotion and true sensitivity to beauty which led him to make his remarkably original appraisal of early Christian art. Already in his book on medals he had discussed the extent to which the Egyptians had continued to carve statues of their gods in a gross, primitive manner, even after they had acquired the skills to produce work of much higher quality, because the earlier idols attracted greater veneration. Now he went much further, and when confronted by a set of figures of the Apostles Peter and Paul painted on glass which had been found in a catacomb and which struck him as being of even lower quality than the other fragments he was forced to reproduce in his book, he claimed that this very feebleness was

a clear argument and certain proof of the great piety of the early Christians. Inasmuch as they were so jealous and so careful of the purity of their religion that they did not want to stain it with even the slightest blemish, we learn from Tertullian that they always refrained from those arts through which they might have run the risk of contaminating themselves with idolatry. And so it was that few or none of them took up painting and sculpture, whose principal aim was to represent the gods and fables of the pagans; so that when the Faithful wished to decorate their vases with symbols of devotion they were for the most part compelled to make use of unskilled craftsmen who were employed on quite different tasks. These men who had no experience of good design fashioned figures guided only by their own natural talents and a crude observation of nature which – as had occurred at the birth of painting and sculpture – presented only its material aspects to them. They were, in fact, unable to distinguish the components of nature or their arrangement and beauty. However, it is impossible to deny that the very crudity of the artists did much to achieve the true purpose of sacred images – that is, to give fruitful instruction to the Faithful. For as these figures are entirely lacking in any beauty or decoration, which usually distract the spirit and the mind from contemplation, and as they are made with natural simplicity and no admixture of external things, they strengthened the feelings of devotion in those who looked at them.

Buonarroti brings his argument to an end by claiming that the very lack of grace and design led to a certain reverential fear and majesty which were well suited to religious art. In other words, that crudity which must hitherto have struck educated connoisseurs as a shameful falling off – to be explained away or apologised for – from the standards of the kind of art which they were accustomed to admire and collect was now affirmed to be its greatest merit. Of course, we can come across many previous examples – even in antiquity – of both connoisseurs and theorists standing up for archaic simplicity in reaction against too much sophistication, but Buonarroti's claims for the edifying value of clumsy artefacts produced by unskilled amateurs do open a new chapter in the appreciation of art. From now on weakness itself could be the best guarantee of purity and devotion, and the impact of this attitude on the interpretation of images was to be profound and long lasting.

It was not only historians of the Early Church who found themselves compelled by the logic of their situation to consider the hitherto despised images of late antique and pre-mediaeval art with greater care than had yet been given to them. Early in the eighteenth century a number of Italian historians, whose views were very different from those of the devout Baronius and his successors, rejected the notion that the supremacy of Rome had always been desirable and that once it had been lost, total barbarism had prevailed. Often in conflict with the pretensions of the papacy, and always in real danger from the Inquisition, these men (of whom Pietro Giannone and Lodovico Antonio Muratori were the most prominent) looked with some sympathy at the 'barbarian' invasions of both the Goths and the Lombards. Neither Giannone nor Muratori was by nature responsive to the appeal of architecture, painting or sculpture, but we will see that Muratori certainly acknowledged in theory that his case would be much strengthened if it could be shown that the distinctive civilisation of mediaeval Italy which he was unveiling to the world had been marked by a flowering of the arts, sciences and letters. And Giannone and Muratori both realised that the obscure and defective chronicles concerning forgotten events which they were bringing to light required far more substantiation than did the familiar and authoritative histories of a Livy or Tacitus. Every additonal piece of confirming evidence was desirable, but the difficulties that stood in the way of getting such evidence were formidable. Years later, when composing his autobiography in prison, Giannone still remembered the complaints made by his teacher, the antiquarian and professor of civil law Domenico d'Aulisio (a man who played a significant part in the life of Vico) about the antiquarians of his day. These men, he had said, carried out

> wonderful researches into the most ancient Greek and Roman medals; they understood, wonderfully well, those coins which had been found, and were still being excavated, of the ancient inhabitants of Asia and Greece and the Greek cities of Italy; they knew their Roman medals, which ones were consular and minted for the tribunes, and which imperial, and everything that belonged to the most remote and recondite antiquity; but as soon as they drew near to the years of the late Empire which were less remote from us, they became silent and utterly ignorant.

Twenty years after the death of d'Aulisio the situation had scarcely improved, and antiquarians were not yet able to elucidate coins of the Lombard kings. Indeed, the only existing set of illustrations purporting to record such coins (two folio sheets devoted to a family tree of the Lombard kings of Italy) carried a warning by the author that the features shown were not in fact derived from actual Lombard coins, but from what were rather vaguely described as 'the coins of other peoples who had lived at the same time'.

None the less, when preparing the second edition of his Neapolitan history (which appeared posthumously), Giannone was able to include a few illustrations of coins and medals from the High Middle Ages (some of which he was able to study in the fine cabinets to be found in Vienna, where he lived for some years under the protection of the Holy Roman Emperor), thanks to the researches of a handful of scholars and collectors who are beginning to share his interest in the topic.

Giannone's interest in coins (and monuments in general) was a historical, not an aesthetic one, and there is not the remotest reason for believing that he could have admired them for their barbaric beauty (and hence challenged traditional notions about the decline of ancient art), even if he did look upon the period of Lombard rule in Italy as a sort of golden age. None the less he certainly played a part in drawing attention to a new range of visual experience, and the same can be said (with rather more conviction) of Lodovico Antonio Muratori, whose life was for a short time to be involved with that of Giannone (whom he was wrongly suspected of trying to protect from his enemies) and who had already been trying for some years to get hold of medallic images of the Lombard kings, including the same inadequate sixteenth-century source that Giannone hoped to draw on – and he asked his correspondents to put him in touch with any publications they knew of. Indeed in his complex relationship to figurative sources Muratori is at once the most typical historian of his time and, to students of today, the most puzzling – although his reluctance, when already famous as one of the most learned and prolific writers, to have his portrait engraved on the grounds that 'people who want to know me will be satisfied with the little I have written', should alert us to the fact that he was not only personally modest but also sceptical concerning the value of visual evidence.

Muratori was four years older than Giannone, and – like him – began his career by studying law. In 1694–5, at the age of twenty-two, he moved from Modena to Milan, and there embarked on a life of scholarship that was to make him one of the most renowned Italians of the eighteenth century. Like Giannone, Muratori was critical of papal pretensions and he deplored the extreme partisanship of historians such as Baronius. He was acutely aware of the restraints imposed by censorship: 'We Catholics constantly complain of the too many brakes which, to tell the truth, are sometimes imposed on us by those who have power,' he wrote warily to a friend, 'so that one can no longer talk or print anything about physics, astronomy, medicine, ecclesiastical history, and other matters, without running the danger of our books being prohibited, or even greater misfortunes.' Even an enquiry about the Lombards was likely to arouse suspicion, and in seeking permission to consult official archives he found it necessary to make clear that he did not intend to pursue his researches beyond the year 1200. The main field of his researches, however, was a potentially dangerous one, for he became particularly interested in the history of the Early Church and of the Middle Ages; and he soon became embroiled in political issues through being commissioned by the Este family, who were Dukes of Modena, to provide documentary justification for the seizure by the Holy Roman Emperor of the papal fief of Comacchio, while at the same time investigating the origins of the Este family itself.

Even before embarking on these studies, Muratori claimed that 'everything concerning customs, religion, clothes, buildings' and so on belonged to the province of history, and he was fully aware of the importance of visual sources for the understanding of periods whose written records were at best patchy. He was in touch with many antiquarians and was always interested in looking at drawings of the artefacts in their possession. He also corresponded with artists such as Nicolas Vleughels and Giuseppe Maria Crespi (who claimed: 'I have learned what it is to be Christian' by reading Muratori's *La Carità Cristiana*), and he was interested in the history of painting, as is shown by his protracted exchange of letters about the life and works of Correggio with the combative artist Lodovico Antonio David.

In the preface to his *Dissertazioni sopra le Antichità Italiane* – the work in eight folio volumes in which he set out to apply the historical programme, which he had drawn up some years before his actual researches, and to discuss the arts along with every other aspect of mediaeval life – Muratori actually compares himself to a guide showing a visitor round some great palace: first the overall plan, then the rooms and staircases, followed by galleries, and the pictures and statues to be seen in them. Yet when he embarks on the dissertations themselves, he indulges in what seems to us to be a surprising reluctance to look directly at just those pictures and statues, not to mention palaces, which would have helped to buttress his arguments. And when he does so, his allusions are of a vagueness that would have been wholly unacceptable to him if applied to a literary text. How much, he tells us, he would have liked to see those large buildings which, though not beautiful in style, continued to be raised under the Lombards but which had long since been swallowed up by time. But such actual buildings and objects as did still survive are barely ever mentioned by him. He expresses the hope that the various 'noble memories of the barbarian age which remain standing' will not be pulled down, because 'although they lack Greek and Roman subtlety yet they do not fail to express venerable majesty and magnificence.' Yet he does not mention what these buildings are. Again and again he insists that the arts constitute essential historical records of the mediaeval world, but what he tells us of late antique and mediaeval art is derived almost entirely from written mediaeval sources.

Muratori's reliance almost exclusively on literary sources is surprising because, soon after he began to embark on his historical researches, he had got in touch with the man who was then doing more than anyone else to reproduce, as well as comment on, some of the principal monuments of early Christian, Byzantine and 'barbarian' artists. Monsignor Giovanni Giustino Ciampini was (despite his very close connections with the papacy) in the forefront of the intellectual revival that marked Roman culture in the last two decades of the seventeenth century through his direction of the *Giornale de' Letterati* and the *Accademia Fiscio-matematica*. He was also a Christian archaeologist of the highest distinction, who had taken a special interest in the mosaics of Ravenna.

The art of Ravenna was, in fact, a central issue for all those concerned with the fate of Italian culture at the hands of the barbarian invaders. It was there that Theodoric, King of the Goths, had made his capital, and ancient sources – particularly Cassiodorus – spoke very highly of the magnificent buildings he had erected. This tradition was, of course, kept alive in Ravenna itself, but the mainstream of Italian art criticism which was based on 'Tuscan' principles had little time for it. Vasari, for instance, had nothing but contempt for the Goths and the Lombards and was in no doubt that the deplorable quality of their civilisation could be gauged by the nature of the buildings which they left behind them in Ravenna. It was true that these might be 'great and magnificent', but he emphasised that their architecture was 'childishly clumsy' (*goffissima*) and that the effect made by them was due to their size and the richness of their decoration rather than to any aesthetic quality.

There was, however, one church, Santa Maria Rotonda, just outside the city, which posed a real problem. Two storeys high and designed to a handsome circular plan, it was covered by a massive vault, made up of a single block of Istrian stone, and it very obviously (and, according to the ancient sources, very self-consciously) echoed the architecture of the Roman Empire. Vasari was extremely impressed by this 'very noble and marvellous' vault, and as he spent two months in Ravenna, it is almost inconceivable that he had not heard of the generally accepted view that the church had originally been the mausoleum which

Theodoric, King of the Goths, had built for himself or which had been built for him by his daughter. However, it would have been difficult for him to acknowledge that that barbaric and ignorant tribe could have managed such an astonishingly skilful feat of engineering – 'it seems almost impossible that a block of stone of that kind, weighing more than two hundred thousand pounds, could have been placed so high' – and he claimed, rather vaguely, that the building had been raised 'after the Lombards had been expelled from Italy'.

Other writers also found it difficult to account for the grandeur of S. Maria Rotonda. Whether Vasari had avoided mentioning the connection with the Goths out of ignorance or out of self-deception or even out of real conviction is not absolutely clear, but there can be no doubt at all that when Scipione Maffei came to write about the church in 1730, its status as the former mausoleum of Theodoric had been established beyond all doubt. Yet Maffei also refrains from acknowledging this – indeed he specifically ridicules the notion – 'a fine job it would have been for the Lombards or the Goths to carve, transport and to place so high a block of this kind.' Like Vasari, Maffei profoundly admired the church, but – in conscious opposition to Vasari – refused to believe that the Goths had been responsible for the corrupting of architecture in Italy. Such a notion derived from 'our pride, according to which we have considered everything bad to be foreign'. On the contrary, argued Maffei with great ingenuity, neither the Goths nor the Lombards had made much impact of any kind on Italy, and the Italians themselves must bear responsibility – or claim the credit – for the buildings to be found on their territory. Indeed, despite many deplorably designed monuments, a grandiose mastery of construction had survived almost uninterruptedly from Roman times, and feats fully comparable to raising the dome of S. Maria Rotonda could be matched in many mediaeval buildings – not least in Maffei's own Verona.

Of the three contemporary Italian scholar-antiquarians who made so great a contribution to the study of history during the first half of the eighteenth century, Maffei was by far the most sensitive to the visual arts (modern as well as ancient), although he too always gave primacy to the written word; and despite the fact that his relationship with his rival Muratori was always uneasy (though marked with respect on both sides) and that he was prepared to be ironical about Giannone, his career had many features in common with theirs, including trouble with the Inquisition – he was even imprisoned for a short time.

Unlike Giannone and Muratori, however, Maffei had no desire to break the continuity between the Italy of his own day and that of the Roman past. Invasions by the Goths, the Lombards and the Byzantines had been purely negative interruptions to the progress of civilisation, but – as has been said – they had left no lasting impact whatsoever: on language or on morals, on clothes or on architecture, on religion or on customs. In one of those sudden references to the present which tend to enliven his pages like those of Muratori, he comments that at the very moment he was writing there were some eighty thousand German soldiers – not to mention their servants, their wives and their children – in those parts of Italy ruled by Austria, which was certainly no fewer than the Lombards who had once dominated much of the peninsula. 'Yet do we now find that the Italians are giving up their own jobs and that the Germans are busy building, painting, inscribing or taking up other employments of the kind? Or that the style of the arts is changing and that the language is undergoing alteration and that the manner of writing is being transformed? Not in the slightest . . .'

Gibbon was to comment that in their attitudes to the High Middle Ages Muratori was 'a plebeian crouching under the impression of the barbarians', whereas Maffei, a great nobleman, exaggerated their injustices. It would have been truer to point out that the Marchese Scipione Maffei, who was as at home in Paris and London (and Oxford) as he was in Rome and Venice, ignored the impact of the Goths altogether. There could be no bad (or good) Gothic or Lombard art because there was no Gothic or Lombard art at all: 'it was soldiers who came to Italy, not architects or stonemasons.' The Italians themselves must bear responsibility for what had happened, and in the true spirit of the Enlightenment he declared that the decline of ancient art had been brought about by exactly the same sort of craving for novelty that was to be found in the Italy of his own day, exemplified by the designs to be seen all around him – in picture frames, altarpieces and saddles as much as in architecture; in the profusion of crystals, mirrors and stucco; in the decoration of libraries which hurts the eye even before one has begun to read. All this had begun to happen in the arts well before the destruction of the Roman Empire. The barbarians had had nothing to do with it, nor (he argues from silence) had the Christian destruction of ancient models. The implication is quite clear. Unless something radical is done, present-day civilisation is as doomed as was the Roman Empire: ominously he refers to Plato's conclusion that the corruption of music can lead to the corruption of behaviour.

All the theories of decadence hitherto mentioned had great importance for nineteenth-century historians, but rather than discussing these, it may be of more interest to bring the story up to our own day. The issue is a delicate and complicated one, and I am not really competent to comment on it, but it is so relevant to the whole argument of this paper that some reference to it is essential. The leading Italian historian of ancient art in our own times, Ranuccio Bianchi Bandinelli, was a man of the utmost distinction, imagination and charm, who died only a few years ago; but like many Italian intellectuals of his generation he had been a Fascist in his younger years and became a Communist later in life. It is my belief that these two allegiances played an important part in influencing the theories that he proposed to account for the problems involved in what we must now call the transformation rather than the decline of later Roman art.

In a very abbreviated and over-simplified form, and allowing for my own errors of interpretation, these theories ran roughly as follows. There had been in Italy – both before and after the rise to power of Rome – a true native style of art, which, although it had once owed a good deal to the example of Greece, had none the less acquired a genuine character of its own. However – during the early Empire especially – this style was driven out of Rome to the remoter provinces because the nouveau riche arbiters of taste in the capital launched a fashion for a slick, Greek-inspired type of sculpture.

Hellenising work of this kind thus became the 'official' style of art and it is usually described as quintessentially Roman, though it should perhaps be thought of as having entered a decadent cul-de-sac because, skilful though it is, it was devoid of true native values. (I need hardly point out that the nationalist, even 'Fascist' implications of opinions such as this were very popular in Bianchi Bandinelli's youth and were expressed with a crudity that was wholly alien to him.) What Bianchi Bandinelli described as 'plebeian' art was, he felt, far more authentically Roman: it had preserved its native roots, and it was the kind of sculpture to be found on monuments erected on the fringes of the Empire to honour magistrates and middle-class officers: crude, powerful, inelegant, unGreek, clumsily expressive, stiff, immobile, fully frontal. Gradually, however, as the Empire aged, it was just such provincial soldiers who increasingly took over its administration even within Rome, and as a direct result commemorative 'plebeian' art necessarily became official. It was thus a 'progressive' force, leading directly to the future, and not (as usually claimed) a degenerate falling away from earlier art – and the Marxist origins of such thinking are obvious.

It is worth turning back once more, for the last time, to the Arch of Constantine. 'We can', says Bianchi Bandinelli, 'find parallels with reliefs from the European provinces . . . But it would be wrong to infer that provincial art-forms had any influence on the capital. On the contrary it was the culture of the capital which, in many respects, adapted itself to the level of that of the provinces, with the political ascendancy of the large administrative and military middle class that dominated provincial life.'

Bianchi Bandinelli's explanation of what happened on the Arch (which – as he acknowledged – owed much to theories earlier proposed by Austrian and German scholars) is, in its own way as dramatic and extraordinary as the very different explanation offered nearly four hundred years earlier by Cardinal Baronius, and I have suggested that this may be partly due to the fact that both men were seeking solutions to problems whose significance was almost as personal to themselves as it was of importance to historical writing in general. The same could be claimed of the other writers who have been discussed here, and of many more who have been omitted.

In his Trevelyan lectures entitled *What is History?*, the late E. H. Carr (who strongly disagreed with Isaiah Berlin on a number of fundamental issues) urged his listeners: 'Before you study the history study the historian . . . Before you study the historian, study his historical and social environment.' Despite the qualifications with which Carr himself elaborated this advice, it has usually been taken to mean that all historical explantion is arbitrary and subjective with no possibility of acquiring any real validity. It has not been my intention to endorse this narrow-minded view: on the contrary, I have wanted to show that by coming to terms with an extremely important historical problem, which carried with it great moral implications and which has not yet (nor ever will be) subject to any single answer, Italian artists, antiquarians and historians of all persuasions during a period of many centuries were indeed significantly – and beneficially – stimulated by their own beliefs into gaining the special insights needed to produce solutions; but that, in nearly every case, these solutions have won some degree of acceptance from researchers who in no way shared those beliefs. In fact the problem of why art declined in Italy has been handled with enviable care and imagination by Italian writers from the fifteenth century until our own times.

(1990)

CHAPTER 13

Naive and Sentimental Opera Lovers
Bernard Williams

In 1966, I went to a concert performance in Oxford Town Hall, given by the admirable Chelsea Opera Group, of Verdi's *La Forza del Destino*. In the interval, I saw Isaiah heading straight for me up the aisle, through numbers of people, his hand raised in greeting – 'You know Schiller's *Ueber Naive und Sentimentalische Poesie*?' I confessed that I did not. He then explained its idea to me, and the view which he was later to publish,[1] that Verdi was the last great artist who was, in Schiller's terms, *naiv*. He went on to mention, as he does in the article, formidable lists of artists who fall on one side or the other of the distinction, Verdi finding himself with Homer, Shakespeare, Bach, Rubens, Pushkin and Dickens, while the *sentimentalisch*, in Schiller's sense of the term, includes, among many others, Euripides, Virgil, Ariosto, Dostoievsky, Flaubert and Wagner.

The distinction is one of self-consciousness. 'The poet is either himself nature: or he seeks her,' Schiller said, and the idea is that the 'naive' artist can take for granted certain unities – of thought and feeling, of man and nature – that the 'sentimental' has to seek as an ideal. Verdi, though a late example of the 'naive', is for Isaiah a paradigm of it in all its aspects: 'perhaps the last complete, self-fulfilled creator, absorbed in his art; at one with it; seeking to use it for no ulterior purpose, the god wholly concealed by his works . . . wholly, even grimly, impersonal, drily objective, at one with his music.' By contrast, the 'sentimental' spirit tries to make art a vehicle for something beyond itself, so that the political outlook of the artist, for instance, may become essential material for appreciating the work, as it is not in Verdi's case, despite the involvement of his life with politics. Verdi does not want opera to be or do anything but what opera is and does; he lacks what Isaiah calls the 'self-conscious, extra-musical, "sentimental" faith in music as a messianic rebirth of the spirit'.[2]

As with all distinctions, there are other discriminations that this one does not help one to make. Intense artistic self-consciousness and a sense of belatedness need not carry with them extra-artistic aspirations: the very idea of art for art's sake, indeed, expresses the one in rejecting the other. There are composers of opera who are paradigmatically 'sentimental' by all the other tests, but whose self-consciousness is precisely engaged with the art itself, to the exclusion of those other aspirations: Berg is surely one, and Debussy another. But it does not matter that the ideas deployed in the distinction can be taken apart and arranged in different ways. What matters is how it is applied to Verdi, and in this, as in any other interesting application of it, the terms of the distinction are not formed simply by some abstract and general idea of the 'sentimental'. Although he is not specifically picked out as doing so, there is surely a particular artist who embodies the other half of the contrast, as Isaiah has expressed it, and represents Verdi's spiritual and artistic opposite. Every mark of the 'sentimental' in Isaiah's characterisation of it might have been expressly formulated to apply to Wagner, from obsessional self-consciousness and the need to reinvent the means of expression, to the urge to issue manifestos and to achieve redemption through art; and the malaise of the nineteenth century from which, as Isaiah says, Verdi was remote, was the condition of much of Wagner's work.

The contrast between Verdi and Wagner is extreme, overdetermined, and just for that reason, it can serve as the occasion of many different discussions – about Italian and German culture, obviously (the contrast that was closest to Verdi's own heart), or about different strains of Romanticism. I should like to use the contrast here as the focus of a more modest set of reflections, about what it is to be an opera lover. I am encouraged to think about the question by Isaiah's love for opera. Someone who has had the good fortune to go to many performances with Isaiah and to talk often about opera with him might reasonably think that Isaiah's love for opera just *is* love for opera, in its purest and best form, and if you understand how he loves it, then you understand what it is for opera, as such, to command the sort of love it commands. This is, indeed, true. But the problem of Wagner leads (as that problem often does) to an interesting question, of the ways in which opera can command love. As the Marschallin says in one of the most *sentimentalisch*, as well as sentimental, of all operas: 'Und in dem "Wie", da liegt der ganze Unterschied' – the 'how' makes all the difference.

The opera lover loves opera as a form of musical and dramatic art, and, from this, several things follow straight away. One is that the opera lover does not love only opera: in particular, he or she enjoys non-operatic music. People who like opera but not, otherwise, music are exposed to the interpretation that what they really like is going to the opera, a taste that can notoriously co-exist with having no interest in operas at all. Again, the opera lover is not simply what is vulgarly called a 'canary fancier', someone who is interested in the talents and achievements of singers, but is as uninterested in what they sing as some of them are themselves. It is certainly possible to combine the two interests, and to take pleasure from collecting in one's experience performances by certain artists, as others collect performances of rare operas. The late Victor Gollancz, for one, certainly had a great love for opera and at the same time was a passionate connoisseur of the countless performances he had heard. He was also an extreme example of a tendency notorious in older opera-goers (from which Isaiah is to a spectacular and saintly degree exempt) of praising as incomparable some artist of the past whom one is not old enough to have heard. This form of bullying by longevity may finally have been put out of business by the fact that recording has now existed for a long time in relatively reliable forms. In V G's day, it was still possible for him to claim that Melba, for example, was very poorly represented by her records (and if half of what he claimed for her was justified, anyone who has heard her records can only agree).

Opera is one case in which love is almost entirely expressed in enjoyment. What you love, you straightforwardly enjoy; you look forward to a performance, or at least one that promises to be tolerably good, with pleasure. 'Rigoletto is the most enjoyable of operas', I have heard Isaiah say. 'Perhaps not the greatest, but the most enjoyable'; and indeed, it is hard to imagine someone who was an opera lover, for whom opera was a special source of pleasure, who would not agree that Rigoletto yielded that kind of pleasure in a very concentrated and effective way. There are a few very basic ways of being held and excited by the operatic stage, and Verdi was a master of some of them: Rigoletto is unusual because the whole work is an example of those, as Figaro is of others. But it is significant that an honest opera lover, asked for examples of what is indisputably compelling as opera, would have to mention some pieces that are suspect in ways that nothing by Verdi or Mozart is: the trio in the last act of Rosenkavalier, for instance, or the end of the first act of *Tosca*, which, with its mounting excitement and the superimposition of a dark baritone declamation on to the rhythm of a tolling bell and religious ritual, is a splendid example of something that real opera lovers really love.

The fact that the powers of opera can be exercised, not just marginally but very typically, by distinctly dubious works, raises a question – a rather unnerving question, perhaps – about the character of opera altogether. Puccini, in particular, despite his great and continuing popular success, has always met critical resistance, and this does not rest only on certain limitations of his range or his musical invention, but more basically on the feeling that there is something manipulative or even cynical about his works. The charge seems to me unanswerable. Yet it is still true that some parts of those works are able to hold us just as much as operas that have no such faults – and those parts are not necessarily less manipulative than other parts, but often more so. If opera is a serious business, how can this be? It is hard to think of a parallel to it in non-musical drama. Indisputably, some great works of music are operas, but the true opera lover loves more operas than those. Is it true, perhaps, as some musicians suggest, that the passion of an 'opera lover' is not really an artistic taste at all, that it has something undiscriminating about it, that it is not too choosy about where it finds its pleasures? (When Dietrich Fischer-Dieskau was given an honorary degree at Oxford, Isaiah introduced me to him, on the steps of the Codrington Library, and said, 'This is Professor Williams, he is a great lover of opera.' 'Ah,' the distinguished artist replied, 'I am not.')

I think that there is an explanation of why opera is peculiar in this way. (It will not satisfy the most intransigently puritanical, but then it is hard for them to be opera lovers.) W. H. Auden once said,[3] 'in a sense, there can be no tragic opera', because singing itself too evidently seems a free and enjoyable activity: 'the singer may be playing the role of a deserted bride who is about to kill herself, but we feel quite certain as we listen that not only we, but also she, is having a wonderful time.' I do not know whether Auden was right about operatic tragedy,[4] but his remark reminds us of something very important, that the enjoyment of opera, particularly Italian opera, grows tightly round the enjoyment of a technique, a manifest technique. It is not only song, and the fact that it is song, that generates excitement, but the singer. At a fine operatic performance, we are conscious of the singers' achievement and of the presence of physical style and vitality; a feeling of performance and of the performers' artistry is more constantly at the front of the mind than with other dramatic arts. It is because of this that outbreaks of applause (if not, these days, the granting of encores) may be appropriate, as they scarcely could be with a play, even one in verse. Yet opera is drama, and the sense of performance, as of musical intensity, reinforces the drama itself. In these respects, there are contrasts not only with non-musical drama, but, in the other direction, with the ballet, where the sense of performance and technique is indeed paramount, but which, in our culture at least, is less committed to being a dramatic art, and has closer relations with both the decorative and the athletic.

Opera, particularly in the Italian style, presents one immediately with musical artistry, and so, more generally, with an obvious artifice – conventions of musical and dramatic form that are not simply transparent, as blank verse may sometimes be, but constantly manifest. It is just because the pleasures of opera are bound up in this way with an artifice of which one remains conscious that Puccini, though a notoriously opportunistic artist, can offer compelling examples of its powers. In the second act of *Tosca*, for instance, Scarpia's arrangement of his treachery gives pleasure through its theatricality, which is displayed in a way that could not be accepted without the music. The instructions to Spoletta tell him, but not Tosca, that the execution of Cavaradossi is to be only a pretended fake, that the 'simulated' killing is to be a real one. 'As we did in the case of Palmieri,' says Scarpia, more than once: 'You understand?' 'Yes,' replies Spoletta, as he leaves, 'like Palmieri.' It is appropriate that the subject of this should be a double falsehood, a pretence of a pretence. It is not just a device that puts us into complicity with them against Tosca. It puts us into complicity with that device itself, with a certain tradition of theatrical effect, and what we enjoy is seeing the wheels of artifice turn.

The acknowledged display of artifice, Puccini's most characteristic device, affects the experience of seeing one of his works with which one is familiar. To see the utterly familiar is the standard experience of opera-goers, and with a very great work, to hear it for the twentieth or the fiftieth time gives the chance, not just to hear something one has missed, but to understand something new, brought out, perhaps, by a fresh interpretation. But this is not the point with Puccini, and everyone knows that it is not the point. The aim is to see him do the trick again; the better one knows the whole thing, and the more familiar the trick, the greater the pleasure, just because the pleasure lies in complicity with his artifice. Puccini carries further than any other opera composer the idea of securing an effect through the audience's consciousness that that is what he is doing. In doing this, he is exploiting something that is inherent, to some extent, in opera and in the performance of opera, and that is why one can acknowledge the truth of his talent to the nature of opera.

Isaiah's feelings about Puccini, and in particular *Tosca*, are, like many people's, ambivalent, but that is not because of Puccini's trickery, the things that his talents can effectively control, but because of the dark elements that defeat those talents: the composer's fascination with violence, what he himself called his 'Neronian instinct'. You have to be far gone in sentimentality and hence in brutality not to find the torture scenes in *Tosca* and in *Turandot* disagreeable. I have known Isaiah to express his rejection of these scenes also by classing them with what he calls 'music that operates directly on the nerves', examples of which he finds equally in *Elektra* and *Wozzeck* and (perhaps more surprisingly) *Peter Grimes*.

The balance between the effective and the repulsive in Puccini is so delicate that one can see how someone who cared for opera might, despite his entirely operatic achievements, want nothing more to do with him. To have nothing more to do with Verdi, on the other hand, would be to have no more to do with opera. Wagner's work, however, this always vexed case, raises issues of acceptance or rejection, attachment and hatred, which are of a totally different order. It also happens to be the subject of the most substantial disagreement between Isaiah's taste in opera and my own. I have been for a long time deeply taken with these works: perhaps I am, mildly and certainly controllably, addicted. What I am not is a Wagnerian, in the sense of someone who is impressed by the pretentious ideology of the *Gesamtkunstwerk* (Wagner's 'music dramas' are no more *Gesamt* than other operas), or who thinks that if you take Wagner's work seriously you must regard most other opera as trivial. The attitude that isolates the appreciation of Wagner in that way, if it still persists at all, is just a remnant of a cult that old Klingsor (as Debussy used to call him) himself encouraged.

What certainly exists is the opposite view, which also isolates Wagner from the rest of opera, not for the Wagnerian reason that it is unworthy of him, but because he is thought to be unacceptable to it. There are, and I am sure there always will be, those who love music and love opera, but find Wagner anything from uninteresting to intolerable – boring, obsessional, assaulting, fraudulent, the original inventor (to borrow a title of Angela Carter's) of the infernal desire machines of Dr Hoffmann. This rejection is not simply a misunderstanding or a limitation – though it takes no depth analysis to detect that in its more passionate forms the rejection sometimes draws its passion from a fascination with Wagner's achievement, or fear of it, or, as in Nietzsche's case, both. The most frequent complaint, that Wagner is boring, can itself, in some of its expressions, attract the same suspicion: as the literary critic David Miller has said, 'boredom, as the example of pornography perhaps best illustrates, overtakes not what is intrinsically dull, but what is "interesting" to excess. Far from the simple reflex-response to banality, boredom hysterically converts into yawning affectlessness what would otherwise be outright panic.'[5]

Isaiah's attitude to Wagner, though negative, is not of these kinds. It is notably cool, firmly rooted among the less passionate forms of rejection. He simply does not like these works. Admires, of course – who could not, in some way? Likes, not. At one time I thought that he did not like them just because he saw them as a prime case of music that acts directly on the nerves, but I decided that this was not all that there was to it, partly because of his attitude to *Parsifal*. He invited my wife and myself to see a performance of it from the Directors' Box at Covent Garden. We very happily accepted, but having it in mind that the music of Amfortas, in particular, operates not just on the nerves but inside them, I did ask Isaiah whether it was not going to be very painful for him. 'No worse than the others,' he replied, and it was obvious, as the evening went by, that he meant it. Again, it is not mainly a matter, for him, of Wagner's anti-Semitism or what is supposed to be the suspect political character of some of the works. Isaiah (quite rightly, in my view) finds the main cause for that sort of concern in *Die Meistersinger*, and for the most part leaves the issue there, being less eager than many critics of Wagner to see Mime, for instance, as a caricature from *Der Stürmer*.

I think that Isaiah's response to Wagner is in some ways like Stravinsky's:[6] not at all the same in the extremity of hostility, and not the same in motivation, but resembling it in a kind of taste that excludes any Wagnerian enthusiasm. Stravinsky's motivations, indeed, and the special colour they give to his hostility, could not be shared by anyone who was not a composer. The function of Stravinsky's views of

Wagner, as with most judgments by artists on artists, is not to render justice, whatever that might be, but to clear a space for his own methods and his own work. It can be a positive help in that task, that the judgments should be downright eccentric. Stravinsky's famous opinion that *Il Trovatore* is a better work than *Falstaff* is barely tenable, but it is at any rate comprehensible. It is a lot weirder than that, to see *Falstaff* as a work that might have been written by Wagner.[7]

Stravinsky openly declares, in fact, his interest as a composer in resisting the Wagnerian impulse, which he equates with an absence of limit, an imminent and implicit disorder.

> As for myself, I experience a sort of terror when, at the moment of setting to work and finding myself before the infinitude of possibilities that present themselves, I have the feeling that everything is permissible to me. If everything is permissible to me, the best and the worst; if nothing offers me any resistance, then any effort is inconceivable, and I cannot use anything as a basis, and consequently every undertaking becomes futile.

This is a problem for a creator, not for a (mere) listener, and no one who does not share his responsibilities and his opportunities need share the judgment. It is possible to share the spirit of his taste, but that spirit is not captured in the formulae that Stravinsky offers when he is describing his own processes of creation. As a composer, Stravinsky says a lot about his own need for constraints, imposed limitations and obstacles. He expresses that need when he says, 'The more art is controlled, limited, worked over, the more it is free.' Taken out of the context of the autobiography of creation, offered as a canon of taste, the statement is absurd – the most crabbed academic exercise would satisfy the test of freedom. In another sense, the statement is of course true, inevitably true, but then it does not lead to a taste for one style rather than another: *Siegfried* is as controlled, limited, worked over, as *The Rake's Progress*.

There is a taste to be shared, however, and I suspect that Isaiah, to some significant extent, shares it. It is a taste sympathetic to Nietzsche's famous anti-Wagnerian remark about *Carmen*, that he liked the music of Bizet because it does not sweat. The taste despises larger spiritual or intellectual objectives (here the definition of the *sentimentalisch* reappears), so long at least as those are the ambitions of an individual rather than the resources of a tradition. It applauds a certain manifest formality, and a displayed desire to please through craft. It would be wrong, though, to say that it is a classical taste, if that is supposed to set it against the Romantic: in opera, it will find a great deal to admire in Weber, for instance, and in Bellini.

Much of what this taste enjoys in opera is Italian, but in its admiration of a certain unpretentious elegance and gaiety, it naturally welcomes many French works. While Isaiah would not, I believe, go to the remarkable lengths of comparing favourably with the works of Wagner, as Stravinsky did, a 'sparkling group of masterpieces' by Delibes, Chabrier and Messager, it is true that as he climbs the path to his house in Italy, what is coming through the headphones of his Walkman may well be, if not some rarity of Rossini, then *La Muette de Portici* or *Le Postillon de Longjumeau*.

It would be wrong to think of this as a taste for good taste. Rather, this view of things defines more than one kind of bad taste. One kind is either naive, like Verdi's, or wilfully assertive, like Mahler's, and both can be entirely creative. The other, however, is the uncontrolled and revealing dissolution of the 'higher' into the banal, and this is variously comical, upsetting or repellent. No one can sensibly deny that Wagner is liable to this kind of disaster. It happens in the truly dreadful march and chorus of the Knights in *Parsifal*; and James Joyce had a point, I am afraid, when he remarked of Siegmund's much admired love song in the first act of *Die Walküre*, 'Winterstürme wichen dem Wonnemond': 'Can you imagine this old German hero offering his girl a box of chocolates?'[8]

There can be no such disasters in Verdi, because his style is always in touch with popular forms, and even with *Aida*, a comparatively late work which uses many sophisticated devices, it is simply not a relevant complaint that the triumphal march could be a large-scale offering by the Busseto town band. It is inherent to Wagner's enterprise, on the other hand, that he should run these risks. For the same reason, he can elicit, at his most effective, a more extreme response. The sense of the limitless, which Stravinsky mentioned in describing his relations as a composer to Wagner's work, is certainly involved in the emotional reactions that it can produce. Feelings of being drowned, ecstatic or immeasurably elated have been mentioned by Wagner's audiences from the earliest performances on: above all, of course, in the case of *Tristan*. There are probably not many people now who would want to find in these experiences the religious or revelatory significance that was once claimed for them by Wagnerians, whose rhetoric of trans-figuration has done almost as much to put off the sceptical as the earlier cult of Bayreuth did (to which the less devotional admirer of Wagner might have applied the remark made by Monsignor Ronald Knox when asked why he never went to Rome, that if you are feeling queasy on a ship, the worst place to go is the engine room).

Whatever is to be made of them, the peculiar effects of Wagner's music, when it works at full power, are undeniable: everyone who cares for it will know what I am talking about. I remember in particular some performances of the *Ring* in English at the English National Opera in the 1970s. It did not always work, but on some evenings, when Reginald Goodall's patiently synoptic vision took hold, and Alberto Remedios showed what it is to be that very rare thing, a truly lyrical *Heldentenor*, all the limitations disappeared, the creaking space-age scenery seemed to dissolve into light, and it was as if there were no tomorrow. There was a performance, too, at Covent Garden by Jon Vickers as Tristan, one of several that he gave at that time, which was extraordinary. While still sustaining the heroic tone, he peculiarly conveyed the sense from the beginning that this was a doomed man who partly understood that he was on the way to disaster. When Tristan confronts Isolde for the first time, near the end of Act I, he greets her with the words 'begehrt, Herrin, was Ihr wünscht'; and as Vickers sang 'Herrin', a descending fifth, his voice took on a hollow tone of acceptance that seemed to prefigure everything, immediately reducing me and others to a virtually uncontrollable state which lasted the rest of the act and most of the evening.

It has often been said that no one but Wagner, at least among opera composers, can cause such extreme responses. In my own experience, it is certainly true. But then one may ask, ingenuously: why should they? This is one, special, form of artistic power; and like all great artistic capacities, there are other very valuable ones that it excludes. It would be an error, perhaps a symptom of real addiction, to suppose that the satisfaction offered by Wagner is one that transcends any other offered by music, and that all opera aspires to the special kind of power that he achieves. No one thinks any comparable thing with respect to the other arts. But equally, it is a question why this power, as opposed to those exercised by other composers, should be so distrusted and resented. Indeed, there is an earlier question, of how this power can even figure in the thoughts of those who reject Wagner: if one does not feel it, how does one know what is supposed to be objectionable? For some people, no doubt, the answer is that they do feel it, and that is why they reject it. For others, it may be that they do not feel it, but they do feel, and resentfully, that something extreme is being demanded of them. For most, perhaps, and especially those who are coolly un-impressed, the answer may be that without the kind of involvement that leads, occasionally, to those extreme responses, the works appear to lack interest in a particularly annoying way: they seem not works of music, but only causes, vehicles, a pharmacopoeia of emotion.

If it were true that Wagner's works lacked musical interest, then it would help to explain why they appear so differently to those who are moved by them and those who are not. But it is not true. It has indeed been said that Wagner wrote 'music for the unmusical', and the intention of the comment, I take it, is that he solved the problems of organising these vast works by principles of dramatic and psychological association rather than in terms of musical form. The *leitmotiv*, above all, is thought to be a less than musical device. There are certainly passages that invite the jokes of Stravinsky, Milhaud and others, where the effect of the motives is indeed like that of a skilfully assembled slide show. But in general, it cannot be right to oppose dramatic and psychological associations to musical procedures in Wagner. His aim was to achieve the associations through the procedures, and it is hard to see how the opening of Act III of *Siegfried*, for instance, charged as it is with the drama, could be thought to fail as a musical achievement, or not to make musical sense.

If the objection is that the musical procedures are dramatically motivated, then this just comes to saying that this is not pure music: indeed, it is opera. In just this way, in his integration of dramatic and psychological processes with musical procedures, Wagner's achieve-ments are essentially operatic, and that is one reason why those who appreciate him see their appreciation as continuous with their re-actions to other opera they admire. Equally, a lot of what excites them is what excites them in other operas – such basic operatic materials as silence or crescendo, or a generous melodic gesture.

Yet there is also a way in which Wagner's art is not typically operatic, and is even an antithesis to that of other operatic composers. He himself said, 'my art is the art of transition', and some of his greatest strengths lie in the capacity, not only to move easily between motives or keys, but to get from one texture or mood or dramatic context to another. A fine example of it is the invention with which, in Act II of *Die Walküre*, he negotiates a particularly difficult change from the testy domestic quarrel, in which Fricka defeats Wotan, to the following scene in which Wotan lays his world-historical concerns before Brünnhilde: Fricka's victory is marked by a beautiful and unexpected passage ('Deiner ew' gen Gattin heilige Ehre . . .') which in a few bars rounds off the first scene and sets the tone for the next.

It is essential to this skill that it conceals itself, that you are conscious of the result rather than of the procedure. Rather similarly, at another level, though great artistry is needed to sing Wagnerian opera well (or, indeed, at all), that artistry is not typically on display – it is deployed in producing, within the conventions of the style, a dramatic voice, which conveys a response or reveals a state of mind. One is conscious, indeed, of physical presence and power (this is a basic excitement that is shared by the experience of Wagnerian operas and others), but vocal artistry as such is less to the fore. The only work of Wagner's in which vocal skill and musical ingenuity repeatedly draw attention to themselves is *Die Meistersinger*, and that is for the special reason that the relation of skill to expression is the subject of the opera – to that extent it is about itself. Wagner is thus the opposite of Puccini, as I earlier described him. The performer's skills, and the composer's, do not stand at the front of the audience's consciousness, and it is not through manifest artifice that he achieves his effects. Yet manifest artifice of that kind is indeed typical of opera, and just as Puccini's exploitation of it brings his melodramas close to the heartland of opera, so Wagner's refusal of it sets his masterpieces apart from that heartland.

It must be in terms of some such account, I think, of the similarities and the equally notable differences between the experience of Wagner's operas and of others, that we should explain the striking asymmetry of taste among people who otherwise share an attachment to opera: those who appreciate both Wagner and other styles of opera find a lot in common between them, while other people find it hard to see how an enthusiasm for opera extends to Wagner at all. Certainly, there is something to explain, and most of the existing explanations, such as they are, are too contemptuous of one party or the other: the disagreement is not one that invites contempt.

But if these, or something like them, are the differences, where are we left with the distinction between the 'naive' and the 'sentimental'? There was never any suggestion that the 'naive' excluded the conventional – on the contrary. In the article from which I started, Isaiah reported the fact that certain progressive Russian composers of the time resented Verdi's work, just because he had succeeded in bringing new life to the dreaded 'formula', the stale conventions of the Italian tradition. There is no puzzle in the 'naive' artist using very conventional means, and the 'sentimental' artist using less conventional means. But what about the operatic audience? They are by the nature of opera conscious of those conventional means, and enjoy them as such. The nature of that consciousness, however, changes over time. Verdi's means are not available now to a popular composer, or to any other, and even if his characters are represented as embodying universal human passions, the conventions of that representation appear to us, now, not just as conventions, but as those particular conventions; just as we also have to allow for some nineteenth-century sentiments about fathers, virgins, respectable sisters and so forth. We may easily accept the conventions, but our sense of them, and our enjoyment, cannot avoid the further turn of historical self-consciousness that all this implies. We can enjoy the 'naive' artist, but only as 'sentimental' listeners.

With Wagner, on the other hand, though some of his concerns belong clearly to the nineteenth century, much of his complexity, perversity and ambiguity is familiar in our world, as is the idea of works as extreme as his. His musical style, because it did so much to form not just the art music of the twentieth century, but (for instance) film music, is close in some ways to what is familiar outside the opera house. Because of their difficulty, their history, and the huge problems of mounting them, his works are only now really meeting the audiences he himself wanted for them: through such productions as those at ENO, and, on an immeasurably greater scale, through TV broadcasts of Chéreau's *Ring*, for instance, they are seen by people who are neither devotees nor experienced opera-goers, and who approach them, not of course without preconceptions, but without the preconceptions of those who love other operas and their artifices. To many people now, despite and because of his oblique devices, Wagner may seem to speak more directly than other opera does. It is the 'sentimental' artist who has the 'naive' public.

CHAPTER 14

*Does Classical Music Have to be Entirely Serious?**
Alfred Brendel

This investigation owes much to Isaiah Berlin's stimulating presence. I started my manuscript, virtually under his eyes, in his Italian summer home. The title is his – a variant, as it seems, of the words from a Max Beerbohm cartoon where Matthew Arnold is asked by his niece: 'Why, Uncle Matthew, oh why, will not you be always wholly serious?'

The essay presented here is a briefer version of my Darwin Lecture, given in Cambridge in 1984, the full text of which is included in my last book, *Music Sounded Out* (Robson Books, 1990). It is offered as a tribute to Isaiah's appreciation of music, and sense of humour.

I

In his remarkable essay on Schubert, Antonín Dvořák[1] makes it clear that he cannot consider Schubert's Masses as ecclesiastical, even though he concedes that the feeling for what is truly sacred music 'may differ somewhat among nations and individuals', as does the sense of humour.

I own a cartoon from Czechoslovakia. In it a pianist is shown sitting on a concert platform. But instead of performing the piece on the music stand in front of him, he is helpless with laughter. The composition that provokes his amusement bears the title 'A. Dvořák – Humoresk'. In the cartoon the faces of the audience are all completely serious; they appear quite unmoved by the mirth of the pianist, who must surely have been the first to discover that Dvořák's Humoresque should be a matter for laughter. Of course, a pianist's audience is not supposed to laugh, but neither is the pianist.

I do not know whether the public in Haydn's time ever laughed during, or at the end of, a performance. For perfectly good reasons, there is a tacit understanding between a civilised audience and the performers that the music should be played, and listened to, without

193

too many additional noises. There is no shortage of evidence that at least some of Haydn's and Beethoven's contemporaries relished a musical sense of humour, and admired it in the works of the two composers. In one of the most important early essays on Haydn, Ignaz Ernst Ferdinand Arnold[2] made an acute comment on Haydn's comic style:

> Being in command of all artistic means, this play of easy imagination endows even the smallest flight of genius with a boldness and audacity [*Keckheit und Dreistigkeit*] that expands the area of aesthetic achievement into the infinite without causing damage or anxiety . . . The last Allegros or Rondos consist frequently of short, nimble movements that reach the highest degree of comicality by often being worked out most seriously, diligently and learnedly . . . Any pretence at seriousness only serves the purpose of making the playful wantonness of the music appear as unexpected as possible, and of teasing us from every side until we succumb and give up all attempts to predict what will happen next, to ask for what we wish for, or to demand what is reasonable.

According to Georg August Griesinger, an early biographer of Haydn, 'a sort of innocent mischievousness, or what the British call humour, was a main trait of Haydn's character. He easily discovered what he preferred – the comical side of things.' Haydn himself confessed (to Albert Christoph Dies) that there is a frame of mind in which, to quote Dies, 'a certain kind of humour takes possession of you and cannot be restrained'. He also thought this was a quality which stemmed from an abundance of good health. About Beethoven, Friedrich Rochlitz writes: 'Once Beethoven is in the mood, rough, striking witticisms, odd notions, surprising and exciting juxtapositions and paradoxes occur to him in a steady flow.'[3] If we apply this statement to Beethoven's comic music, we have a valuable list of characteristics that bear musical scrutiny.

There is widespread confusion about the meaning of humour, irony and wit. Not only does it differ from language to language; in the sense of Dvořák's remark quoted above, it turns out to be a deeply personal matter, as indeed religion should be. (According to one of Jean Paul's definitions, humour is 'the sublime in reverse' – *das umgekehrte Erhabene*.) I can therefore only relate to a choice of pieces outside the realm of opera and song that I personally find funny, amusing, ludicrous or hilarious, and I have settled for the word 'comic' to signify an ingredient that is common to all of them. Whether oddities and incongruities of a purely musical nature will strike the listener as hilarious, strange or disturbing must depend on the psychological climate of each piece, but also on the psychological disposition of each listener.

In the third movement of Haydn's C major Sonata, Hob. XVI:50, the teasing avoidance of classical four- or eight-bar patterns, the abortive storm in D minor that peters out almost before it begins, and its laughing and bouncing staccatos contribute towards making it comical. But it is the 'wrong' B major chords in bars 20 and 69 that come as the most memorable surprise, presenting the listener with an intriguing problem. How should one 'understand' them?

To me, these B major chords are arbitrary and unjustified, an insult veiled by apparent innocence, an act of splendid nonsense that is all the more delightful because it cannot be explained away. As Schopenhauer said in his analysis of laughter: 'It is diverting to see the strict, untiring, troublesome governess, Reason, for once convicted of inadequacy.'

Summing up the comic traits in Haydn's piece, I find: (1) breaches of convention; (2) the appearance of ambiguity; (3) proceedings that masquerade as something they are not, for instance as lacking professional knowledge or skill; (4) veiled insults; and (5) nonsense. All of these distinctions belong to the stock-in-trade of the comical in general.[4]

A comic feature that is specific to music is the evocation of laughing and leaping, familiar manifestations of playfulness and high spirits that can be musically suggested by short staccato, leaps of large intervals, and short groups of fast notes separated by rests, as in the scherzos of two A major sonatas: Beethoven's Op. 2 No. 2 and Schubert's D.959. In Kandinsky's late painting *Scherzklänge* (*Jocular Sounds*), such musical effects become visible by means of abstract art: short staccato is represented by wedges, while hopping or skipping is suggested by arched shapes. Though musical laughing and leaping may not be sufficient to make a piece of music comical, it can greatly contribute towards setting a mood from which comic surprise will emerge.

II

To become apparent, breaches of order need a framework of order. In other comical contexts, the framework is given by words and their meaning, by human situations and reactions, and by the kind of thought that is connected with language. In music, the framework relies on the established musical forms and expectations, and on the logic of purely musical thought. Such a framework is indeed available to the musical layman; the musical experience that is needed is comparable to the verbal experience a child needs to understand a joke. Of course, there are also sophisticated jokes for grown-ups.

Why does classical music lend itself so readily to comic effects? Because it seems to me to reflect, in its solid and self-sufficient forms and structures, the trust of the Enlightenment in rational structures that rule the universe. The spirit of classical music seems to imply the belief that the world is good, or at least that it could become so. For the Romantics, there was no sense of order to rely upon; it had to be found and created in oneself. The open and fragmentary structures of romantic music, as epitomised by the fantasy, aimed to be as personal, and exceptional, as possible. Where, as with Berlioz, surprise becomes the governing principle of composition, and music a succession of feverish dreams, comic effects have little chance; they have to be achieved as an assault on what is proper and predictable.

Cadenzas of classical concertos were allowed, and supposed, to be unpredictable. The final trill, however, traditionally leading from the dominant seventh into the tonic and the orchestral tutti, was something that could be relied on, for listeners and orchestral players alike. Beethoven, one of the supreme musical architects, wrote cadenzas that make Mozart's look like models of restraint. In the marathon cadenza for his own C major Concerto, the trill is the special target of his mockery. It never happens as it should.

In the end, it does not happen at all. When the dominant seventh has been let loose in a frenzy of vehemently repeated scales, there is a last, truly bizarre surprise: the two final chords are, 'unnecessarily', interrupted by a soft, short, arpeggiated one. To play the end of the cadenza without this soft chord and lead directly into the orchestral tutti helps to realise the degree of Beethoven's mischief. If this chord could speak an aside to the public, or the orchestra, we might well make out something like: 'Are we really coming to an end?', 'Wouldn't you like the cadenza to be over?', 'What a ridiculous frenzy!', 'Heavens, didn't we forget the trill?', 'As it didn't work before, why should it work now?', or simply 'Am I fooling you well?'

III

Comic irreverence in classical music has a rational and an irrational significance. The rational side may be illuminated by a quotation from Francis Hutcheson: 'Nothing is so properly applied to the false Grandeur, either of Good or of Evil, as ridicule.' And, according to Schiller, the comic writer has 'continuously to amuse reason', 'shun pathos' and 'defend himself against passions'. Comic music has no other use for the solemn, the rapturous, the pastoral, the heroic or the frenzied than to make fun of it. On the other hand, irrationalism, that had started to undermine the 'certainties' of reason, is musically manifest as a mockery of what is normal, worthy and well-behaved. What rationalism does to grand emotions, irrationalism does to the civilised procedures of musical form. Diderot likened great artists, in their defiance of rules, to great criminals, and he conceded that the dark forces in man had their share in the creation of works of art. Nowhere have these dark forces surfaced more cheerfully than in several of Haydn's finales, and more disquietingly than in some of his works in minor keys.

It needs to be said that the formal peculiarities of a piece are not sufficient evidence for its comic leanings. Form and psychology have to interact. Two hallmarks of Haydn's eccentricity, his sudden rests and fermatas at unlikely places, and his extended repetitions of the same soft chord, or note, over several bars, can have a very different psychological impact on the listener in pieces of different character. To suspend, interrupt or freeze the flow of music can be purely hilarious, or purely disturbing. If it is both at once, or oscillates between the two, the effect may be called grotesque. (Ligeti's *Aventures et Nouvelles Aventures* is grotesque music, and so is much of the comic music of this century.) Generally, the same devices that make music amusing can also make it strange, eerie, disturbing and macabre. The psychological climate of a piece will finally decide whether they are one or the other, or both. In classical music, they are likely to be one *or* the other. Incidentally, the colloquial use of the word 'funny' takes care of both the comical and the strange.

The basic key of a basically comic piece is a major key. There is, outside the field of opera or song, only one comical example in a minor key that comes to my mind: Beethoven's C minor Bagatelle from Op. 119. The piece is comical because a cheerful dance that should be in a major key is used to express grim resolution. Communication of comic resolution or comic anger is generally reserved for episodes in Beethoven's earlier Rondo movements. A well-known example is the A minor section in his C major Piano Concerto.

This seems a good moment to introduce another area of comic music: that of the excessive and obsessive, of overstatement and *idée fixe*. There is an 'as if' character about such music. It may resemble comic acting, caricature and *opera buffa*. The composer seems to imply: 'This is not really me. I am just turning into somebody choleric or absent-minded, into a pedant, a naughty child, or a very, very innocent child, to amuse you.'

At the beginning of Beethoven's Variations Op. 35, there is a juxtaposition of excessive contrast: pianissimo and fortissimo. One may call it an alternation of whispering and stentorian laughter, or of tiptoeing and stamping. Other comic elements are in evidence: the bass alone pretending to be the complete theme (that in effect is only presented later); the rests before and after the fortissimo B flats; and the following B flat, marked *piano*, that appears to me like an actor putting a finger to his lips, and going 'shhhh'.

In the course of these variations, Beethoven plays with the contrast of soft and loud, of changing and repeated notes. In Variation I, he makes fun of the loud strokes, brings them in too soon, and thereafter cunningly subdues the middle section. In Variations IX and XIII, the loud B flats take over the whole variation as furious grunts, or tear it apart as hysterical shrieks. In Variation VII, there is a series of grim belly-laughs in the bass register, while the rest of the piece is provided with odd accents.

Odd, misplaced, bizarre, obsessive accents are another tool of the composer in a comic frame of mind. The Rondo of Beethoven's Second Piano Concerto starts with accents against the grain which later, before the coda, are misplaced in a parody.

The alternation of fast and slow can also generate results of a comical, and highly theatrical, kind, like two different characters who speak *to* one another, or *past* one another. In Variation XXI of Beethoven's Diabelli Variations, the utterances of the two characters, one coarsely energetic, the other whining, remain incompatible, and the unity of musical context is startlingly broken up. Before the end of Beethoven's G major Sonata Op. 31 No. 1 there is a succession of different tempi, with adagios almost too slow, and rests almost too long, for comfort – only to be followed by a presto that tries to make up for the wasted thirty seconds by comic haste. The pianist who has not succeeded in making somebody in his audience laugh at the end of this sonata should become an organist.

The sarcastic Hans von Bülow once shouted to a female pupil who tried to play the third movement of Beethoven's 'Lebewohl' Sonata: 'Stop! In the joy of reunion, you rush off, get entangled in the train of your dress, crash down, and smash all the flowerpots in the garden!' I think certain classical pieces should communicate a whiff of such a state of mind, with the player in ironic command. Musicians like Bruno Walter, Edwin Fischer and Artur Schnabel had more courage to turn such movements into an exhilarating romp than most of us today.

One of the pieces that can only be appreciated in terms of the obsessively comical is the first movement of Beethoven's Sonata Op. 31 No. 1. If one looks at this piece from a purely formal perspective, and without any psychological insight, one might dismiss it as incompetent, repetitious and unworthy of Beethoven. It would, however, be naïve to assume that Beethoven, in the course of this movement, brought in the same opening idea seven times in the same G major, and in an identical position, without doing so on purpose.

There are further clues to his comic intentions: the two hands that seem unable to play together; the short staccato; the somewhat bizarre regularity of brief spells of sound interrupted by rests. The character that emerges is one of compulsive, but scatterbrained, determination. The piece seems unable to get anywhere except where it should not go. What a nice surprise to find oneself, for the second theme, in the key of B major instead of the dominant, or in E major instead of the tonic; a surprise that, within a sonata form in a major key, must have been a novelty of an almost exotic flavour. Only Beethoven's String Quintet Op. 29 had made use of the mediant – the related third – before, but in its exposition alone. What, in Op. 31 No. 1, sounds jocular and provocative, must have signalled to some of Beethoven's contemporaries a delicious disregard of rules, while simply bewildering others. (It took Beethoven's later 'Waldstein' Sonata, as Tovey has pointed out, to establish the same harmonic progressions as a natural part of widely extended harmonic perspectives.) The coda indicates to anybody who may have missed the point that nothing in this piece was meant to be taken at face value. As for the second movement, Adagio grazioso, it sounds like a Beethoven parody produced by Rossini – who, when this sonata was completed, was ten years old. In Beethoven's Adagio, a complicated balance is achieved between sympathy and mockery, the graceful and the bizarre, nostalgia and anticipation, lyricism and irony. What is Beethoven being ironic about? His own style of the early Rondos? The manner of coloratura embellishment? The demeanour of a prima donna on stage? Or the slightly grotesque suppleness of a Taglioni or Fanny Elssler, indicated by the well-oiled mechanism of trills, staccato quavers and musical pirouettes? One might call this movement the first neoclassical piece of music. It is an irony in itself that Op. 31 No. 1 seems to have been the only Beethoven sonata Stravinsky did not enjoy.

IV

The combination of incongruous elements is generally regarded as a distinguishing feature of wit. In another example of musical wit, Beethoven's F major finale from the Sonata Op. 10 No. 2, the solemn technique of fugal writing is 'abused' for burlesque purposes. Adolf Bernhard Marx likened the movement to 'a child that plucks an old man's beard'. Of course, there is never a serious attempt to present a proper fugal exposition and the listener is left wondering what the composer's intentions were, wittily torn between counterpoint and homophony, sonata and rondo, bristling energy and musical laughter. Already Haydn had been commended (by Griesinger) for his ability 'to lure the listener into the highest degree of the comical by frivolous turns and twists of the seemingly serious'. Devices of musical style that were supposed to suggest such elevated emotional states as 'magnanimity, majesty, splendour, rage, revenge, despair, devotion, delight or virtuousness' (to quote from C. P. E. Bach's friend Christian Gottfried Krause, whose book *Von der musikalischen Poesie* impressed Lessing) were applied by Haydn to the lowest category of poetics, the comical. The 'mescolanza di tutti generi' of which Salieri spoke in connection with Haydn's Masses is evident also in his comic music. There is a strong theatrical element in some of Haydn's works, not surprising in a composer who over a period of fifteen years organised performances of opera at Eszterháza, and was acquainted with all comical genres of the musical theatre, marionette opera included. Haydn himself turned his incidental music to Jean-François Regnard's *Le Distrait* into a capriciously humorous symphony in six movements known as 'Il distratto'. The success of this symphony shows how fluid the borderlines were, how readily such music was appreciated without the stage, and how eagerly the contemporary public, particularly in France, tried to find out what music 'expresses' or 'represents'.

The promotion of the comical in string quartet, sonata and symphony is one of Haydn's great innovations. Carl Friedrich Zelter explains in a letter to his friend Goethe (9 March 1814) that Haydn's art was criticised in earlier years 'because', as he says, 'it immediately made a burlesque of the deadly seriousness of his predecessors', J. S. Bach and C. P. E. Bach. Haydn certainly did not set out to parody C. P. E. Bach, whom he revered, in the way early *opéra comique* had parodied some works of Lully. Rather, the listener was stimulated to take the comical more seriously, and accept it as part of one's own life. The term 'the elevated comical' (*das hohe Komische*) had been used, and may have been coined, to characterise Haydn's music, including even, as the *Musical Almanac of 1782* states, the Adagios, 'during which people actually, and properly, are supposed to weep'.

Beethoven's F major finale from Op. 10 No. 2 starts with what one may call a 'laughing theme', and the dominating impact of the movement remains that of laughter. (Nobody seems to doubt that music can 'sigh', metaphorically speaking, but I have read denials that music can 'laugh'.) To some people, the noise of laughter is contagious. To the depressive, laughter may be painful and unavailable. To others, laughter is vulgar, seriousness a sign of maturity, and everything that is hilarious a desecration of loftier states of mind. To step down from one's elevated platform would mean to lose one's self-respect.

The Austrian Emperor Joseph II disapproved of what he called 'Haydn's jests' (*Haydns Spässe*). Laughter poses a danger to state and religion. Plato wanted to ban it. Laughter is incompatible with the holy and the absolute. Or rather, it is the privilege of the Deity, whether sardonic (as in Indian mythology, and the *Iliad*) or serene (as in Hegel's 'unquenchable laughter of the Gods'). Umberto Eco, dealing with the significance of laughter in his novel *The Name of the Rose*, quotes Pliny the Younger: 'Aliquando praeterea rideo, ioco, ludo, homo sum' ('Sometimes I laugh, I joke, I play, I am human'). The laughter of man is not the laughter of gods. Anybody who has witnessed a little child recognising a parent, relishing a new toy or embarking on an exciting adventure, knows that there is laughter that does not originate in catastrophe, or represent superiority.

In a German musical encyclopaedia of 1875 (*Musikalisches Conversations-Lexikon*, Verlag R. Oppenheim) I found an admirable article on humour (the *New Grove* has none); it sets humour apart from other modes of the comical in that it is a world view, a complete outlook on life. 'For the humorist,' the article says, 'there are no fools, only foolishness and a mad world.' (This, again, is a formula borrowed from Jean Paul.) 'He will therefore perceive man and the world to be not ridiculous or revolting but pitiable.' Humour relates to the dark undercurrent of life, and prevails over it. If we understand humour in this comprehensive sense, Beethoven's Diabelli Variations are one of its musical paradigms.

V

You may have noticed that the name Mozart has hardly been mentioned.[5] In looking for examples in his works, I found myself to be the victim of prejudice. I wrongly assumed that his absolute music should be a mine of the comical because his letters abound in hilarious word-play and nonsense and because the music of his operas makes such superlative use of all comical resources. Haydn and Beethoven, with all their love for cantabile, were predominantly instrumental composers; sensual beauty of sound was not an innate quality, or a primary concern. The imagination of Mozart or Schubert, however, was predominantly vocal, even in their instrumental works, and the style of Mozart's symphonies had been castigated accordingly as too operatic by Nägeli. Singing, like sensuality, is hardly funny. It constitutes an area of beauty that opens itself to the comical only by means of words and comic acting. Singing itself can become comical where it turns into grotesque utterance; the music of our time has seized upon such sounds or noises, suggestive of the absurd and the crudely physical.

Mozart's beauty of cantabile is matched by the beauty of his musical proportion and balance, that singular illusion of complete formal perfection at any time. Next to Mozart's truly classical sense of order, Haydn often appears whimsical. Where Mozart somehow manages to surprise us with what we expect, Haydn excels in the unexpected. The sudden fortissimo chord in the Adagio of his 'Surprise' Symphony is only one of many examples.

Writing about 'The Comical in Music', Schumann claims that Beethoven and Schubert were able to translate any state of mind into music. 'In certain Moments Musicaux,' so he says, 'I imagine I recognise unpaid tailors' bills.' This would undoubtedly have come as a surprise to Schubert who, according to Eduard Bauernfeld, asked a certain Josef Dessauer whether he knew any funny music when Dessauer pronounced one of Schubert's songs to be too melancholy. Whatever 'lustig' may have meant to Schubert, his music bears out the fact that it hardly aspires to be comical. Schumann's sometimes does; of the important Romantic composers, he was the only one to be influenced by those German Romantic writers to whom humour and irony were a major concern. But Schumann's 'Humor', wherever indicated in his music, is too good-humoured and warmly lyrical to be comic, and his capriciousness does not come from a light-hearted disposition. I cannot find a trace of humour in the music of Chopin, or Liszt. And Wagner is reported to have turned Schiller's line 'Ernst ist das Leben, heiter die Kunst' on its head: art must be serious, while life may be cheerful. The only excuse for the Romantic composer to write funny music seems to have been the use of a funny text, in opera or song.

For most performers and virtually all concert audiences of our time, music is an entirely serious business. Performers are meant to function as heroes, dictators, poets, seducers, magicians or helpless vessels of inspiration. The projection of comical music needs a performer who dares to be less than awe-inspiring, and does not take him- or herself too seriously. Comic music can be ruined, and made completely meaningless, by 'serious' performance. It is much more dependent on a performer's understanding than an Allegro di bravura, a nocturne, or a funeral march. To manage to play a piece humorously is a special gift, yet, I am afraid, it is not enough: the public, expecting the celebration of religious rites, may not notice that something amusing is going on unless it is visibly encouraged to be amused.

I admit that to expect a player to radiate amusement while performing is a tall order. The trouble is that many performers, on account of their concentration and nervous tension, look unduly grave or grim, no matter what they play. The first bars of a classical piece set its mood. To sit down and start Haydn's last C major Sonata with a tortured look is even worse than to embark on the so-called 'Moonlight' Sonata with a cheerful smile. Nobody will mistake the first movement of the 'Moonlight' for a cheerful piece, whereas the hilarious beginning of Haydn's C major Sonata can easily sound wooden, and pointless. Before the first note, a discreet signal has to pass from the performer to the audience: 'Caution! We are out for mischief.'

When the English notion of 'humour' arrived in Germany, Lessing translated it as 'Laune'. *Laune*, according to Kant, means, in its best sense, 'the talent to voluntarily put oneself into a certain mental disposition, in which everything is judged quite differently from the ordinary method (reversed, in fact), and yet in accordance with certain rational principles in such a frame of mind'. This sounds to me like an apt description of the quality that a perfomer of comical music should be able to summon up. 'But this manner,' as Kant further says, 'belongs rather to pleasant than to beautiful art, because the object of the latter must always show a certain dignity in itself'.[6]

For my part, I am perfectly happy to enjoy the 'sublime in reverse', and leave Kant's dignity behind where Haydn and Beethoven took such obvious pleasure in doing so.

CHAPTER 15

*Isaiah Berlin: A Tribute**
Joseph Brodsky

It is almost a rule that the more complex a man is, the simpler his billing. A person with a retrospective ability gone rampant often would be called an historian. Similarly, one to whom reality doesn't seem to make sense gets dubbed a philosopher. Social critic or ethical thinker are standard labels for somebody who finds the ways of his society reprehensible. And so it goes, for the world always tries to arrest its adolescence, to appear younger than it is. Few people have suffered this fear of grown-ups more than Sir Isaiah Berlin, who is frequently called all these things, at times simultaneously. What follows is not an attempt to redress the terminological chaos: it is but a tribute by a simpleton to a superior mind from which the former for a number of years has been learning about mental subtlety but apparently hasn't learned enough.

A study in genealogy normally is owing to either pride in one's ancestry or uncertainty about it; our history of ideas is no exception. Given the fruit this century came to bear, however, there are additional reasons for such scrutiny, which have nothing to do with attempts to brandish or ascertain the origins of our nobility. These reasons are revulsion and fear.

The quest for universal social justice that preoccupied European thought for, roughly speaking, the last four centuries has too often in our era resulted in its exact opposite. Considering the number of lives this quest has claimed, its Holy Grail proved to be the fixture of a literal dead end, and with a total disregard for the individual in its wake. A subject for revulsion, this effect should also be perceived as a cry from the future, given the rate of population growth throughout the world. After all, the temptation of social planning has turned out to be irresistible even for relatively humble social units.

That is what instils fear. In a manner of speaking, every bullet flies from the future. A mass society is natural prey for any presumption, but above all to a socialist one, which may eventually yield only to that of a computer. For this reason, poring over the genealogical chart of European philosophical thought through the last four centuries is not all that different from scanning the horizon: in either case, though, one looks out not for the cavalry but for an Indian scout.

There are not many of these scouts, and few of them are much good. The invention of ethical and political doctrines, which blossomed into our own social sciences, is a product of times when things appeared manageable. The same goes for the criticism of those doctrines, though as a voice from the past this criticism proved prophetic. All it lacked was the appropriate volume, but then one of the main distinctions between Indian scouts and cavalry is their discretion.

They were always discreet, as well as few in number – those opponents of political certitude, doubters of social blueprints, disbelievers in universal truths, exiles from the Just City. It could not be otherwise since for them to be shrill in social discourse would have been a contradiction in terms. Even systematisation often seemed to them contradictory because a system would entitle them to mental privilege over the very subjects of their ponderings.

Their actual lives and careers were diverse but not spectacular. Some of them would advance their views in magazines. Others would do so in a treatise or, even better, in a novel. Still others applied their principles to the offices they held or disciplines they were mastering. They were the first to shrink from being called philosophers; above all, they never tried to shout anyone down.

This posture had little to do with either humility or modesty. In fact it could and perhaps should be perceived as an echo of a polytheistic notion of the world, for these people firmly believed in the multiplicity of the human predicament, and the core of their social formula was, essentially, pluralism. This of course drew fire or silence from social reformers of every stripe, both democratic and autocratic, whose most high-minded common contention would even today be that pluralism is pregnant with moral relativism.

It is. But then moral absolutism is not so hot either. Its main attraction is that it is unattainable and, for a social reformer, that it provides an attractive embellishment for his designs. Yet the bottom line of every social order is not the moral superiority of its members but their safety, which, in fact, moral superiority doesn't necessarily guarantee.

Every discourse on social matters boils down, of course, to the issue of free will. This is something of a paradox, however, since regardless of whether the will is free or not, in any outcome of such discourse it will be curbed. One's curiosity regarding the nature of the will is therefore either sadistic or academic or both. ('Let's see how free is what we are curbing.')

In any case, with pluralism one would think a danger far greater than moral relativism (which is the reality of the world anyway) or shackling the will, is the implicit dismissal of the metaphysical properties of the species: the short shrift that pluralism, like nearly any other social formula, gives to the notion that man can be driven as much by his appetite for the infinite as by necessity.

The pluralist formula shares this danger with every form of social organisation, including theocracy. Man's metaphysical instinct (or potential) is substantial enough to overshoot the confines of any creed, not to mention ideology. At the very least, that is what is responsible for the emergence of art, music, and, particularly, poetry. In many ways, this is both a self- and world-negating instinct and its exercise may easily make the finest social tapestry fade. Whether a society benefits from this humbling effect is another matter. One suspects that it may.

On the basis of this suspicion one perceives the equating of man's metaphysical potential with its absence as a danger. Everything that reduces man's spiritual tenor is a danger. The antihierarchical pathos of pluralism may render society's senses dull to the pitch of the human maximum, which is always a solo performance. Worse still, it may perceive this solo as a subject for applause, exacting no obligations from its audience.

But if it were only a matter of the quality of the applause, that would be fine. Regrettably, what passes for social pluralism is echoed in the life of cultures and even civilisations. For they and their values, too, are conflicting and diverse enough to make up society, especially given their current Biblical proximity (we are literally only a stone's throw from one another), especially given the world's emerging ethnic composition. From now on when we are talking about the world we are talking about a society.

The need for a common denominator, for a universal set of values, is dictated by our concern for our safety (and one wouldn't be wrong to regard Herder as a precursor of the League of Nations). Alas, the development of this common denominator is fraught with a cultural realignment so enormous that one is not keen to ponder it. We already hear, for example, about equating tolerance (this high-pitched solo of Christianity) with intolerance.

Alas, the trouble with ethics is that it always answers the question 'How to live?' not, 'In the name of what?' or even 'What for?' It is clear that it tries to supplant those questions and their answers with its own; that moral philosophy tends to operate at the expense of metaphysics. Perhaps rightly so, given the world's population prospects; perhaps it's time to bid the Enlightenment farewell, to learn an inflected guttural tongue and step into the future.

One is almost ready to do so when in walks Isaiah Berlin, carrying under his arm seven not very long books: *The Age of Enlightenment, Four Essays on Liberty, Vico and Herder, Against the Current, The Hedgehog and the Fox, Russian Thinkers* and *Personal Impressions.* And now it is nine books. (Since this essay was written for his eightieth birthday he has added two more: *Concepts and Categories* and *The Crooked Timber of Humanity.*) He does not look like an Indian scout; his mind, however, has been to the future. The volumes under his arm are its map, where the East overlaps with the West, where the North flows South.

This is not how I first saw him, though, nineteen years ago, when he was sixty-three and I thirty-two. I had just left the country where I'd spent those thirty-two years and it was my third day in London, where I knew nobody.

I was staying in St John's Wood, in the house of Stephen Spender, whose wife had come to the airport three days before to fetch W. H. Auden, who had flown in from Vienna to participate in the annual Poetry International Festival in Queen Elizabeth Hall. I was on the same flight, for the same reason. As I had no place to stay in London, the Spenders offered to put me up.

On the third day in that house in the city where I knew nobody the phone rang and Natasha Spender cried, 'Joseph, it's for you.' Naturally, I was puzzled. My puzzlement hadn't subsided when I heard in the receiver my mother tongue, spoken with the most extraordinary clarity and velocity, unparalleled in my experience. The speed of sound, one felt, was courting the speed of light. That was Isaiah Berlin, suggesting tea at his club, the Atheneum.

I accepted, although of all my foggy notions about English life, that of a club was the foggiest (the last reference I had seen to one was in Puskhin's *Eugene Onegin*). Mrs Spender gave me a lift to Pall Mall and before she deposited me in front of an imposing Regency edifice with a gilded Athena and Wedgwoodlike cornice, I, being unsure of my English, asked her whether she wouldn't mind accompanying me inside. She said that she wouldn't, except that women were not allowed. I found this puzzling, again, opened the door, and announced myself to the doorman.

'I'd like to see Sir Isaiah Berlin,' I said, and attributed the look of controlled disbelief in his eyes to my accent rather than to my Russian clothes. Two minutes later, however, climbing the majestic staircases and glancing at the huge oil portraits of Gladstones, Spencers, Actons, Darwins *et alia* that patterned the club's walls like wallpaper, I knew that the matter with me was neither my accent nor my turtleneck but my age. At thirty-two I was as much out of sync here as if I were a woman.

Presently I was standing in the huge, mahogany-cum-leather shell of the club's library. Through high windows the afternoon sun was pouring its rays on to the parquet as though testing its resolve to refract light. In various corners two or three rather ancient members were sunk deep in their tall armchairs, in various stages of newspaper-induced reverie. From across the room, a man in a baggy three-piece suit was waving to me. Against the sunlight, the silhouette looked Chaplinesque, or penguinish.

I walked toward him and we shook hands. Apart from the Russian language, the only other thing we had in common was that we both knew that language's best poet, Anna Akhmatova, who dedicated to Sir Isaiah a magnificent cycle of poems, *Sweetbriar's Bloom*. The cycle was occasioned by a visit Isaiah Berlin, then secretary of the British embassy in Moscow, paid to Akhmatova in 1946. Aside from the poems, that encounter provoked Stalin's wrath, the dark shadow of which completely enveloped Akhmatova's life for the next decade and a half.

Since in one of the poems from that cycle – spanning in its own turn a decade – the poet assumed the persona of Dido, addressing her visitor as Aeneas, I wasn't altogether surprised by the opening remark of that bespectacled man: 'What has she done to me? Aeneas! Aeneas! What sort of Aeneas am I really?' Indeed, he didn't look like one, and the mixture of embarrassment and pride in his voice was genuine.

Years later on the other hand, in his own memoirs about visiting Pasternak and Akhmatova in 1946, when 'the world's strength was all spent / and only graves were fresh', Sir Isaiah himself compares his Russian hosts to victims of a shipwreck on a desert island, inquiring about the civilisation which they've been cut off from for decades. For one thing, the essence of this simile echoes somewhat the circumstances of Aeneas's appearance before the queen of Carthage; for another, if not participants themselves, then the context of their meeting was epic enough to endure subsequent disclaimers.

But that was years later. Now I was staring at a face I saw for the first time. The paperback edition of *The Hedgehog and the Fox* that Akhmatova had once given to me to pass onto Nadezhda Mandelstam lacked a picture of its author; as for a copy of *Four Essays on Liberty* it came to me from a book shark with its cover torn off – out of caution, given the book's subject. It was a wonderful face, a cross, I thought, between a wood grouse and a spaniel, with large brown eyes ready at once for flight and for hunting.

I felt comfortable with this face being old because the finality of its features alone excluded all pretension. Also, in this foreign realm where I had suddenly found myself, it was the first face that looked familiar. A traveller always clings to a recognisable object, be it a telephone or a statue. In the parts I was from that kind of face would belong to a physician, a schoolteacher, a musician, a watchmaker, a scholar – to someone from whom you vaguely expect help. It was also the face of a potential victim, and so I suddenly felt comfortable.

Besides, we spoke Russian – to the great bewilderment of the uniformed personnel. The conversation naturally ran to Akhmatova until I asked Sir Isaiah how he had found me in London. The answer made me recall the front page of that mutilated edition of *Four Essays on Liberty*, and I felt ashamed. I should have remembered that that book, which for three years served me as an antidote to all sorts of demagoguery in which my native realm was virtually awash, was dedicated to the man under whose roof I now stayed.

It turned out that Stephen Spender was Sir Isaiah's friend from their days at Oxford. It turned out that so, though a bit later, was Wystan Auden, whose 'Letter to Lord Byron' had once been, like those *Four Essays*, my daily pocket companion. In a flash I realised that I owed a great deal of my sanity to men of a single generation, to the Oxford class, as it were, of circa 1930; that I was, in fact, also an unwitting product of their friendship; that they wandered through each other's books the way they did through their rooms at Corpus Christi or University College; that those rooms had, in the end, shrunk to the paperbacks in my possession.

On top of that, they were sheltering me now. Of course, I wanted to know everything about each one of them, and immediately. The two most interesting things in this world, as E. M. Cioran has remarked somewhere, are gossip and metaphysics. One could add, they have a similar structure: one can easily be taken for the other. That's what the remainder of the afternoon turned into, owing to the nature of the lives of those I was asking about, and owing to my host's tenacious memory.

The latter of course made me think again about Akhmatova, who also had this astonishing ability to retain everything: dates, details of topography, names and personal data of individuals, their family circumstances, their cousins, nephews, nieces, second and third marriages, where their husbands or wives were from, their party affiliations, when and by whom their books were published, and, had they come to a sorry end, the identities of those who had denounced them. She, too, could spin this vast, weblike, palpable fabric on a minute's notice, and even the timbre of her low monotone was similar to the voice I was listening to now in the Atheneum's library.

No, the man before me was not Aeneas, because Aeneas, I think, remembered nothing. Nor was Akhmatova a Dido to be destroyed by one tragedy, to die in flames. Had she permitted herself to do so, who could describe their tongues? On the other hand, there is indeed something Virgilian about the ability to retain lives other than your own, about the intensity of attention to others' fates, and it is not necessarily the property of a poet.

But, then again, I couldn't apply to Sir Isaiah the label 'philosopher', because that mutilated copy of *Four Essays on Liberty* was more the product of a gut reaction against an atrocious century than a philosophical tract. For the same reason, I couldn't call him a historian of ideas. To me, his words always were a cry from the bowels of the monster, a call not so much for help as *of* help – a normal response of the mind singed and scarred by the present, and wishing it upon nobody as the future.

Besides, in the realm I was from, 'philosophy' was by and large a foul word and entailed the notion of a system. What was good about *Four Essays on Liberty* was that it advanced none, since 'liberty' and 'system' are antonyms. As to the smart-alecky retort that the absence of a system in itself is a system, I was pretty confident that I could live with this syllogism, not to mention in this sort of system.

And I remember that as I was making my way through that book without a cover I'd often pause, exclaiming to myself: How Russian this is! And by that I meant not only the author's arguments, but also the way that they were presented: his piling up of subordinate clauses, his digressions and questions, the cadences of his prose which resembled the sardonic eloquence of the best of nineteenth-century Russian fiction.

Of course I knew that the man entertaining me now in the Atheneum was born in Riga – I think Akhmatova told me so. She also thought that he was a personal friend of Churchill's, whose favourite wartime reading had been Berlin's dispatches from Washington. She was also absolutely sure that it was Berlin who arranged for her to receive an honorary degree from Oxford and the Etna Taormina Prize for Poetry in Italy in 1963. (Having seen something of Oxford dons years later, I think that making these arrangements was a good deal rockier than she could have imagined.) 'His great hero is Herzen,' she would add with a shrug and turn her face to the window.

Yet for all that, what I was reading wasn't 'Russian'. Nor was it Western rationalism marrying Eastern soulfulness, or Russian syntax burdening English clarity with its inflections. It appeared to me to be the fullest articulation of a unique human psyche, aware of the limitations imposed upon it by either language, and cognizant of those limitations' perils. Where I had cried, 'Russian!' I should have said 'human'. The same goes for the passages where one might have sighed, 'How English!'

The fusion of two cultures? Reconciliation of their conflicting values? If so, it would only reflect the human psyche's appetite for and ability to fuse and reconcile a lot more. Perhaps what could have been perceived here as faintly Eastern was the notion that reason doesn't deserve to have such a high premium put on it, the sense that reason is but an articulated emotion. That's why the defence of rational ideas turns out sometimes to be a highly emotional affair.

I remarked that the place looked positively English, very Victorian, to be precise. 'Indeed so,' replied my host with a smile. 'This is an island within an island. This is what's left of England, an idea of it, if you will.' And, as though not sure of my fully grasping the nuance, he added, 'a Herzen idea of London. All it lacks is fog,' And that was itself a glance at oneself from the outside, from afar, from a vantage point which was the psychological equivalent of the mid-Atlantic. It sounded like Auden's 'Look, stranger, on this island now . . .'

No, neither a philosopher nor a historian of ideas, not literary critic or social utopian, but an autonomous mind in the grip of an outward gravity, whose pull extends its perspective on this life insofar as this mind cares to send back signals. The word, perhaps, would be *'penseur'*, were it not for the muscular and crouching associations so much at odds with this civilised, alert figure comfortably reclining in the bottle-green leather armchair at the Atheneum – the West and the East of it mentally at the same time.

That is where an Indian scout normally is, that's where one would be looking for him. At least in the beleaguered fort I was from one learns not to look in one direction only. The sad irony of all this is of course that, so far as I know, not a line of Berlin's writings has been translated into the language of the country which needs that intellect the most, and which could profit from those writings enormously. If anything, that country could learn from him a lot more about its intellectual history – and by the same token about its present choices – than it seems capable of thus far. His syntax, to say the least, wouldn't be an obstacle. Nor should they be perturbed by Herzen's shadow, for while Herzen indeed was appalled by and sought to change the mental climate of Russia, Berlin seems to take on the entire world's weather.

Short of being able to alter it, he still helps one to endure it. One cloud less – if only a cloud in one's mind – is improvement enough, like removing from a brow its 'tactile fever'. An improvement far greater is the idea that it is the ability to choose that defines a being as human; that, hence, choice is the species's recognised necessity – which flies into the moronic face of the reduction of the human adventure to the exclusively moral dimensions of right and wrong.

Of course, one says all this with the benefit of hindsight, sharpened by what one could have read of Berlin since. I think, however, that nineteen years ago, with only *The Hedgehog and the Fox* and *Four*

Essays on Liberty on my mind, I could not have reacted to their author differently. Before our tea at the Atheneum was over I knew that others' lives are this man's forte, for what other reason could there be for a sixty-three-year-old knight of England to talk to a thirty-two-year-old Russian poet? What could I possibly tell him that he didn't already know, one way or the other?

Still, I think I was sitting in front of him on that sunny July afternoon not only because his work is the life of the mind, the life of ideas. Ideas of course reside in people, but they can also be gleaned from clouds, water, trees; indeed, from a fallen apple. And at best I could qualify as an apple fallen from Akhmatova's tree. I believe he wanted to see me not for what I knew but for what I didn't – a role in which, I suppose, he quite frequently finds himself vis-à-vis most of the world.

To put it somewhat less stridently, if not less autobiographically, with Berlin the world gets one more choice. This choice consists not so much of following his precepts as of adopting his mental patterns. In the final analysis, Berlin's notion of pluralism is not a blueprint but rather a reflection of the omniscience of his own unique mind, which indeed appears to be both older and more generous than what it observes. This omniscience in other words is very man-like and therefore can and should be emulated, not just applauded or envied.

Later the same evening, as we sat for supper in Stephen Spender's basement, Wystan said, 'Well, how did it go today with Isaiah?' And Stephen immediately asked, 'Yes, is his Russian really good?' I began, in my tortured English, a long story about the nobility of old Petersburg pronunciation, about its similarity to Stephen's own Oxonian, and how Isaiah's vocabulary was free of unpalatable accretions of the Soviet period and how his idiom was so much his own, when Natasha Spender interrupted me and said, 'Yes, but does he speak Russian as fast as he speaks English?' I looked at the faces of those three people who had known Isaiah Berlin for much longer than I had lived and wondered whether I should carry on with my exegesis. Then I thought better of it.

'Faster,' I said.

Notes

1 Sidney Morgenbesser and Jonathan Lieberson, *Isaiah Berlin*

* A version of this essay appeared in the *New York Review of Books*, 10 March 1980 and was reprinted in Jonathan Lieberson, *Varieties*, Farrar, Straus, Giroux, 1989.

1 Isaiah Berlin, *Against the Current: Essays in the History of Ideas*, Viking, 1980.
2 Bryan Magee, ed., *Men of Ideas*, Viking, 1979, p. 31.
3 In his essay on Alexander Herzen, but more eloquently in intellectual portraits of Ivan Turgenev and Herzen in his *Russian Thinkers*, Berlin has explored the fascinating ramifications of value conflict in the personal sphere, in the dilemma of the Russian 'superfluous men' of the mid-nineteenth century, who could not fit in their society, who lived continually in the shadow of a prodigious decision about what they were to do, to be, to become; or who, like Turgenev, could not 'simplify' themselves, who 'held everything in solution', remaining outside their cultural situation 'in a state of watchful and ironical detachment'.
4 Isaiah Berlin, *Four Essays on Liberty*, Oxford University Press, 1969, p. 169.
5 Ibid.
6 Isaiah Berlin, *Vico and Herder*, Hogarth Press, and Viking, 1976, p. 23.
7 *Four Essays on Liberty*, p. 205.
8 Alan Ryan, ed., *The Idea of Freedom: Essays in Honour of Isaiah Berlin*, Oxford University Press, 1979.
9 *Four Essays on Liberty*, p. 8.
10 *Vico and Herder*, p. xxxii; for the origin of the word 'Nationalismus', see p. 181.
11 Reprinted in *Four Essays on Liberty*.
12 Other problems about Berlin's distinction between positive and negative liberty have been raised by John Rawls, Ronald Dworkin and G. MacCallum. Taylor's essay in *The Idea of Freedom* contains useful discussion of various other issues raised by Berlin's distinction.
13 *Four Essays on Liberty*, p. vi.
14 *Four Essays on Liberty*, p. 39.
15 The appreciation of this fact (if it be one) is what lends poignancy to Berlin's more abstract essays on freedom and knowledge, his '"From Hope and Fear Set Free"', in *Concepts and Categories*, Viking, 1979, and his earlier 'Historical Inevitability' (reprinted in *Four Essays on Liberty*). It may be, he says in these works, that our current mode of interpreting the 'facts', other persons, the

world, is one according to which men are 'free' – in some sense of this ambiguous term, he never makes clear exactly which sense – free to form new ideas, to take new paths in life, to make choices among values and forms of life. But, he asks, might not the growth of knowledge change all this?

> If a great advance were made in psycho-physiology, if, let us suppose, a scientific expert were to hand me a sealed envelope, and ask me to note all my experiences – both introspective and others – for a limited period – say half-an-hour – and write them down as accurately as I could; and if I then did this to the best of my ability, and after this opened the envelope and read the account, which turned out to tally to a striking degree with my log-book of my experiences during the last half-hour . . . we should then have to admit, with or without pleasure, that aspects of human behaviour which had been believed to be within the area of the agent's free choice turned out to be subject to discovered causal laws.

Indeed, haven't psychology and other social sciences shown us repeatedly that many of the actions we commonly assume to be under our control (or that of our parents, or our statesmen, or other authorities) are in fact owing to heredity or have biological or psychological causes, or are owing to our educational history, or our social and environmental background – at least to a larger degree than we had previously thought? And might it not be that the growth of such knowledge will increase rapidly over time, increase the range of explainable and predictable events taking place in a human being and eventually snuff out entirely our ordinary concept of a 'free' agent? Further, Berlin asks, would such discoveries not radically alter our way of approaching the world? Would it not shake our estimation of the worth of political liberty? Or would we trade rational analysis and science for our established convictions and repudiate such knowledge, cease the research that generated it, and reaffirm what is now 'common sense'? These are brave and absorbing questions that deserve fuller treatment by contemporary thinkers.

16 Isaiah Berlin, *Russian Thinkers*, Viking, 1978, p. 300.
17 See 'Political Ideas in the Twentieth Century', in *Four Essays on Liberty*.
18 *Russian Thinkers*, p. 297.
19 *Four Essays on Liberty*, p. 40.
20 'The Hedgehog and the Fox', in *Russian Thinkers*. For further discussion of the history and meaning of the distinction between hedgehogs and foxes, see our exchange with John S. Bowman, *New York Review of Books*, September 25, 1980, and a letter from Isaiah Berlin, *New York Review of Books*, October 9, 1980.
21 'The Origins of Israel', in Walter Z. Laqueur, ed., *The Middle East in Transition*, Routledge & Kegan Paul, 1958.

3 Charles Taylor, *The Importance of Herder*

1 See his 'Herder and the Enlightenment', in *Vico and Herder*, Hogarth Press, and Viking, 1976.
2 Cf. *Hegel*, Cambridge University Press, 1975.
3 *Philosophical Investigations*, Part I, para. 1.

4 This is the term I used in 'Language and Human Nature', in *Human Agency and Language*, Cambridge University Press, 1985.

5 Condillac, *Essai sur l'Origine des Connoissances Humaines* Part II, Section I, chap. I.

6 In Erich Heintel, ed., *Herder's Sprachphilosophie*, Hamburg, Felix Meiner Verlag, 1960, pp. 12–13. Herder, *Abhandlung über den Ursprung der Sprache).*

7 Condillac, loc. cit., para. 3.

8 See Donald Davidson, *Inquiries into Truth and Interpretation*, Oxford University Press, 1985, Essays 1–5, 9, 13.

9 See 'The Very Idea of a Conceptual Scheme', in op. cit., Essay 13. This question is bedevilled by the confusion of two issues. One concerns the claim that arises out of the Cartesian-empiricist tradition, that I grasp my own thoughts, including my understanding of language, directly, in a way my interlocutor can never match. The other is the issue about subjective understanding I've been discussing here. The two are quite distinct. Subjective understanding is usually elaborated between people, members of the same culture. Indeed, that is what makes them members of the same culture. The phenomenon of incommensurable conceptual schemes arises between cultures, and is more than a mere logical possibility here; rather it is a continuing source of historical tragedy. But if we run the two issues together, then the discredit under which Cartesian-empiricist privileged access justly labours blinds us to the real differences of subjective understanding. I have tried to show why meaning can't be understood exclusively in terms of truth conditions in 'Theories of Meaning', in *Human Agency and Language*.

10 See Hans Aarsleff, *From Locke to Saussure*, University of Minnesota Press, 1982. Aarsleff's dismissal of Herder as an innovator is a good illustration of how easily the two sides in the debate can talk past each other. If we take no account of Herder's shift in perspective, then he can indeed seem to be recapitulating a number of themes from Condillac, while confusedly protesting his disagreement with him.

11 See Vicki Hearne, *Adam's Task*, Heinemann, 1987.

12 See W. van O. Quine, *Word and Object*, Wiley, 1960, chap. 2.

13 George Herbert Mead, *Mind, Self and Society*, University of Chicago Press, 1934, pp. 46–7.

14 J. L. Austin, *How to do Things with Words*, Oxford University Press, 1962; see also J. R. Searle, *Speech Acts*, Cambridge University Press, 1969.

15 Herder, op. cit., p. 23.

16 Herder, op. cit., pp. 24–5.

17 Condillac, op. cit., Part I, Section I, chap. IV, para. 45.

18 Loc. cit. Locke is the great source of this reifying language. He often uses images of construction out of materials when speaking of the mind. See *An Essay Concerning Human Understanding*, 2.2.2.

19 David Hume, *An Enquiry Concerning Human Understanding*, chap. VII.

20 The reference, in the by now canonical form, is to page 104 of the first edition of Kant's *Kritik der reinen Vernunft*, in the Berlin Academy edition, in *Kants Werke*, vol. IV, Berlin: Walter de Gruyter, 1968.

21 For the suspicion towards unthinking custom, see Locke, *Essay*, 1.2.22–6. I have discussed this connection between disengagement and modern epistemology at greater length in 'Overcoming Epistemology', in Kenneth Baynes, James Bohman and Thomas MacCarthy, eds, *After Philosophy*, in *Sources of the Self*, Harvard University Press, 1989, chap. 9; and in '*Lichtung* or *Lebensform*: Parallels between Wittgenstein and Heidegger' (forthcoming).

22 Herder, op. cit., p. 21.

23 See also Maurice Merleau-Ponty, *La Phénoménologie de la Perception*, Paris, Gallimard, 1945, Part I, chap. 6.

24 See, e.g., *De la Grammatologie*, Paris, Éditions de Minuit, 1967. Derrida's almost obsessive attempt to deny altogether any special status whatever to speech in the human language capacity raises the question whether he doesn't have more in common with the Cartesian tradition than he would like to admit. 'L'écriture' and 'la différence', while embedded in culture (or constitutive of it), are peculiarly disembodied functions. See also *L'Écriture et la Différence*, Paris, Le Seuil, 1967.

25 See Maurice Merleau-Ponty, op. cit.

26 Herder, op. cit., pp. 24–5.

27 See for instance, in *Ideen zur Philosophie der Geschichte der Menschheit*, Book IX, chap. 2: 'Wie sonderbar, dass ein bewegter Lufthauch das einzige, wenigstens das beste Mittel unsrer Gedanken und Empfindungen sein sollte! Ohne sein unbregreifliches Band mit allem ihm so ungleichen Handlungen unsrer Seele wären diese Handlungen ungeschehen.' And a little later: 'Ein Volk hat keine Idee, zu der es kein Wort hat: die lebhafteste Anschauung bleibt dunkles Gefühl, bis die Seele ein Merkmal findet und es durchs Wort dem Gedächtnis, der Rückerrinerung, dem Verstande, ja endlich dem Verstande der Menschen, der Tradition einverleibt; eine reine Vernunft ohne Sprache ist auf Erden ein utopisches Land.'

28 Herder, op. cit., p. 25.

29 Loc. cit.

30 Ferdinand de Saussure, *Cours de Linguistique Générale*, Paris, Patot, 1978, p. 166.

31 See, for instance, *Philosophical Investigations*, Part I, para. 257.

32 Thomas Hobbes, *Leviathan*, chap. 4, Michael Oakeshott edition, Blackwell, 1955, p. 21.

33 Wilhelm von Humboldt, *On Language*, trans. Peter Heath, Cambridge University Press, 1988, p. 49.

34 These terms were made famous by C. K. Ogden and I. A. Richards in their *The Meaning of Meaning*, New York, Harcourt, 1923. This is a magnificent example of a hold-out, well into the twentieth century, of the old designative theory, in all its crudity and naïveté, quite oblivious of any of the insights generated in the aftermath of Herder.

35 I borrow the term from Ernst Cassirer, *The Philosophy of Symbolic Forms*, Yale University Press, 1953.

4 Richard Wollheim, *The Idea of a Common Human Nature*

1 This point has its personal relevance. On the evening when Isaiah Berlin and I gave our papers on 'Equality' to the Aristotelian Society, which in those days met in the large dusty conference room of the Royal Anthropological Society, which occupied the first floor of a Bedford Square house, John Findlay, then professor of philosophy at King's College London, sat through the discussion visibly dissatisfied. Towards the end of the discussion he got to his feet. His jacket was tightly buttoned across his chest and stomach, and, as happened when he was provoked, his face had gone brick red while his nose and hooded eyelids were a powdery white. He had, he said, looking round, been listening to what had been said, but no one had made the obvious point. Equality was a drab doctrine, there were far nobler, grander ideals, but they all require us to be different from what we are. 'We believe in equality, we have to, because we're all just – just two peas in a pod. What I don't understand', and his voice rose, and, opening the palm of his left hand, he began methodically striking it with his right forefinger, 'what I don't understand . . .' and then he suddenly gave up and sat down, for, whenever he started on the things that he couldn't understand other people's believing, the list stretched ahead indefinitely. He gave a sigh of exhaustion, he shut his eyes and smiled.

2 Donald Davidson, *Essays on Actions and Events*, Oxford, 1980, passim.

3 This second way of denying a common human nature is broadly characteristic of the views of Michel Foucault and his followers. Foucault is a thinker sometimes subtler, sometimes less subtle, than one would expect.

4 Norman Malcolm, *Ludwig Wittgenstein: A Memoir*, Oxford, 1958, p. 32.

5 Stephen Spender, *World Within World*, London, 1950, p. 71.

6 See Isaiah Berlin, 'Empirical Propositions and Hypothetical Statements', *Mind*, vol. LIX, no. 235, July 1950, pp. 289–312, reprinted in *Concepts and Categories*, Oxford, 1980.

7 See Muriel Gardiner, ed., *The Wolf-Man and Sigmund Freud*, London, 1972.

8 David Hume, *The Natural History of Religion*, section III.

6 Ronald Dworkin, *Two Concepts of Liberty*

1 Berlin, *Four Essays on Liberty*, Oxford Paperbacks, 1969, p. lvi.

2 *American Booksellers Association, Inc. et al.* v. *William v. Hudnut, III, Mayor, City of Indianapolis et al.*, 598 F. Supp. 1316 (S.D. Ind. 1984).

3 771 F.2d 323 (US Court Appeals, Seventh Circuit).

4 That court, in a confused passage, said that it nevertheless accepted 'the premises of this legislation', which included the claims about a causal connection with sexual violence. But it seemed to mean that it was accepting the rather different causal claim considered in the next paragraph, about subordination. In any case, it said that it accepted those premises only *arguendo*, since it thought it had no authority to reject decisions of Indianapolis based on its interpretation of empirical evidence.

5 See *Daily Telegraph*, 23 December 1990.

6 Frank Michelman, 'Conceptions of Democracy in American Constitutional

Argument: The Case of Pornography Regulation', 56 *Tennessee Law Review* 291, 1989, pp. 303–4.

7 G. A. Cohen, *Isaiah's Marx, and Mine*

1 In 'Does Political Theory Still Exist?', which first appeared in 1961, Isaiah Berlin remarked that 'no commanding work of political philosophy has appeared in the twentieth century' (Isaiah Berlin, *Concepts and Categories*, Hogarth Press, 1978, p. 143).

2 'Benjamin Disraeli, Karl Marx, and the Search for Identity', in Isaiah Berlin, *Against the Current*, Hogarth Press, 1979, p. 252.

3 Marranos were Spanish Jews who pretended to be Christians in order not to be targets of the Spanish Inquisition.

4 *Karl Marx: His Life and Environment*, 4th edn. Oxford University Press, 1978, p. 116.

5 'Herzen and Bakunin on Individual Liberty', in Isaiah Berlin, *Russian Thinkers*, Hogarth Press, 1978, p. 86.

6 'Benjamin Disraeli . . .', p. 284.

7 In conversation with Ved Mehta, as reported by the latter in *The Fly and the Flybottle*, Little, Brown, 1962. For an unnervingly effective demonstration of that power, see Berlin's exposition of the views of Joseph de Maistre in 'The Counter-Enlightenment', *Against the Current*, pp. 62–3. In the course of reading it you have to remind yourself of where you stand in order not to be recruited to de Maistre's view.

8 *Karl Marx*, pp. 62–3.

9 Ibid., p. 98.

10 Ibid., p. 99.

11 For Berlin, 'every thought belongs, not just somewhere, but to someone, and is at home in a context of other thoughts, a context which is not purely formally prescribed. Thoughts are present to Berlin not just, or primarily, as systematic possibilities, but as historically and psychologically actual, and as something to be known and understood in these concrete terms' (Bernard Williams, Introduction to Isaiah Berlin, *Concepts and Categories*, p. xii).

12 'Benjamin Disraeli . . .', pp. 276–8.

13 Ibid., p. 260.

14 *Karl Marx*, p. 15.

15 'Herzen and Bakunin', p. 99.

16 'Alexander Herzen', in *Russian Thinkers*, p. 209.

17 'Speech on the Hague Congress', 1872, in D. Fernbach, ed., *The First International and After*, Penguin, 1974, p. 324. Marx also said, a year earlier, that 'insurrection would be madness where peaceful agitation would move swiftly and surely do the work'. I see no warrant for the judgment of Jon Elster, from whose *Making Sense of Marx* (Cambridge, 1985, p. 445) I draw the latter quotation, that such comments 'may not have corresponded to [Marx's] inner beliefs' (ibid., p. 446).

18 'The Future Results of British Rule in India', in Marx/Engels *Collected Works*, Volume 12, Lawrence & Wishart, 1979, p. 222.

19 *Karl Marx*, p. 24.

20 Ibid., p. 206.

21 Ibid., p. 76.

22 Ibid., p. 6.

23 The nature of all that arduous theory construction also makes it impossible for me to accept that Marx was 'scarcely interested' in truth in the ordinary sense of correspondence of proposition to fact (ibid., p. 114).

24 *Capital*, Volume I, Penguin Books, 1976, p. 815.

25 Ibid., p. 728.

26 Ibid., p. 761.

27 'Two Concepts of Liberty', in *Four Essays on Liberty*, Oxford University Press, 1969, p. 167.

28 Ibid., p. 168.

29 Karl Marx, Preface to *A Contribution to The Critique of Political Economy*, Lawrence & Wishart, 1971, p. 21.

30 *Karl Marx*, p. 179.

31 'Two Concepts of Liberty', p. 169.

32 I have, indeed, defended him on that score, against the late Gerald McCallum, in 'A Note on Values and Sacrifices', *Ethics*, Volume 79, 1969, pp. 159–62.

33 See my review of Allen Wood's *Karl Marx* in *Mind*, vol. 92, 1983, p. 444.

34 'Herzen and Bakunin', p. 105.

35 For it is a distinct contention, and one on which I do not here comment, that it is unachievable and that the attempt to achieve it has disastrous consequences for liberty.

36 'Political Ideals in the Twentieth Century', in *Four Essays on Liberty*, p. 31. (I have criticised the phrasing of this praise of Roosevelt in 'Capitalism, Freedom and the Proletariat', in Alan Ryan, ed., *The Idea of Freedom: Essays in Honour of Isaiah Berlin*, Oxford University Press, 1979, p. 13.) See too, 'Two Concepts of Liberty', pp. 169–70.

37 *Karl Marx*, p. 6.

38 'Benjamin Disraeli . . .' pp. 280–1.

39 Ibid., p. 281–2, my emphasis.

40 Ibid., p. 281.

41 See *Karl Marx.*, pp. 135, 183.

42 Ibid., p. 5.

43 *Capital*, Volume III, Penguin Books, 1981, p. 368.

44 *The Grundrisse*, Penguin Books, 1973, p. 325: for a number of other relevant texts, see the citations in sections (5) and (6) of chap. VII of my *Karl Marx's Theory of History: A Defence*, Oxford University Press, 1978.

45 *Karl Marx*, p. 113.

46 For further discussion, including an attempt to explain why there is a tendency to misinterpret Marx in the way just quoted, see my *History, Labour, and Freedom*, Oxford University Press, 1988, chap. IV, section 8.

47 *The Critique of the Gotha Programme*, in *Marx/Engels Selected Works* in Two Volumes, vol. II, Moscow, 1958, p. 24.

48 *Karl Marx*, p. 112.

49 Ibid., p. 113.
50 *Zur Kritik der Politischen Oekonomie* (Manuscript 1861–3), *Marx–Engels Gesamtausgabe*, Dietz, Berlin, 1982, vol. 6, p. 2287. As Jon Elster points out (*Making Sense of Marx*, p. 106), the same passage appears in the earlier *Grundrisse* manuscript of 1857–8, with the very significant difference that Marx replaced *'ungehörig'* (improper) by *'ein Unrecht'* (an injustice) in the revised version of his manuscript.
51 I am grateful to Arnold Zuboff for incisive criticism of drafts of this piece. And, for constructive suggestions, I thank Charlotte Brewer, Maggie Cohen, Jon Elster, Ted Honderich, Will Kymlicka, John McMurtry, Avishai Margalit, Mike Otsuka, Bill Shaw, Seana Shiffrin and Jo Wolff.

9 Michael Ignatieff, *Understanding Fascism?*

* In writing this review essay of *The Crooked Timber of Humanity*, I am particularly indebted to Bernard Williams for his comments and criticisms. I also learned much from John Dunn's review, 'Our Insecure Tradition,' *TLS*, Oct. 5–11, 1990, pp. 1053–4.
1 Isaiah Berlin, *Karl Marx: His Life and Environment*, 4th ed., Oxford University Press, 1978, pp. 1–16.
2 Isaiah Berlin, *The Crooked Timber of Humanity: Chapters in the History of Ideas* (hereafter *Crooked Timber*), John Murray, 1990, p. 161.
3 Isaiah Berlin, 'Does Political Theory Still Exist?', in *Concepts and Categories: Philosophical Essays*, Oxford University Press, 1980, p. 170.
4 *Crooked Timber*, p. 18.
5 Ibid., p. 205.
6 Bernard Williams, Introduction to *Concepts and Categories*, p. xvi.
7 Isaiah Berlin, *Four Essays on Liberty*, Oxford University Press, 1969, p. 192; see also Richard Wollheim, 'John Stuart Mill and Isaiah Berlin', in Alan Ryan, ed., *The Idea of Freedom: Essays in Honour of Isaiah Berlin*, Oxford University Press, 1979, pp. 253–71.
8 *Crooked Timber*, p. 18.
9 Ibid., p. 192–3.
10 Bernard Williams, Introduction to *Concepts and Categories*, p. xviii.
11 *Crooked Timber*, pp. 7–10.
12 Ibid., p. 62.
13 Ibid., p. 60.
14 *Four Essays on Liberty*, p. 116.
15 *Crooked Timber*, p. 121.
16 Ibid., p. 111.
17 Ibid., p. 194.
18 Ibid., p. 204.
19 Ibid.
20 Ibid., p. 180.

10 Yael Tamir, *Whose History? What Ideas?*

1 I would like to thank Edna Ullman-Margalit, Avishai Margalit and Yossi Malli for their helpful comments.

2 Blacks and members of other non-white groups endure a surprisingly similar sense of subjection.

3 I. Young, 'Impartiality and the Civic Public: Some Implication of Feminist Critiques of Moral and Political Theory, in S. Benhabib and D. Cornell, eds., *Feminism as Critique*, Polity Press, 1987, p. 76.

4 Such claims are particularly powerful in immigrant societies such as the U.S., Australia and Israel.

13 Bernard Williams, *Naive and Sentimental Opera Lovers*

1 'The "Naïveté" of Verdi', *Hudson Review*, 21, 1968, pp. 138–47; reprinted from *Atti del 1º Congresso Internazionale di Studi Verdiani, 1966* (Istituto di Studi Verdiani, Parma, 1969); reprinted in *About the House* 3:1 (March 1969), pp. 8–13.

2 *Hudson Review*, pp. 140–1, 143.

3 'Notes on Music and Opera', in *The Dyer's Hand*, Faber, 1963, pp. 468–9. Auden agreed, however, that opera could be the ideal vehicle of 'tragic myth'. See also 'The World of Opera' in his *Secondary Worlds*, Faber, 1969. I have taken some sentences in this and neighbouring paragraphs from my article, 'Manifest Artifice', in *Tosca*, ENO/ROH Opera Handbook 16, London, John Calder; New York, Riverrun Press, 1982.

4 It may be that the discussion of this subject is distorted by a bad assumption, that if there are operatic tragedies, *Otello* must be one of them. *Otello* is a tremendous opera, but it is as much a melodrama as *Il Trovatore*. If there is a tragedy by Verdi, it is *Don Carlos*.

5 D. A. Miller, *The Novel and the Police*, California University Press, 1988, p. 145. He is actually discussing a markedly different case: Trollope.

6 As expressed in *Poetics of Music* (the Charles Eliot Norton Lectures 1939/40), translated by Arthur Knodel and Ingolf Dahl, Harvard University Press, 1970. I have no reason to think that Isaiah's views were actually influenced by Stravinsky: it is only a matter of resemblances.

7 *Poetics of Music*, p. 61; the quotation in the next paragraph comes from p. 63.

8 Richard Ellmann, *James Joyce*, revised ed., Oxford University Press, 1983, p. 460.

14 Alfred Brendel, *Does Classical Music Have to be Entirely Serious?*

1 Antonín Dvořák: 'Franz Schubert' (In co-operation with Henry T. Finck), *The Century Illustrated Monthly Magazine*, New York, 1894.

2 'Joseph Haydn', *Bildungsbuch für junge Tonkünstler*, Erfurt, 1810.

3 *Für Freunde der Tonkunst*, Leipzig, 1868, IV, p. 235.

4 I am especially indebted to D. H. Munro's survey of comical tendencies in his book *Argument of Laughter*, Melbourne University Press, 1951.

5 Mozart's 'Musical Joke', usually regarded as a prize example of musical wit, is a work in which, as far as I can see, a catalogue of musical blunders is

distributed with little kindness, along with some blatantly wrong notes that the performers are made to play on purpose.
6 Immanuel Kant, *Critique of Judgement*, 1790, section 54.

15 Joseph Brodsky, *Isaiah Berlin: A Tribute*
* This essay was first published as 'Isaiah Berlin at Eighty' in the *New York Review of Books*, 17 August 1989.

INDEX